Stock Market Efficiency, Insider Dealing and Market Abuse

To Sue and Edward

Stock Market Efficiency, Insider Dealing and Market Abuse

PAUL BARNES

Routledge
Taylor & Francis Group
LONDON AND NEW YORK

First published 2009 by Gower Publishing

Published 2016 by Routledge
2 Park Square, Milton Park, Abingdon, Oxon O14 4RN
711 Third Avenue, New ork, N 10017, USA

Routledge is an imprint of the Taylor & Francis Group, an informa business

British Library Cataloguing in Publication Data
Barnes, Paul
Stock market efficiency, insider dealing and market abuse
1. Stock Exchange (London, England) 2. Stock exchanges - Great Britain 3. Stocks - Great Britain 4. Insider trading in securities
I. Title
332.6'4241

ISBN: 978-0-566-08849-0

Library of Congress Cataloging-in-Publication Data
Barnes, Paul.
Stock market efficiency, insider dealing, and market abuse / by Paul Barnes.
p. cm.
Includes bibliographical references and index.
ISBN 978-0-566-08849-0 1. Efficient market theory. 2. Securities fraud. 3. Insider trading in securities. 4. Stock exchanges. I. Title.

HG4915.B37 2008
332.64'2--dc22

2008022328

ISBN 978-0-566-08849-0 (hbk)

Contents

List of Figures

List of Tables

Acknowledgements

There are many people that need to be thanked in the publication of a book of this kind. First, I would like to thank my joint authors, referees and editors in respect of the articles I have written over the years on this topic and on which the book is based. I would particularly like to thank Dave Snutch, a great friend, who has so kindly read earlier versions of the script for me. I would also like to thank John Simon for allowing me to use some of his graphs in Chapter 4, John Billot for his assistance in some of the figures and Jonathan Norman, Fiona Martin and Mike Brooks at Gower for their support. Finally, I would like to thank Dario Crispini at the FSA for helpful comments on certain technical aspects. I hasten to add that the opinions and mistakes are mine.

Introduction

We are interested in this book in 'equities' and the market in the UK for risk capital of 'listed' companies. That is, companies whose shares are traded on the London Stock Exchange (LSE) and its subsidiary market, known as the Alternative Investment Market (AIM) for smaller, growing companies. AIM's membership and reporting rules are less onerous than for the main market. As a result, investment in AIM companies is riskier but can yield higher returns. AIM started in 1995 with just a few companies but has grown steadily.

Equities are sometimes referred to as 'ordinary' or 'common' shares or stock. There is no difference between a stock and a share, nor is there a difference between ordinary shares or common stock. These are also referred to as 'securities', a wider term to include stocks, shares and bonds. We are also interested in, but limited to, certain equity 'derivatives': that is options (to buy or sell equities), spread betting (on equities) and contracts for difference (CFD) (on equities). These are defined in Chapter 2. There are other markets with similar properties (for example efficiency) which are outside our scope, for example futures and commodities.

Chapters 6 and 7 relating to the law and cases were up to, and as at, the beginning of 2008. Much of the remaining chapters were put together, and certainly the academic research was published, before the Credit Crunch that began in the second half of 2007. In the light of the subsequent events and the traumas experienced by the stock markets, the theories discussed in Chapters 3 and 4 will appear poignant and are more relevant today than ever before. Unfortunately, both Kindleberger and Minsky died a few months before the spectacles occurred about which they had developed theories. It is sad that their theories and insights are not better known. I hope this book will help.

Why the Stock Market and its Efficiency are so Important

CHAPTER **1**

This chapter attempts to answer the following questions: What is stock market efficiency? What is market abuse? Why is stock market efficiency so important for the economy and why is stock market abuse so bad that people are imprisoned for it? First, however, why are the stock market and its efficiency so important? In a sentence: because the stock market channels our savings, and those from other nations, if we have a good and well-run exchange, into production and productive services and, if it is efficient, the stock market channels this money into those areas that most require it.[1]

Today, we take the stock market very much for granted. The creation of an economy in which limited liability companies could easily be formed and their shares freely sold and transferred between investors dates from, and very much underpinned, the Industrial Revolution in Great Britain. To take advantage of the new opportunities for automation and economies of scale, businesses needed to operate on a much larger scale than hitherto. For the first time, companies with limited liability and transferable shares enabled entrepreneurs to raise funds on the scale they needed and from people who were not involved in the running of their businesses (Barnes and Firman 2002). The concept of shares being easily transferable was a brilliant idea. It enables investors to invest in a business for just as long as they wish. When they wish to end their interest, they are able to sell the shares without harming the company whatsoever. An open and free market allows them to sell shares easily. From the company's point of view, it has long-term capital in the form of shares for as long as it wishes. Also, it is an easy mechanism through which the company can raise new capital.

The price of a share is determined by supply and demand. It is what investors are prepared to pay for it – at that time – and what others are prepared to sell it for. Its price is, therefore, what an investor believes it is worth. A share

1 This directly relates, of course, to new issues (or initial public offerings – IPOs). Indirectly, however, it results in invested funds staying within the market and enables companies traded on the LSE to raise new funds.

price reflects all known information and represents the collective beliefs of all investors about the business' future prospects. When an investor is considering buying a company's shares, they will attempt to assess how much the shares are worth by determining how much money they will receive in future dividends from those shares and how much the shares are likely to be worth when the investor comes to sell them. The investor will also consider how risky the shares are, and can only do this by attempting to place a value on the company's business and its ability to earn profits in the future. Table 1.1 provides a list of examples of information likely to affect a company's value and, therefore, its share price.

In this sense, the stock market is 'efficient'. If an investor thinks a share is worth more than the current market price, they will buy it – or at least they should – and as many as possible, if they have the money. Similarly, if they think the value of a stock they own is less than the market price, they should consider selling

Table 1.1 Examples of new pieces of information likely to affect a company's share price according to their type

	The company	Other related companies in the same industry, competitors etc.
General	Significant changes in indices related to raw material prices, property, goods and services etc. Interest rate changes Significant change in the political situation	Economic forecasts Analysts' predictions General stock market changes
Specific	Financial results Top management changes Major acquisitions and disposals Major changes in financial structure Business news, for example large contracts Analysts' forecasts Credit ratings	Mergers, takeovers and bankruptcies Financial results Major changes in financial structure Business news, for example large contracts Analysts' forecasts Credit ratings

it. If they think the value of a share is about the same as the market price, then they should do nothing. In other words: if they think a share is 'undervalued' they will hold those they already have and buy more but if they think it is 'overvalued', they will sell it and invest their money elsewhere. Therefore, if there are enough investors interested in the share, with enough money to buy and sell in large quantities, its market price will soon adjust to their collective beliefs. It is sometimes said that a speculator performs a useful and valuable role in the market by buying what they consider to be undervalued shares and selling overvalued shares. Most large stock exchanges, certainly the LSE, are regarded as being efficient because most listed companies' shares are traded in sufficiently large volumes. There may be a few stocks in relatively small companies that are not sufficiently traded – or there is not a sufficient amount of interest in them – for this to not to occur. The market in these 'thinly traded' stocks may be inefficient at times and it is open for speculators to profit from such situations. Nevertheless, the large exchanges are regarded as efficient, both internally and across exchanges. That is, the price of a company's shares is likely to be the same, or about the same, across other exchanges as otherwise investors (known as arbitragers) will buy on one exchange and sell on another at a profit. The action of these arbitragers, or even the prospect of it, is sufficient to ensure that the prices across these exchanges are about the same.

Also contributing to its efficiency is the fact that the stock market is dominated by large financial institutions and investment funds that are managed and advised by 'professionals' – financial analysts. Part of their job will be to seek out under- and overvalued shares and inefficiencies in the market from which they may be able to profit. It is also true that the abler investor makes more money in the longer term because they make consistently better choices and decisions compared with the less able investor who makes weaker decisions and less money. The consequence of this is that the financial markets will be dominated by the decisions of the best investors because it is they who are strong and powerful. (Later parts of this book illustrate how 'the fool and his money are soon parted'.) In practice, therefore, the prices of the vast majority of companies will not only reflect the collective opinions of investors but that of the professionals and ablest investors. Given the speed of information in today's world, the ease of access that so many people have to it, and the amount of money that stands to be made or lost in the market, it is very difficult to imagine how it can be anything other than efficient.

What has been said so far relates solely to informational efficiency. The stock market adjusts to new information very quickly. Some say that this is instantaneous, although we will see in later chapters it is quite sluggish. At any time, therefore, a share price reflects all that is known relating to the prospects of the company and the collective judgement of the market as to what it is worth. This has a number of implications.

The first relates to decision-making by individuals and organizations. If the information available to a shareholder is completely up to date, full, fair, reliable and freely available (that is: easily accessible and at zero or negligible cost) then we can truly say there is a fair market in the shares, in which case all investors will have similar information (or at least if they do not, it is their own fault) and market prices will move to reflect these. It follows that not only does an investor have all the information available to make a good decision, they do not have to read, analyse and digest all the information about and affecting the company, because the market has done it for them! Even if they do this and are skilled at analysing such data, they will simply arrive at a similar value for the company as professional analysts – the market price! They have had what economists describe as a 'free ride'. In fact, we may argue that studying a company's accounts, analysts' reviews etc. is pointless because they will (or should) simply lead the investor to the conclusion that the market price is correct and it equals the value of the share. It also follows, therefore, that an investor does not need to read the company's financial statements but can choose any firm, even at random, and the price will represent the security's correct value. Some academics argue that the best way of selecting a portfolio of shares is to take a newspaper containing a list of publicly traded shares and stick pins in it at random to select which companies to invest in!

At first glance, this implies that all an investor can do is choose the companies in which to invest in at random, hold them and not trade as there is no point in trading as they cannot beat the market and earn a higher return. By trading, the investor will simply incur unnecessary trading costs. This is incorrect. A better investor will usually earn higher returns than a poor investor – certainly in the long term. Whilst the prudent investor may be able to obtain the same level of returns as the market as a whole by simply holding a representative sample of companies, the bad investor may earn low returns by continually trading, for example, by taking a profit on what had proved to be a good investment and putting the proceeds into a bad investment. Also, the abler investor may earn high returns by making better judgements than others and beating the market by identifying companies that are likely to be successful.

The second implication of informational efficiency relates to the role of the stock market within the economy. Informational efficiency assists in the efficient allocation of resources within the economy. 'Allocative efficiency' refers to a situation in which scarce resources are allocated between competing requests in a way that maximizes the net benefit to society in accordance with the wishes of consumers. A company whose products are not in demand, or whose productive processes are inefficient, will not make as much profit as a company whose goods are in demand or which is very efficient. As a consequence, its returns to shareholders will not be as high and it will find raising new capital difficult. A stock market that is allocatively efficient will allocate new funding to the most profitable companies – those most able to provide goods that are most needed and those that are most efficient at providing them.

A good example of this is the rise of hi-tech and Internet-related companies in the USA and UK in the late 1990s. Many new companies were formed that promised huge profits from the information technology revolution and investors clamoured to invest in them in anticipation of the high returns. In the early 2000s the situation was reversed when it was found that not all companies were able to provide the promised returns, and investors became very sceptical about investing in these kinds of companies without certain assurances of a return. As a result, even well-run companies in the sector found it difficult, if not impossible for a period, to raise new funds.

Informational efficiency is a necessary, but not a sufficient, condition for allocative efficiency. The market may adjust quickly to news but the information may not be perfect or complete. It is well known that not all costs of production are incurred by the producer and are included in their financial statements. I live both close to a huge power station and the runway of an international airport. I pick up some of their costs (in the sense that the operating costs they actually incur are less than the total cost to society of their operations). They do not have to pay, directly anyway, for my hospitalization and shortened life expectancy from air pollution. As a result, their contribution to society and their profits are both overstated. If airlines incurred the true and total societal costs, not only would they no longer make such large profits, they may actually make losses and certainly would be unable to offer cheap flights in the way they are doing. In short, a capitalist system is not perfectly allocatively efficient. Its merits lie in the speed of allocation.

Also, as with any other market, its participants (in particular, those companies whose shares are traded) will want to exploit their own positions as they pursue their own objectives. Businesses have better information about their business investment opportunities than savers. Invariably, management has an incentive to overstate the value and performance of the business, if only to maximize their salaries and rewards. That is human nature. One need look no further than the collapse of Enron, Worldcom and Arthur Andersen to see how even very large organizations may be brought down if such behaviour goes unchecked.

Savers have an 'agency problem' as they wish to know how their investments are faring and the returns they are making (Healy and Palepu 2001). Their agents – the managers who are managing the company on their behalf and the auditors who are checking that those managers are acting properly and accounting fairly – have their own interests at heart. They both have an incentive to provide owners with information that implies the company is doing well. Owners, on the other hand, need to know when it is not.

This problem may lead to a breakdown in the functioning of the capital markets. Say a number of businesses came to the stock market to raise funds. Half of them had good proposals yielding profits to investors and the others had weak proposals with no likely profits. If investors are unable to distinguish between the two groups, they will be unable to identify what are good and bad investments and probably assume they are similar. The result is the good investments are undervalued and the bad investments are overvalued. Clearly, this is a 'bad thing'. It is bad for investors because they do not know where it is best to invest. It is bad for businesses because those that are more deserving of the new funds are not prioritized but stand alongside those businesses that do not deserve the new investment. Most of all, it is bad for society because scarce investment resources are not directed to those areas most in need. Further, it does not encourage individuals (and, therefore, a nation as a whole) to save and invest. In short, it is allocatively inefficient.

A similar result occurs if we substitute into the illustration 'honest' and 'dishonest' for 'good' and 'bad' businesses. Investors may stand to lose their money by being unable to distinguish between honest and dishonest investments. I remember once speaking with a wealthy student from a poor African country. I asked her why she did not invest money on her country's stock market. She laughed with derision remarking something along the lines that 'you must be joking; they are all corrupt'. As a result, her family invested its money in more secure and (probably, therefore) more prosperous countries. The economic consequences for her country (once rich but now poor) are obvious.

This is a well-known problem in economics. It is known as the 'market for "lemons" problem' (Akerlof 1970), a reference to the US second-hand motor vehicle market where buyers are unable to distinguish between good cars and bad ones – lemons. The result is that buyers presume that all second hand cars are bad and prices are driven down as a result. The effect is that sellers of good cars do not get a good deal and good cars are driven out (excuse the pun) of the market by the bad cars. The problem has several solutions. The two most important are relevant here. The first is to ensure that, by means of regulation, full and necessary information is provided by businesses to investors to enable them to distinguish between good and bad investments. Hence the need for accounting, the regulation of accounting, and auditors. The second relates to the creation of a demand for information intermediaries, such as financial analysts and credit rating agencies who are expert in interpreting business information and are judged on the independence and quality of their assessments. As we will see in later chapters, whilst both solutions help to resolve the essential problem, they bring with them their own problems.

Market abuse

Market abuse is a general term to describe actions by investors that unfairly take advantage of other investors. It includes not only insider dealing but various actions attempting to mislead the market, such as providing false information about a company's performance or giving a misleading impression of the market in the shares.

I have argued that it is in the public interest that investors are provided with reliable and trusted information as it is only then that they will be prepared to invest and businesses will be provided with the necessary funds and the money channelled into the most worthy areas. For this reason, the law and regulations related to the informational aspects of the UK stock market are considered to be very important. Not only must the markets be fair, they must be seen to be fair, thereby encouraging investment. An individual should not be able to profit from inside information, nor should they be able to manipulate financial information because not only is society losing out but so are individuals. It is sometimes said that market abuse and insider dealing are not immoral and they are victimless crimes. I have argued why they are crimes against society. It is less obvious why they are morally wrong. We live in an information-led society. We are bombarded with information to help us make decisions. It is a fact of life that if we do not seek out information we risk being disadvantaged. We also acknowledge that to be first with information or knowledge is likely to confer an advantage. So why should insider dealing be such a deadly sin as to warrant imprisonment? Most laws are formed when there is general agreement that certain actions are morally wrong. It is unlikely that there would be such unanimity about insider dealing.

On closer inspection, it clear that there is both a winner and a loser. An investor holding inside information is able to profit either by buying or selling before the release of the new information depending on whether it is good or bad news, respectively. The corresponding seller or buyer who does not have that inside information and is, therefore, prepared to trade at the existing price is losing. Consider Figure 1.1 which shows a rise in a share price at the time of an announcement of good news through the Regulatory Information Service. Here, Investor B decides to buy, because they have inside information and know that when it becomes public, the shares will rise in price. Investor A decides to sell at that price because they do not have inside information. Investor B makes a profit from the increase in the share price. Investor A makes a corresponding loss in the sense that had they had been in possession of the same information as B, they would not have sold to B at that price.

It should not be thought that an inside dealer can only make money from inside information that is good news: they may profit by selling ahead of the announcement of bad news; for instance, prior to an earnings or profits warning (a statement by the company that its profits will not be as high as expected. Earnings and profits are synonymous and used interchangeably throughout). The dealer may sell their existing shares prior to the announcement, thereby benefiting from selling at a higher price than it would be after the announcement

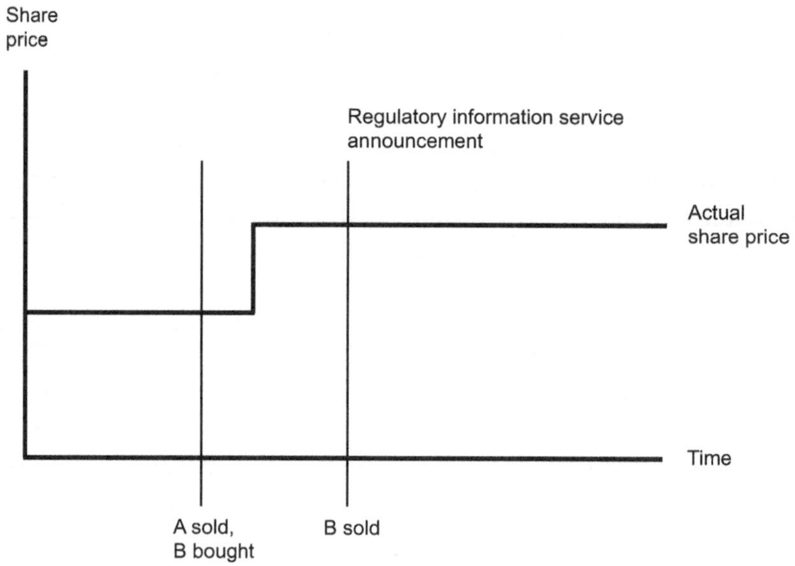

Figure 1.1 Insider dealing prior to a rise in a share price arising from the announcement of good news

has been made. If the dealer does not own shares in the company but has received the inside information and wants to profit from it, they may 'sell short' – sell now and buy later, that is sell before the announcement and buy afterwards. (The practice of short selling is explained in Chapter 2). In Figure 1.2, by means of short selling the inside dealer (B) makes a profit on the fall in the price of the shares.

There are other ways in which an individual with inside information may profit from either good or bad news, which may involve less initial investment enabling them to maximize the profit (although at an increased risk) from the share price change. These are spread betting, CFDs, and the purchase of options and are also explained in Chapter 2.

An individual may attempt to make a profit by inflating a share price. This is known as 'share ramping' or in the USA as 'pump and dump'. It may be done in a number of ways. They may try to influence the share price by broadcasting new information that will affect the share price. This can be done for example on the Internet through a chat room, notice board or simply emailing investors. This news may or not be true – it doesn't matter. It may be news of a possible

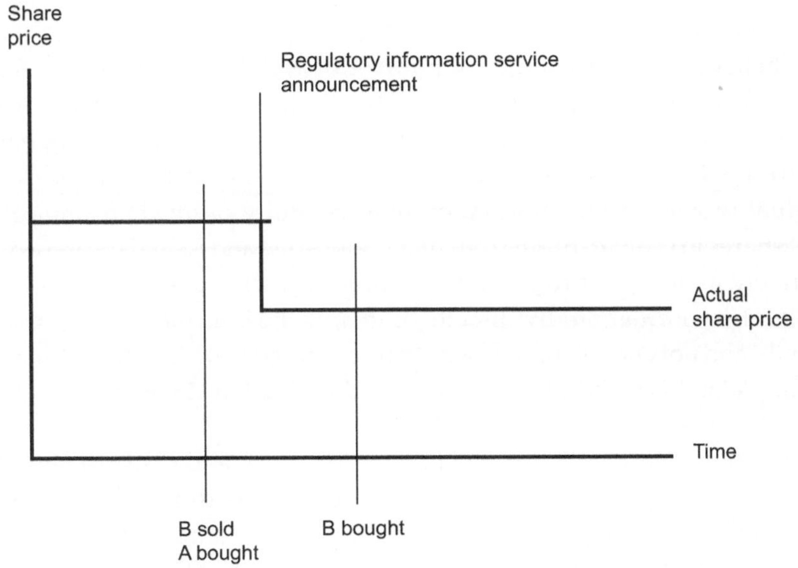

Figure 1.2 Insider dealing prior to a fall in a share price arising from the announcement of bad news

takeover bid, a new contract the company has entered into or anything likely to push up the share price: see Box 1.1 for an example.

Box 1.1

Williams' share price leapt 59p to 284p in brisk early morning trading last month when *The Times* reported that the Barclay brothers, who own the private Ellerman lines, had built a 3 per cent stake and were considering a bid for the industrial and consumer products group.

The report was untrue and was based on information provided as part of what appears to be an elaborate and determined fraud. The man behind the scam contacted a number of newspapers over a week claiming to have detailed information of the bid. He even sent *The Independent* a number of documents purporting to be from the takeover papers. The documents were little more than extracts from previously published financial information.

The International Stock Exchange's surveillance unit launched an inquiry into share dealings in Williams Holdings. There was significant trading in the company's shares on the day the newspaper report appeared. Some dealers were left with heavy losses as the Williams share price fell back to 238p once the story had been denied. Others made significant profits as approaching 4 million shares changed hands.

The Independent, 11 December 1989.

The important point is not whether the information is correct but that the market believes it – and a sufficient number of individuals believe it – for it to affect the share price. If it is untrue, eventually the market will realize that the information is false and the share price will revert to what it was originally, as in Figure 1.3. If it is true, the actual share price will not fall. In either case, the individual providing the information may be guilty of inside dealing if they bought shares in order to profit from that knowledge and issued the information deliberately in order to profit from it in this way. Of course, it would be very difficult for an ordinary individual to do this, as the information may not have credibility and not enough people would be prepared to believe the information. An example of this is the City Slickers case described in Chapter 7.

The investor may also profit from bad news by 'trash and cash', the inverse of pump and dump. Here, instead of releasing false good information to push up the share price, the investor releases false bad information ('trashing' the company) to force the share price down. The trader (A in Figure 1.4) then buys the shares at the artificially low price with a view to profiting from them when the market recognizes the information is wrong and the share price rights

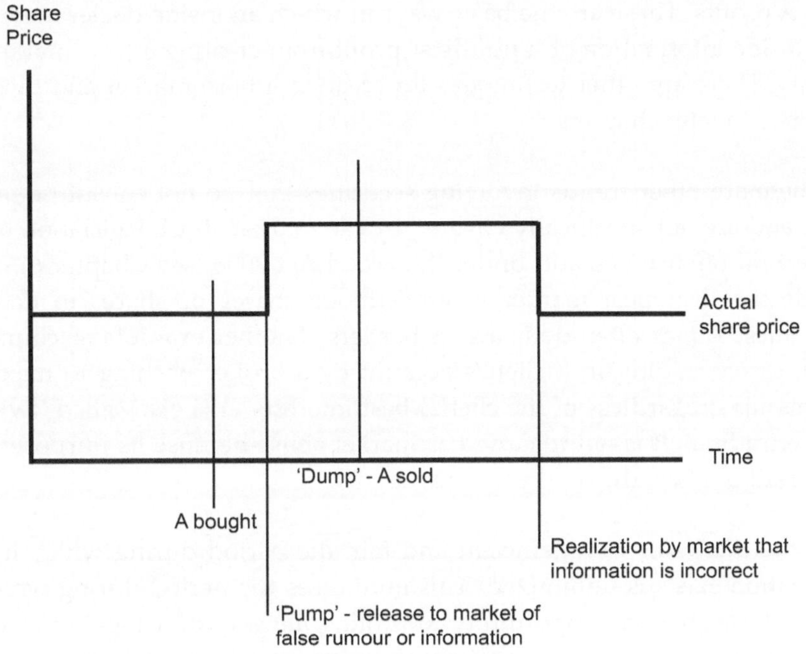

Figure 1.3 Pump and dump or share ramping

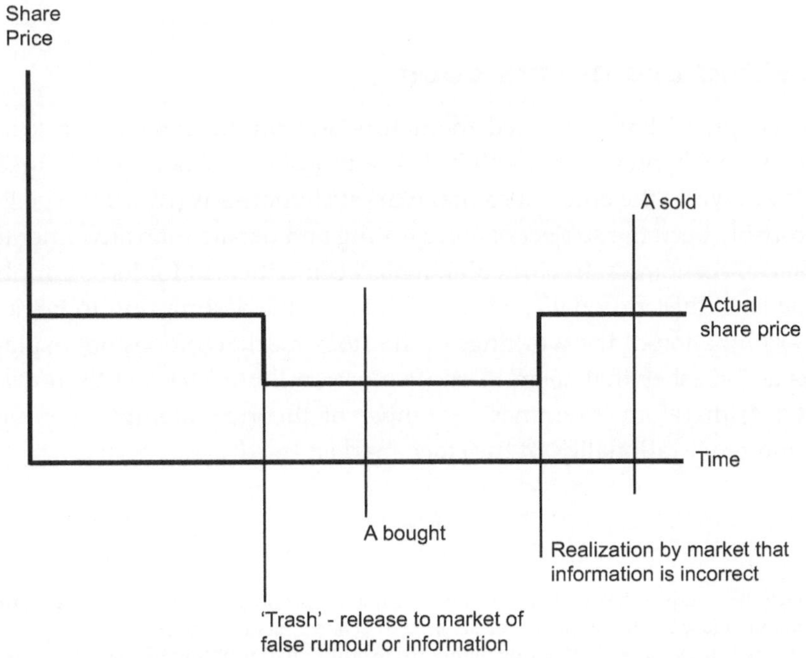

Figure 1.4 Trash and cash

itself. A profits. These are the basic ways in which an inside dealer may profit from inside information or a fraudster profit from creating a false market in a security. There are other techniques for creating a false market and these are described in later chapters.[2]

There are other frauds involving securities that do not constitute market abuse and are not specifically covered by the market abuse legislation but by the general offence of fraud under the Fraud Act 2006 (see Chapter 6). These include the dishonest marketing of fictitious shares or shares in fictitious companies. This is often done across borders. Another example is 'churning', the excessive trading in a client's account by a broker wishing to maximize commissions regardless of the client's best interests. It is also called 'twisting' or 'overtrading'. It is not regarded as market abuse because its purpose is not to mislead or affect the market in the security.

If the market is to be efficient and fair, the period during which insider information exists is minimized. This minimizes the period during which an insider dealer has the opportunity to profit. One way of achieving this is to make insider dealing and market abuse unlawful and place an obligation on companies and their advisers of ensuring that a proper market exists in their shares by releasing price-sensitive information as soon as possible.

The structure of this book

In this chapter, I have outlined the nature and implications of stock market efficiency. In Chapter 3, this will be more thoroughly examined by means of what is known as the efficient capital markets hypothesis (ECMH). The ECMH has probably been the subject of more testing and debate than any other theory in financial economics. In particular, it has been criticized for its assumption of rationality. Whilst rationality may be a reasonable assumption to begin with in an examination of the workings of the stock market, it does not explain the booms and crashes that seem to occur more and more frequently nowadays. Chapter 4, therefore, examines a number of theories attempting to explain these and the 'irrationality' of the stock market.

---

2 In fact, the fraudster has two opportunities to make a profit. In addition to profiting from the pump in Figure 1.3, he could short sell, use a CFD or a spread bet, to profit from the fall in the share price at the time of the dump. Similarly, in addition to profiting from the trash as shown in Figure 1.4, he could short sell, use a CFD or a spread bet to profit from the fall in share price at the time of the trash if he thought it would affect the share price.

The most important single area of the market in which huge profits (and losses) are made by both investors and companies, where egos are stretched and tested, muscles are flexed, lies are told, and laws and regulations broken is undoubtedly the area of mergers and acquisitions. Chapter 5 is devoted to this. If a market, principally comprising players who are all trying to make money out of one another, is to be fair in any meaningful way, it needs to be regulated. Chapter 6 provides a brief coverage of the law and how it attempts to ensure that information is properly released to the market and insider dealing and market abuse are outlawed and curbed. The remaining chapters examine the extent of this abuse. First we need some background information – how the market works and how you can work out what the price of a share should be. These are the subject of Chapter 2.

References

Akerlof, G.A. (1970) 'The Market for "Lemons": Quality Uncertainty and the Market Mechanism', *Quarterly Journal of Economics,* 84(3): 488–500.

Barnes, P and R. Firman (2002) 'The Loss of Popularity of Limited Liability Companies in Great Britain in 1866 and the Role of Financial Information: A Case Study', *Financial History Review,* 8(2): 143–161.

Healy, P.M. and K.G. Palepu (2001) 'Informational Asymmetry, Corporate Disclose and the Capital Markets: A Review of the Empirical Disclosure Literature', *Journal of Accounting and Economics,* 31(1–3): 405–440.

How Shares are Traded and Valued

CHAPTER **2**

This chapter examines how shares are traded, how the market is created and how an investor may make decisions as to whether to buy, sell or continue to hold stocks. It discusses the alternative approaches as to how the investor may calculate how much a security is worth. There are various approaches to valuation, ranging from a purely rational economic approach to a behavioural – but not necessarily irrational – one in which the investor attempts to forecast share price movements based on the psychology of the market using price movements and trends.

The 'market' for stocks and shares

The London Stock Exchange (LSE) provides a market for the trading of shares. Its stringent admission conditions must be met before allowing a company's shares to be traded on the market (such companies are termed 'listed') and imposes continuing obligations for the conduct of a listed company. If these are not met, the LSE may suspend trading on the market. Whilst a shareholder may assume certain things about the conduct of the company's affairs and the provision of information about it, listing provides no assurance of the future financial performance of the company or its share price.

The actual market principally comprises a number of 'market makers'. A market maker is a bank or brokerage company that facilitates a market in a company's shares. Each listed company will have at least one market maker dealing in its shares. The market maker is obliged to deal at the prices they are quoting (subject to certain size limitations) so anyone wishing to buy or sell will be able to do so without attempting to contact a potential seller or buyer. The market maker will offer a buying and a selling price. These are known, respectively, as a 'bid' price and an 'offer' price. For instance, the market maker may agree to buy a company's shares at 95p per share (the bid price) and sell them at 100p (the offer price). It will adjust its prices in order to balance the current supply and demand for the company's shares (see Figure 2.1). The price of a share changes frequently as the market maker attempts to balance its books and be able to continue to provide shares to buyers and buy them from sellers yet hold a reasonable number in reserve to meet future commitments. The market maker attempts to make a profit on its dealing. This is known as the 'bid–offer' spread which is the difference between the buying and selling price. In our numerical illustration, it is 5p. This is not only compensation for the market-maker's risk and effort in creating and maintaining the market, it also reflects the volume of trade in the company's shares. The spread would be relatively small for shares in a well-known company whose shares are regularly traded but larger for a company whose shares are less frequently, that is 'thinly' traded, where it is more difficult for the market maker to guarantee a market in those shares. The price newspapers quote is the mid-price between the bid and offer price for the stock at the end of a working day.

The development of electronic trading technology in recent years has led to an alternative to what has just been described, that is an 'order-driven' as opposed to a 'quote-driven' system of trading has emerged. Here, members, acting either on their own behalf or for customers, input their buy and sell orders into a central computer system known as the Stock Exchange Electronic Trading Service (SETS). The SETS computer system informs the market of details of all orders and matches buyers and sellers automatically, cutting out the need

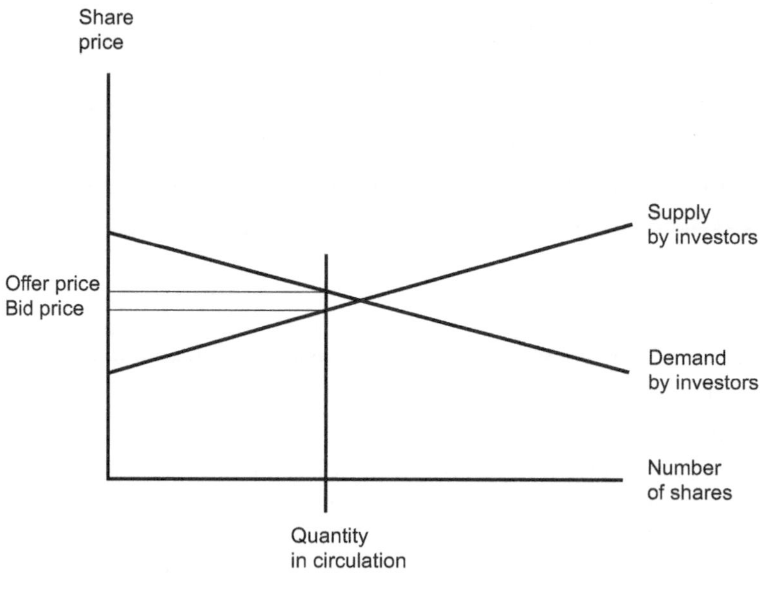

Figure 2.1 The supply and demand of a company's shares showing the bid–offer spread

for a market maker. Theoretically, this means a narrower bid–offer spread. At the moment, this service only exists for the largest companies quoted on the main list of the LSE. Smaller companies continue to use the Stock Exchange Automated Quotation (SEAQ) 'quote' book system, with market makers quoting prices to brokers and trades being done on a semi-automatic rather than fully automatic basis. All AIM and listed UK equities whose turnover is insufficient for the market-making system or Stock Exchange Alternative Trading System (SETS) are handled by a trading system known as SEAT Plus.

Market makers are actually relatively new, dating back to 1986 and the deregulation of the markets, what was known as the Big Bang. Big Bang principally involved the abolition of the dual capacity system and the creation of a single capacity system. Under the dual capacity system, jobbers acted as market makers, merely dealing with other jobbers and brokers. An individual who wished to buy or sell shares dealt with a stockbroker who would contact a jobber to execute the trade. Since the passing of the Financial Services Act 1986, all brokers and jobbers are able, if they wish, to operate in a dual capacity – as an agent or as a principal. As a result, trading soon moved from being conducted face to face on the floor of the Stock Exchange to being performed via computer or telephone. Very quickly, the existing firms of brokers and jobbers were bought up by large financial institutions, usually merchant banks, leading to the formation of 'one-stop shops'. More recently, they have become the property of a small number of foreign-owned, mostly US, investment banks. All high street banks have a stockbroking arm.

Ways of trading

It is a very simple task (and now a relatively cheap one) to buy and sell shares. We do not need to discuss the mechanics of this further here other than to say the investor needs to decide whether they wish to buy or sell through a 'full service' broker who will provide them with some advice about the decision or, if they wish to minimize costs and feel they do not require advice, they may look for an 'execution only' stockbroker. Execution only means that the broker will simply take an investor's order and execute it for them. These brokers cannot legally offer any advice on decisions and, to keep costs down, they usually operate over the phone or the Internet.

Alternatives to actually owning equities exist, and may be particularly useful to the investor who wishes to attempt to profit from a fall in price of a share. These include: the purchase of options, Contracts for Difference (CFD) and the use of spread betting. There are many forms of options and these relate to many types of investment, not merely ordinary shares. Essentially an option is the right, but not the obligation, to buy or sell something at some time in the future at a given price. A 'call' option confers on the buyer the right to buy a fixed quantity of an underlying asset (for example, shares) at a fixed price (the 'exercise price' or 'strike price') on or before a specified date in the future (the 'exercise date' or 'expiry date'). A 'put' option confers on the buyer the right to sell a fixed quantity of an underlying asset (for example, shares) at a fixed price on or before a specified date in the future. Options that allow the holders to exercise the right to buy or sell up to and including the expiry date are known as 'American-style' options. 'European-style' options allow the holders to exercise the option only on the exercise date. A market exists in options and an investor who wishes to maximize their profit relative to the sum paid may decide to buy an option rather than the stock. However, after the expiration date, the option is worthless. An option, therefore, is nearer to gambling than investment.

Spread betting is similar to the acquisition of an option in the sense that it is simply betting whether a share price is going to rise or fall beyond a specified level within a specified period. Spread betting companies quote two prices, which they call a 'spread'. A punter may make a bet on whether the outcome will be above or below the spread, and the profit or loss depends on the level of the relevant index (for example of the share price) at the end of the period. Therefore, by means of spread betting, a punter can take a 'short' position and make a profit from a falling price.

CFDs are very similar to spread betting. A CFD is an agreement made between two parties to exchange, at the closing of the contract, the difference between the opening and closing prices of the underlying share, multiplied by the number of shares stated in the contract. CFDs are designed to make a profit or avoid a loss by reference to movements in the price of a security, which is, itself, not bought or sold. CFDs are becoming popular as an alternative to actual share trading as they allow the maximum amount of money to be made from the share price movement and avoid stamp duty. Typically, a quoted CFD price will track the underlying share price very closely.

Short selling refers to selling a block of shares before buying them. It is done by an investor if they think the price of a security will fall significantly very soon. In practice, short selling involves arranging to borrow shares from a long-term holder (for example, a financial institution such as an insurance company or pension fund) and paying a fee to 'rent' the shares for the relevant period. For example, assume that shares in Z plc currently sell for 100p per share. A short seller would borrow 1,000 shares, and sell them immediately for

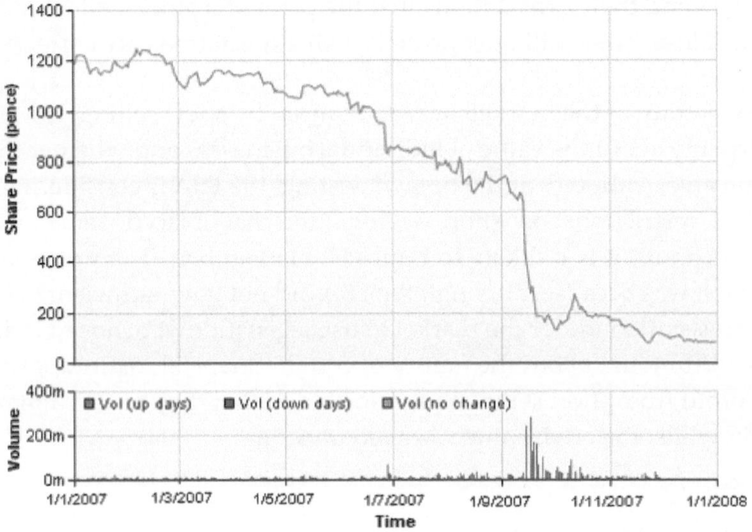

Figure 2.2 Northern Rock's share price during 2007

£1,000 in anticipation of a fall in their price. Say the price of shares in Z plc fell to 80p per share. The short seller would then buy 1000 shares back for £800, return the shares to their original owner, and make a £200 profit.

The recent case of the Northern Rock is a good example of this activity. It was reported that during the crisis of September 2007, Northern Rock's share price had fallen not only because of the uncertainty about its future and viability but because of short selling.[1] What is likely to have happened is this. Some investors thought that its price would continue to fall quickly and that they could profit from the situation by selling short. They therefore sold first and bought later. Their very act of selling, by increasing the supply of unwanted Northern Rock shares, helped to force the share price down further.

For this reason, it was argued that short selling contributed to the instability and volatility of the stock market during late 2007 and 2008. It was also regarded as distasteful that speculators should be able, and allowed, to profit from business failures. However, as I argued in Chapter 1, it is in the public interest that the markets are efficient and short selling only acts to help a share price to more quickly move to its new value, i.e. it contributes to market efficiency. If

1 *The Financial Times*, 'Rock's short-selling stock runs out', 21 September, 2007. Page 3 reported that the stock of shares in Northern rock available for short selling had run out. As supplies ran out, fees to 'borrow' shares had risen from typically 0.3 to 0.4 per cent annually to 3 per cent.

short sellers and their expectations that the price of a stock will fall are wrong in they will lose. They will only profit if their expectations are correct.

The volatility of the markets was not caused by short selling, It was caused by uncertainty about the value of individual businesses and whether they were able to survive. Although at the time of writing, the FSA is considering placing permanent restrictions on short selling (and has placed some temporary restrictions on it), it is unlikely to impose a blanket ban. The principal reason for its action was because, although the FSA did not have sufficient evidence to make a prosecution under the market abuse legislation, it believed individuals had placed rumours about the failure of certain financial institutions enabling them to profit from short selling those stocks and that they would attempt to do this again whilst the environment was so uncertain.

Market participants

Most people do not invest directly in securities on the LSE but indirectly through intermediaries – financial institutions such as pension funds, insurance companies, investment trusts and unit trusts. The aggregate percentage of institutional ownership of UK shares has increased from 35 per cent in 1963 to 70 per cent in 2004 and is about the same today. During the same period, the percentage of individual or private investor investment fell from 54 to 14.1 per cent.[2] This is despite the privatizations during the 1980s, such as British Telecom and British Gas and the demutualization of friendly societies and building societies such as the Abbey National, when individuals were actually given shares. This is also despite the fact that, as a result of Big Bang, commission paid to brokers and market makers for the purchase and sale of shares has fallen considerably.

In order to encourage business, most merchant banks depend on their investment analysis services. They employ large teams of financial analysts to study companies and make recommendations – internally, for themselves and externally, for their clients and to investors considering purchasing or selling shares.

The processing of raw and often biased information,[3] into informed and independent judgements and forecasts by means of the best possible analysis

2 Office for National Statistics. This is as a percentage of total UK equities owned by UK bodies and organizations.

3 The possibility that accounting and other financial data may often not be independent but, instead, biased and even deliberately misleading is taken up in Chapter 8.

and research is likely to have a considerable impact on – and improve – market efficiency. However, it is very difficult for a financial institution to consistently outperform the market as a whole because of its size. The purchase or sale of a large block of shares is likely to affect the share price by significantly increasing the demand for, or supply of, the number of shares available on a particular day. For an institution even to achieve average performance, it will have to earn greater returns to compensate for this.

It is often argued that some analyses and recommendations given to customers or the public are not independent but flawed because of conflicts of interest. A merchant bank may perform many different roles. In addition to providing investment recommendations, it may also be acting for, or advising, companies. For instance, it may be handling an Initial Public Offering (IPO). It would not be in its client's interests for it to recommend investors to sell. The only safeguard is that it is not in the merchant bank's interests to be known to offer poor or biased recommendations or analysis.

It is useful to distinguish between institutional and private investors according to their investing characteristics. As we have discussed, institutional investors are able to rely on the professional advice provided by financial analysts. They will attempt to estimate the value of a stock objectively (subsequently referred to as its 'intrinsic' or 'fundamental' value) and trade accordingly. An institutional investor will have different objectives relating to a stock's growth, risk and level of dividend payout according to its needs. For example, a pension fund may be very conscious of its need to have a steady and regular income to meet its payment commitments. An investment fund will also have clearly defined objectives and will invest in accordance with them. For instance, it may be a 'growth fund' committed to looking for companies in which to invest that have particularly promising growth expectations. Most institutional funds also have legal and regulatory constraints that determine the types of stock in which they are allowed to invest.

In addition to investment funds managed by financial institutions for the general public, other 'high-risk' funds operate, notably hedge funds and private equity funds. A hedge fund, contrary to its name,[4] is a fund used by wealthy individuals and institutions, which aims to earn high returns by investing in high-risk investments and uses aggressive strategies such as short selling, leverage, arbitrage, and derivatives that are inappropriate to

4 'Hedging' (as in 'hedging one's bets') implies investing in securities that have the effect of reducing an investor's overall risk. The concept of risk reduction by means of diversification is discussed later in this chapter.

conventional funds such as unit trusts. Hedge funds are exempt from many of the rules and regulations governing conventional funds, allowing them to adopt aggressive investing goals. A private equity fund is an investment fund that invests in both listed and unlisted companies. It is often their plan to obtain a controlling interest in a company (usually by becoming a majority shareholder) delisting it (that is removing it from the LSE as a listed company), reorganizing its financial structure, management, and investment, and then relisting it through an IPO.

In contrast to the institutional investor, it is more difficult to make assumptions about the level of financial ability and research by the private or 'small' investor prior to investing or selling. They may have very little understanding of the working of the financial system and would not have the ability to interpret financial information in order to arrive at an independent assessment of a stock's intrinsic value. Even if they did have that ability, they may take the view that the size of their investment does not warrant the time and trouble involved in computing it. The small investor may conclude that they are unable to better the market's estimate of the stock's value and 'free ride' on the effort exercised by financial analysts and the effects of market efficiency. On the other hand, the private investor may have a definite view about the company, and may believe that, for whatever reason, the market as a whole has 'got it wrong' and so decide to invest in the stock because it is currently undervalued.

Market efficiency is helped by the actions of all investors. Trading takes place if one investor thinks a stock is worth more than what another person considers it to be worth. Assuming they have sufficient funds, an investor will buy if $V_S > V_M$, where V_S is. That is, the investors subjective value of the stock and V_M is its market value. An investor will sell if $V_S < V_M$. The resultant price will reflect the collective and informed opinion of the market.

Investors buy or sell when the difference between a stock's market price and what they consider to be its intrinsic value is sufficient to cover the 'transaction costs'. These include not only the fees incurred in the purchase or sale, but probably more importantly, the difference between the bid and offer price – the spread, mentioned earlier. The spread will be sufficiently large to make it difficult for an investor to buy and sell regularly. As a result, they will only do this if the market price significantly departs from the investor's intrinsic value. Figure 2.3 shows how a share price will move on a day to day basis as market makers adjust their prices to supply and demand and how these fluctuate around the intrinsic value. Trading occurs because investors disagree as to the

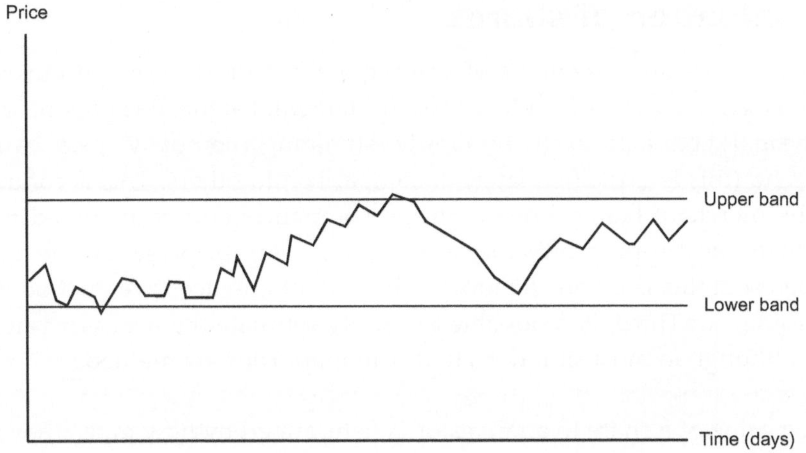

Figure 2.3 The movement of a share price around its intrinsic value

intrinsic value. There will not necessarily be any unanimity in the market about what this should be. The value inferred from the mid point of the two limits can only be interpreted as the average of investors' estimates of its intrinsic value or, to be more precise, by the investor at the margin.[5] If the share price meets the upper band the investor will sell; if it meets the lower band, they will buy. This action will itself help the price stay within the bounds determined by transactions costs and contribute to the efficiency of the market. We will discuss later in this chapter how this may be computed.

This activity is known as 'arbitrage'. An arbitrageur is a trader who attempts to profit by exploiting price differences. For example, an arbitrageur will look for price differences across international exchanges. If the price of a share is different on the LSE (say 100p) to the price quoted on the New York Stock Exchange (120p), the arbitrageur will continue to buy these shares on the LSE and sell them on the NYSE until his actions have caused supply and demand to narrow the difference between the two exchanges such that it is no longer worth his while. Ivan Boesky is probably the most famous arbitrageur who looked for situations from which he would be able to profit. Although some of his activities were later shown to be illegal, there is no reason to believe that all arbitrage is always unlawful or dishonest or that it serves no useful purpose. On the contrary by exploiting inefficiencies, and thereby closing them, the arbitrageur is helping to make the market more efficient.

5 The investor at the margin is the last person to trade; the next would not because it is too costly.

The valuation of shares

There are three main methods of valuing a share or, in terms of our earlier terminology, calculating its intrinsic or fundamental value. It is possible to free ride the market to some extent by simply estimating a company's price:earnings (P/E) ratio (this is explained later) in comparison to others. This is commonly used by merchant banks when advising companies and is discussed first. A more theoretical approach that is based on a discounted present value method may be used: this is by far the most independent and accurate method and is discussed next. Third, it is possible to simply estimate the net asset value per share, although in most situations this is an inappropriate method.

The value of a share to an investor is determined by how much they think they will receive in the future from purchasing the share. A share, unlike most objects, has no beauty or utility and provides no benefit or enjoyment to its owner other than the income it produces and the price it would make when it is sold. Therefore, its value and price should be based on three main factors: its expected future returns, that is dividends per share, its eventual sale value and the certainty of these. Valuation is easier said than done. A company's past performance is likely to have been mixed. Sometimes it did well, sometimes not so well and its future is uncertain. Its future dividends are dependent on its future profitability which, in turn, is dependent on its financial and business performance. In order to value a share, therefore, it is necessary to forecast the likely future growth of profits and dividends and assess the certainty of these. All things being equal, investors would prefer a company that is able to offer relative certainty of its future dividends compared to a company that is unable to offer this – but would investors be prepared to accept a lower growth rate of future dividends for greater assurance?

THE P/E RATIO APPROACH

Because of the difficulty of forecasting those variables affecting the value of a share directly, an investor may decide to see how the market is actually valuing other similar companies and, after studying these, may be able to arrive at an assessment of the value of the company in question relative to others. Alongside the Stock Exchange list of the previous day's closing share prices, the serious newspapers provide a company's P/E ratio and other data to do this. The purpose of these is to help the investor estimate future returns from current data relating to current returns and the uncertainty of these being continued in the future.

A company's P/E ratio provides an investor with an indication of how the market rates the company and its future earnings and prospects. The higher the P/E the more the market (that is investors) is willing to pay for the company's earnings. This indicates that the market has high expectations about the company's future in terms of its growth in profits and, therefore, dividends. Conversely, a low P/E indicates that the company's shares are effectively cheap. This suggests that the market has low expectations about the company's future. It has low growth of profits and dividends expectations. A low P/E ratio could suggest that the company is undervalued in the same way that a high P/E ratio could suggest it is overpriced. There is no such thing as a 'right P/E'. It is simply determined by the market's expectations of the company's growth of earnings and dividends. Companies in different industries may have very different P/E ratios, not only because the market's expectations are different but because the market also believes their riskiness is different. All things being equal (including growth expectations) a riskier company will have a lower P/E ratio than a company believed to be safer.

A P/E ratio may be used to value a company's shares. It is the company's expected earnings per share multiplied by its expected P/E ratio[6] (see Table 2.1). Here, a company's next earnings per share are expected to be 25p and similar companies have a P/E ratio of 14.0. If so, its share price should be 350p. The variable that is critical to the calculation is the expected P/E ratio. Tables 2.2 and 2.3 show the variation in P/E ratios both across sectors and across firms within the same sector. Therefore, whilst the calculation may be easy to do, it may be difficult to do accurately because it is difficult to arrive at a good estimate of the company's P/E value without an intimate knowledge of its business and prospects. The published data relating to other companies' and sectors' yields, cover, and P/E provide the investor with an insight into what it should be.

Table 2.1 The valuation of a share by means of its estimated P/E

Expected earnings per share 25p
Estimated P/E 14.0 from the average of a sample of similar companies
Estimated share value 14 × 25p = 350p

6 Let 'P/E' = P/E where 'P/E' is the price earnings ratio, 'P' is price and 'E' is earnings. Multiply this equation by E. In which case P/E × E = P.

Table 2.2 Published financial data relating to some large general retailers as at 23 October 2007

	Actual yield (%)	Share price (p)	P/E	Beta	Estimated growth rates (%)*
Debenhams	4.7	103.5	8.1	0.92	2.5
Marks and Spencer	3.0	612	15.1	0.81	4
Morrison	1.4	297.2	24.2	0.75	5.6
J. Sainsbury	1.7	577.5	32.0	0.74	5.2
Tesco	2.2	464	17.9	1.05	5.9
Woolworths	8.9	20	21.0	1.11	−1.2

* These are calculated by means of the equation $g = r_M - (D_1/P_0)$. In the case of Marks and Spencer, this is 0.01029 = 0.043362 – 0.033333 where 0.043362 = 0.04 + 0.81(0.0815 – 0.04) where 0.04 is the risk free rate, beta is 0.81 and 0.0815 = 0.034 + (6459.3 – 6166.1)/6166.1 where 6166.1 and 6459.3 are the FTSE 100 indices on 23 October 2006 and 2007 respectively and the before-tax dividend yield is 0.03333 = 0.3/0.9 where the after-tax actual yield is 0.03 and tax is deducted on dividends at 10 per cent.

Table 2.3 UK average P/E ratios 23 October 2007

Oil and gas	12.16
Chemicals	25.76
Mining	10.04
Construction and materials	17.88
Aerospace and defence	18.95
General industrials	15.13
Electronic and electrical equipment	17.10
Health care equipment and services	29.53
Pharmaceuticals and biotechnology	13.60
Food and drug retailers	20.30
General retailers	16.93
Travel and leisure	12.41
Media	19.13
Utilities	13.97
Financials	10.11
FTSE 100	12.01

Source: *The Financial Times.*

Most of these data relate to 'yields': a yield is similar to a return. If you have money deposited in a bank or building society at, say, 5 per cent, this is its yield or return. The important point about yields for shares is that they are expressed as a percentage of the current market price in an attempt to make the return as real as possible by measuring it as the return the investor would receive if they had bought the shares that day at that price.

Let us take an example. As at 23 October 2007 the FTSE 100 Index stood at 6459.3. The FTSE Actuaries Share Indices showed that for the FTSE 100 that the P/E ratio was 12.01, the 'actual yield' was 3.06 per cent, and the 'cover' was 2.72.[7] The actual yield is the average across companies of dividends paid per year as a percentage of their share price that day. This is also known (and referred to in textbooks) as the 'dividend yield'. Cover is the number of times the earnings per share 'covers' the dividend per share. It is a measure of the security of the current level of dividends as it provides an indication of how much earnings would have to fall in order that they would have to be reduced. The actual yield (or dividend yield) may be contrasted with the 'earnings yield'. Whilst the actual yield relates to actual dividend receipts (hence its title according to *The Financial Times*), the earnings yield measures that yield an investor would receive if *all* the profits made that year and available to ordinary shareholders were paid to them as a dividend. It is, therefore, the earnings per share as a percentage of the share price. This ratio is not usually published as it is simply the reciprocal of the P/E ratio which is published. It follows from a simple piece of algebra that the actual yield multiplied by the cover will equal the earnings yield.[8] That is: $3.06 \times 2.72 = 8.32$ in our illustration where the actual yield as a percentage is the reciprocal of 12.01; that is $1/12.01 = 8.32$.

There is another yield measure. This computes the total return on the shares – both the dividends received during the year and the increase (or decrease) in the share price over the period. We will refer to this as the 'return', r, which, of course, can be negative. It is calculated as $\{[D + (P_1 - P_0)/P_0]\}$ where P represents the share price, the subscripts 0 and 1 refer to the beginning and end of the year, respectively and D refers to the dividend paid per share. This formula simplifies to $\{[(D_1 + P_1)/P_0)] - 1\}$. For the return to be expressed as a percentage, we simply multiply these formulae by 100. Clearly, an increase in the share price is an important component of the return on the share and, therefore, the return is a more appropriate measure than the actual yield. Some investors may regard it as the most important, especially if the dividend is quite low and they are investing in the company because they expect it to do well in the future. Nevertheless, it should be remembered that in order to actually

7 These are averages across companies.

8 If E and P are the same as in the previous footnote and D represents dividends then $(D/P) \times (E/D) = E/P$.

realize the return, the shares would have to be sold at the end of the year – and repurchased at the new price, of course.

THE PRESENT VALUE APPROACH

The value of a share is the same as that for any other investment: the present value of its future income. In the case of a share, its future income is its dividend stream. The present value of a future receipt is computed by reference to 'the time value of money'. Say interest rates are 10 per cent per annum. If I invested £1000 at 10 per cent it would have accumulated to £1100 in a year's time. In which case we could say that £1000 received today is equivalent to £1100 received in one year's time. Therefore, we may convert that £1100 back to its present value by the formula X/(1 + r) where X represents the future receipt and r represents the annual interest rate. Here £1100/(1.1) = £1000. Let us assume that later receipts are received at the end of a year. Let us also assume that the interest is also received at the end of a year and is reinvested at the same rate. Therefore, a receipt at the end of two years has a present value of $X/(1+r)^2$, a receipt at the end of three years has a present value of $X/(1+r)^3$ and so on. That is: £1000 received at the end of year one has a present value of £909 being 100/1.1; £1000 received at the end of year two has a present value of £826 being $1{,}000/(1.1)^2$; and £1,000 received at the end of year three has a present value of £751 being $100/(1.1)^3$. In other words, the present value of a sum of money received at the end of one, two and three years based on an interest rate of 10 per cent may be computed by multiplying it by 0.909, 0.826 0.751. These are sometimes referred to as 'discounting factors' and tables listing these for a range of interest rates and time scales exist for those unable or unwilling to calculate them by means of a pocket calculator.

We may now proceed to the calculation of the value of a share. Based on what we have said, this is:

$$V_0 = \frac{D_1}{1+r_e} + \frac{D_2}{(1+r_e)^2} + \frac{D_3}{(1+r_e)^3} + \cdots + \frac{D_n}{(1+r_e)^n} \qquad (1)$$

where V_0 represents the intrinsic value of the share now (point in time 0), r_e represents the required rate of return on the shares by investors (given the returns available elsewhere and the company's risk) and n as both a subscript and superscript represents infinity. In this model, the income stream continues for infinity. Why should the model assume this when an investor is only going to hold the stock for a finite period – perhaps, even for a very short period? Why doesn't the valuation model include the profit or loss made on the shares when the investor comes to selling them? It is assumed here that the investor will eventually sell them; that a new investor will similarly buy and hold them for a period and then sell them on to a new investor who will do likewise, and so on, and that this will continue for infinity – or at least, if not for infinity, for a very long time.[9] In which case, the returns to each investor will be the dividends plus the disposal value. This disposal value will be based on the present value at that time of future dividends to the next investor and so on. Therefore, the value of a share is simply the present value of all future dividends per share and Equation 1 above which contains dividends going into infinity is equivalent to a model which merely contains the dividends for a number of finite periods and the disposal value of the shares at the end of these.

It is unrealistic to assume that the dividend stream is constant. Let us assume that it grows at a constant rate, g. In which case:

$$P_0 = \frac{D_0(1+g)}{1+r_e} + \frac{D_0(1+g)^2}{(1+r_e)^2} + \frac{D_0(1+g)^3}{(1+r_e)^3} + \ldots + \frac{D_0(1+g)^n}{(1+r_e)^n} \qquad (2)$$

This simplifies to $P_0 = \dfrac{D_1}{r_e - g}$

For a proof of this see the Appendix at the end of this chapter. This is known as the Gordon growth model (Gordon 1962). It should be noted that the growth rate is compound. This may be estimated from the growth of previous dividends, say over the last four years. For example, say the dividends were 6.8p, 7.3p, 7.7p and 8p. So, over the four year period, dividends have grown from 6.8p to 8p. That is $6.8(1 + g)^4 = 8$; hence g = 4.1 per cent. Let us also say that an investor requires a return of 6 per cent; in which case the share price should be 438p which is (1.041 × 8)/(0.06 – 0.041).

If, of course, the expected growth of dividends is zero, the model simplifies to $P_0 = D/r_e$. A more likely problem in practice is that the model does not allow for changes in expected growth rates. This may be unrealistic. If it is necessary to adjust for such changes, the following variable growth model may be used:

$$P_0 = \underbrace{\frac{D_0(1+g_1)}{1+r_e} + \frac{D_0(1+g_1)^2}{(1+r_e)^2} + \ldots + \frac{D_0(1+g_1)^n}{(1+r_e)^n}}_{\text{present value of dividends during initial growth period } (g_1)} + \underbrace{\left[\frac{1}{(1+r_e)^{n+1}} \times \frac{D_{n+1}(1+g_2)}{r_e - g_2}\right]}_{\text{present value of stock relating to second growth period } (g_2)} \qquad (3)$$

9 As long as it is a reasonably long period, the calculation will not be impaired for not being based on infinity as after a few years, the discount factor quickly becomes infinitesimal.

This adjusts for one change in the growth rate. If this is still unrealistic, each expected dividend will have to be discounted individually in the same way that the present value of future £1000 receipts was calculated in the early part of this section. There is no simple model available as the future dividends are no longer constant or grow at a constant rate.

How should r_e be computed? The rate of return required by an investor on an investment depends on at least two things: the level of interest rates generally and the riskiness of the investment to the investor. An investor would require a return of the rate of interest payable on a risk-free investment plus a premium for risk. Figure 2.4 shows the required rate of return required by an investor for a specified level of risk.

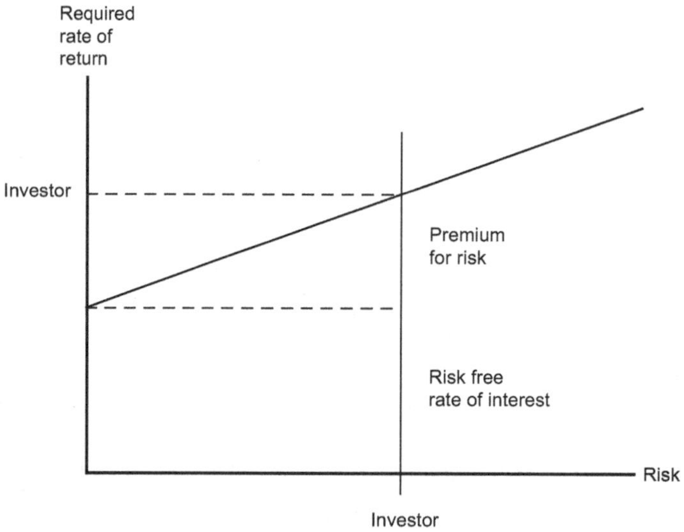

Figure 2.4 The risk-free rate of interest and the premium for risk

We have already discussed how a return or yield is computed. How is risk computed? The simplest way to do this reasonably properly is to estimate all the possible future returns for a particular period attaching a probability to each. It will then be possible to estimate the risk associated with that return in terms of its overall likelihood by computing the 'variance' or 'standard deviation' as a measure of the dispersion of that probability distribution. Using the usual notation, the variance is σ^2_E where σ represents the standard deviation and:

$$\sigma_E = \sqrt{\sum_{i=1}^{N} P_i \, (E_A - E_1)^2}$$

and p_i is the probability of estimate E_i and:

$$E_A = \sum_{i=1}^{N} (p_i . E_1)$$

is their weighted average. For example, say the estimates of the dividends per share for a particular period together with their probability are:

dividend	probability
20p	0.1
25p	0.2
30p	0.3
35p	0.3
40p	0.1

In which case, their average, E_A, is 30.5p and their standard deviation, σ_E, is 15.85.

An alternative, in the case of shares, is to take a similar measure of the historical returns, say over the last few years, of the dividends per share. That is:

$$\sigma_E^2 = \sum_{i=1}^{N} \frac{(E_A - E_i)^2}{N - 1}$$

where N represents the number of years for which we are computing the average and standard deviation and:

$$E_A = \sum_{i=1}^{N} E_1$$

is the dividends per share for year i. In the earlier example where there were dividends over four years, the average and standard deviation are, respectively, 7.45 and 0.519615.

Of course, there is no such thing as a completely risk-free investment and, therefore, a purely risk-free rate of interest cannot exist. Even the most secure investment is not entirely risk-free. The World may end tomorrow and the Bank of England, the City of London and the British Government could all be demolished. Nevertheless, we can get reasonably close to a risk-free rate by examining the rates offered on government securities, say Treasury bills.

Usually, this is about 4.0 per cent. Historical studies have shown that it has been consistently about that figure for most of the last century.

We have seen how an investor can measure the level of risk they are taking on by purchasing a particular security. By comparing this with similar data for other investments they are considering, they may choose how much risk to take on. It is also possible for an investor to combine investments to reduce their overall risk. Stock market risk can be reduced considerably simply by diversification, that is investing in more than one stock. If you invest in a single stock, you are exposed to a greater risk than if you invest the same amount of money spread over many stocks. By investing in more than one stock, an investor is avoiding 'putting all their eggs in one basket'. Consider Figure 2.5 which shows the fluctuations in profit of two companies, Abc plc and Xyz plc. When Abc plc does relatively well, Xyz plc does relatively badly and vice versa. The effect is that if an investor holds a portfolio comprising one half of his money in Abc plc and the other half of his money in Xyz plc, the riskiness of each stock is totally eliminated and, as a result, the riskiness of the investor's portfolio is negligible. Of course, this is an extreme example and the likelihood of two stocks' returns being perfectly negatively correlated over time is very low. It is also rare that they are perfectly positively correlated. Nevertheless, by diversifying in this way as far as possible, an investor is able to eliminate a large amount of risk, simply because the success and failure of different stocks are usually dependent on different factors. It is possible to reduce risk simply by choosing stocks at random. As their returns are unlikely to be perfectly positively or negatively correlated under all conditions, by simply

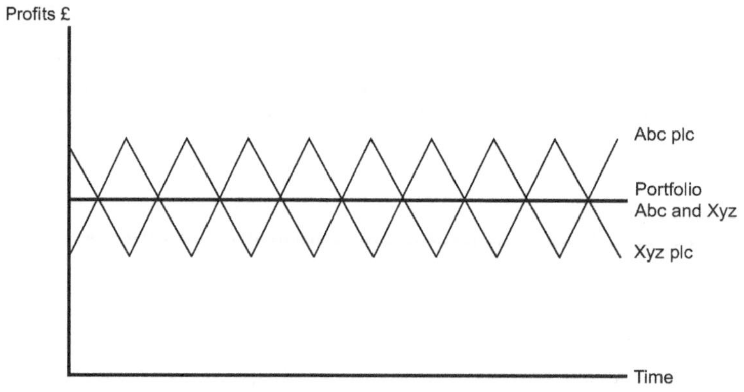

Figure 2.5 Diagram to show the variable earnings per share of two companies, Abc plc and Xyz plc, and how this may be eliminated by an investor who holds a portfolio comprising equal amounts invested in each

holding as many different stocks as possible, an investor is able to reduce the total portfolio risk. It has been estimated that by choosing fourteen stocks at random, an investor is able to eliminate a large proportion of their individual risks (see Figure 2.6).

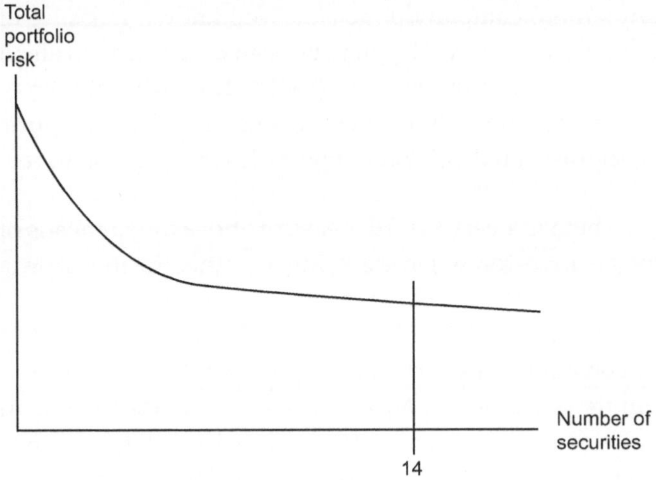

Figure 2.6 Diversification and portfolio risk

The amount of risk that an investor may eliminate by holding other stocks is known as 'diversifiable' risk or 'unsystematic' risk. These derive from the specific risks involved in investing in a particular stock. By investing in a number of these, the specific factors affecting individual companies tend to cancel one another out. Having diversified away as much of the portfolio's total risk as possible, the investor is left with the 'undiversifiable' risk or the 'systematic' risk. Systematic risk relates to that part of the riskiness of a stock that is common across all stocks. For example, all stocks are affected, but by different amounts, by changes in general economic conditions, interest rates and other general factors affecting the financial system.

This is an area of finance which has been the subject of much debate and analysis. The upshot of this as far as we are concerned is that the correct measure of the riskiness of an individual stock is the impact its individual risk has on the investor's portfolio as a whole. This may be computed by means of what is known as the Capital Asset Pricing Model (CAPM) which is:

$$r_{j,t} = \alpha_t + \beta_{j,}(r_{m,t} - \alpha_{j,t}) + e_{j,t}$$

where r represents return, the subscripts j and m represent company j and the market as a whole, α represents the risk-free rate of return, and e is an error term whose expected value is zero. It is assumed that α_t is constant across companies but not necessarily across time as interest rates change; hence the subscript, t, representing a specified time period. $\beta_{j,}$ does vary across companies and is known as the company's (here company j) 'beta', a well-known measure of the risk of investing in a company's stock. This may be seen diagrammatically in Figure 2.7 which shows the securities market line (SML). The SML may be estimated by plotting the returns for individual stocks against their betas. Figure 2.7 may be seen as a more sophisticated version of Figure 2.4 relating risk to return.

A company's beta is a very useful measure of risk and a means of predicting future risk for an investor when deciding whether to invest in a particular company. Betas are so often used that they are regularly published and readily available. However, their use is founded on one major assumption: that betas are reasonably constant across time. A company's published beta will have been estimated from its share price performance over the last few years. It is then proposed to be used to make an investment decision relating to that company's returns over the next few or more years. In other words, a measure of past risk is being used as an indicator of future risk. This is a major assumption and not surprisingly, the empirical evidence does not necessarily support this. In fact, it suggests that betas are unstable across time as to undermine their reliability (for a review see Fama and French 1992).

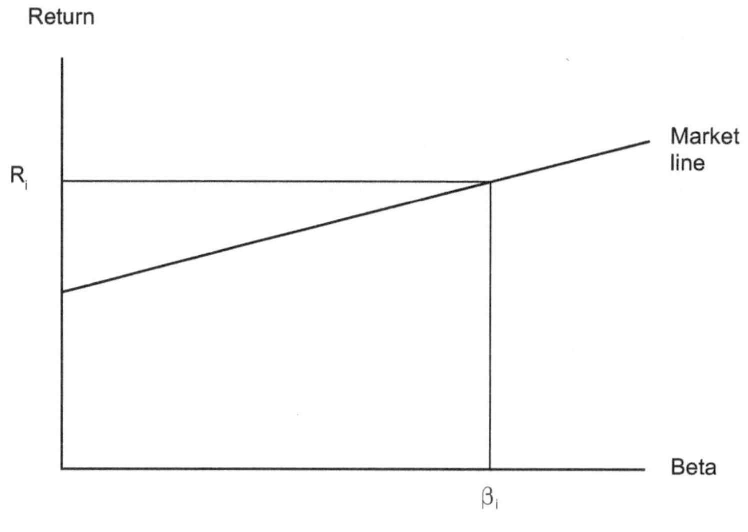

Figure 2.7 The securities market line showing the relationship between a company's beta and its required return

Let use the CAPM to calculate a stock's required rates of return and compute an intrinsic or fundamental value. Table 2.1 used earlier also lists the six retailers' betas. Because their share prices are available, it is possible by making further simplifying assumptions to estimate the growth rates built into these as at 23 October 2007. These are shown in the last column of Table 2.1 and are calculated by means of the Gordon growth model equation, $g = r_e - (D_1/P_0)$. For instance, Marks and Spencer's growth rate is computed as 4.0282 per cent. This is derived from the formula $g = r_e - (D_1/P_0)$. r_e may be computed using the CAPM where 0.04 is the risk free rate and Marks and Spencer's beta is 0.81. That is:

$$r_e = 0.073615 = 0.04 + 0.81(0.0815 - 0.04)$$

where r_m, the return on the market as a whole, is computed from published data relating to the before-tax dividend yield and the increase/decrease in the share price over the period. The before-tax dividend yield for the market as a whole is 0.034 = 0.0306/(1 – 0.1) where the published after-tax actual yield is 0.0306 and tax is deducted on dividends at 10 per cent. The increase in the FT index is computed from the FTSE 100 indices on 23 October 2006 and 2007 which are 6166.1 and 6459.3, respectively. Therefore:

$$r_m = 0.0815 = 0.034 + (6459.3 - 6166.1)/6166.$$

The final stage is to compute D_1/P_0, the company's before-tax actual yield. Its published after-tax actual yield is 0.03. This gives a before-tax yield of 0.033333 if tax is deducted on dividends at 10 per cent. That is:

$$0.033333 = 0.03/(1 - 0.10)$$

Marks and Spencer's growth rate, r_e, may now be computed as:

$$g = r_e - (D_1/P_0) = 0.073615 - 0.033333 = 0.040282$$

Having computed the growth rates underpinning the current prices, it is also possible to estimate values for these shares based on different growth expectations using the formula $P_0 = D_1/(r_e - g)$. For example, say you expected Marks and Spencer's growth rate to be 5 instead of 4 per cent. This puts a value on the shares of 864p. That is:

$$864 = 20.4/(0.073615 - 0.05)$$

where the next dividend is still assumed to be 20.4p. (These calculations will change slightly if the change in the growth rate is applied to the value of the next dividend D_1.) The existing share price of 612p is arrived at as 20.4/(0.073615 – 0.040282).

NET ASSETS PER SHARE METHOD

A common way of valuing shares that are not traded is to simply calculate the realizable value of the company's net assets and divide that total by the number of shares. Say a company had assets with a total disposal value of £1 200 000, debts of £300 000 and 200 000 shares. Its net assets per share are therefore 450p, that is (£1 200 000 – £300 000)/200 000. This figure may be particularly important when its financial performance is very poor and its value based on its future profitability and dividends is very low. It may also be particularly relevant for a takeover target when a bidder is considering buying a company and breaking up its assets (see Chapter 5 and Tobin's t).

The use of net assets per share is generally an inappropriate valuation, for two reasons. It is usually assumed that a company is a going concern and plans to continue trading. If so, a valuation of the business based on it being closed down and its assets being sold off is inappropriate. Second, this method probably significantly undervalues the company's worth if its assets are valued at their disposal value as opposed to their contribution to the value of the business as a going concern. Disposal values are often very low, even negligible in some cases, if the assets are specialized, whereas their value as part of a successful and continuing business may be much higher and, of course, more realistic.

That method is basing the calculation on the assets' disposal values. An alternative approach is to use their book values (that is the values at stated on the company's balance sheet) which are likely to be their historical cost. The historical cost of an asset is unlikely to equal its disposal value or its value as contributing to a continuing business. Therefore, the value of a share based on the book values of net assets is also unlikely to accurately or correctly indicate a reasonable price at which it should be bought or sold by an investor. However, it is likely to fall somewhere between these extremes and provide a preliminary indication of the share's worth.

'Technical analysis' or 'chartism', as opposed to fundamental analysis

So far we have looked at a 'rational' approach to buying and selling shares: computing a share's intrinsic value and comparing this to the market price. This is sometimes referred to a 'fundamental analysis'. Calculating what a stock should be worth is not the only basis on which an informed or sophisticated investor may decide to buy or sell shares. He may use a very different approach – 'chartism'. A chartist is someone who studies charts in the hope of predicting future changes in stock market prices instead of calculating their fundamental values. This is often referred to as 'technical analysis' and represents a behavioural as opposed to a rational approach.

Despite the evidence suggesting that this is an impossible task, chartists openly try to predict future share price movements purely from past performance. They look for patterns within charts created from share price movements and use them as buy or sell signals. Chartists believe that all the significant information about a company's performance is already reflected in the share price. Therefore, the study of price movements will itself provide the key to investment decisions.

It is not possible to fully explain their techniques here. Chartism is an art. It involves intuition, experience and skill and, given the same graph, two chartists may interpret it in different ways and, more importantly, make different buy and sell decisions. However, we can examine some of their tools. Chartists do not believe that share prices follow a random pattern. On the contrary, they look for patterns. Having identified a known pattern, they are able to forecast how that pattern will continue from their past experience.

Let us take some examples. Earlier we looked at the relationship between the upper and lower bands and how daily share price movements fluctuated between these two to reveal its intrinsic value. We rationalized this in terms of transaction costs and the point at which it would be worthwhile for an investor to buy or sell given the intrinsic value. However, we can just as easily rationalize such behaviour in chartist terms and the principle that a share price will remain within these 'tramlines'. If it significantly departs from these, there will have been a revision of some kind, that is that the fundamental value has changed or that it is in the process of changing.

Chartists believe that investors are very conscious of the price at which they bought a share. For example, say a share sold for about 100p for a long time during which many investors bought. Suppose the share price fell to 80p.

Chartists believe that those investors who had bought at 100p would not be prepared to take a loss. They would not sell but simply wait (and wait and wait if necessary) for it to rise to above 100p. As a result, the price of 100p becomes a resistance area. Each time the share price turns down again to 100p, the theory holds that the resistance level becomes even harder to cross as more investors will have bought at that price or above.

An extension of this psychology is the 'support level' or 'support area'. A chartist may argue that those investors who sold shares when the market was low and saw the share price rise, would be keen to buy it again at the price at which they sold. If this is so, the original level (100p) also becomes a support area which becomes stronger on each successive fall. Therefore, if a share price falls to a support area and then begins to rise, other traders may soon join in forcing the share price up leaving the old resistance area behind.

So far we have assumed that these tramlines are horizontal. They may not be; share prices rise and fall. We have just considered the possibility of a share price breaking out of these and upward. If so, there will be pressure for it to continue upward. If the trend continues, there will be expectations for it to continue to do so and a rising tramline will be the result with similar reasons as before for the share price not straying outside the two tramlines (see Figure 2.8 for an example). However, share prices rises do not continue for ever. Each time the share price reaches the tramline, the question arises: will the share price fall back and continue to rise or fall in accordance with the existing tramlines or will it break out and go in a new direction, forming a new set of tramlines? The answer to that depends on the opinion and skill of the chartist.

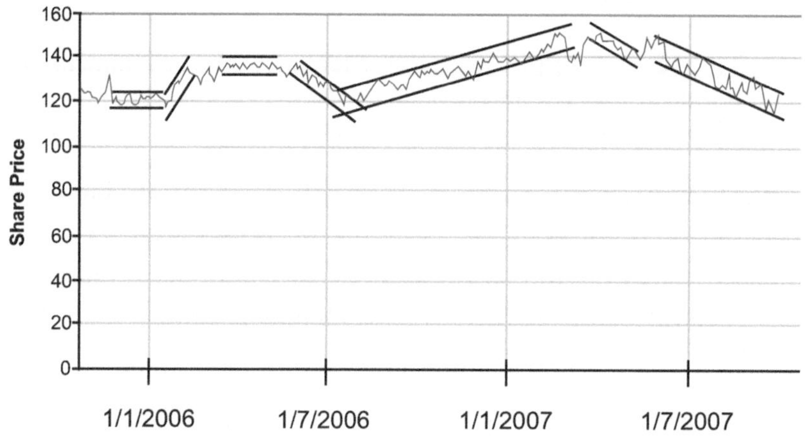

Figure 2.8 Share prices and tramlines – Aegis Group plc

There are other recognizable patterns. Probably the most famous is the 'head and shoulders'.[10] This is a large rise in the price that is halted at some stage, perhaps by profit taking by existing shareholders. The share price falls for a short period before continuing its steep rise again. This is the first shoulder. The steep rise in the share price cannot continue for ever and eventually it will peak. A similar situation may occur on the way down as it did on the way up. The shoulder in this case represents a temporary halt in the fall in the share price. Of, course, at each of these points when the share price changes direction, it is not known in which direction the new tramlines will go, or even if for certain, the existing one has ended. Again, the identification of a pattern to form the basis of a buy/sell decision is left to the skill of the chartist.

Why should such patterns exist? There is one very good reason. If a sufficient number of investors believe that a pattern exists and, as a result, trade on it, then it will occur – their behaviour will make it occur. If a share price is three-quarters of the way through a head and shoulders (say at the second shoulder), and it is recognized as such by enough investors, they will sell in the belief that the share price will soon fall dramatically. Their selling will cause this to happen. Perhaps, for that reason, the second shoulder is often not so pronounced as the first, as in the graph of Bisichi Mining plc share price in Figure 2.9.

In retrospect, of course, the head and shoulders pattern is recognizable. It may not have been so during its formation (say mid way through the price hike when the price was about 350p) and chartists who were presented with the graph at that time may have disagreed about its outcome. Some may correctly recognize it as a developing head and shoulders whilst others may simply interpret the tramlines in other ways. For instance it could have turned out differently – as it did earlier for Bisichi when the price peaked at about 275p and there was a downward movement to about 210p without a head and shoulders.

One final word: there is very little empirical evidence for chartists being able to outperform the market and earn above average returns. The ECMH evidence which is discussed fully in Chapter 4 implies that they cannot. The reason for a lack of evidence is because the chartist does not use mechanistic buy and sell rules but uses his skill and intuition in making such decisions. It is therefore not possible for a researcher to know and model what a chartist would have

10 This is a variation on the rise and fall of a share in line with Keynes' 'biggest fool theory'. See Chapter 4.

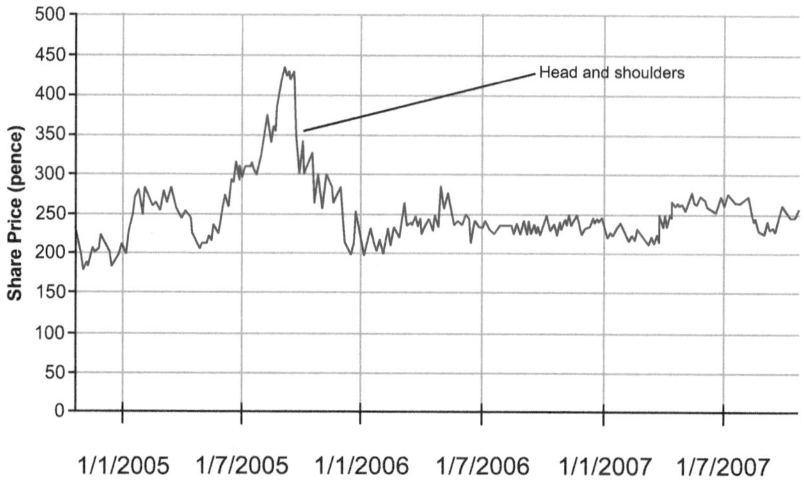

Figure 2.9 Bisichi Mining plc – share price

done. As a result, chartism cannot be said not to work and it remains an open question. Whilst this is so, many will still be persuaded that chartism can.

Conclusions

It was the purpose of this chapter to provide some background information. The way by which shares are traded was discussed together with recent developments brought about by advances in new technology and deregulation. It was also shown how shares may be valued based on their future dividends. This approach should be seen in stark contrast to the approach of chartists who totally ignore these and look to price changes alone. It is in the context of these that market moods, irrationality, bubbles and irrational exuberance by the market should be seen. These are the subject of the next chapter.

References

Fama, E.F. and K. French (1992) 'The Cross-section of Expected Returns', *Journal of Finance,* 47: 427–465.

Gordon, M.J. (1962) *The Investment, Financing and Valuation of the Corporation,* Irwin, Homewood, Ill.

Appendix
Derivation of Gordon Growth Model

Equation 2 simplifies to:

$$P_0 = D_0\left[\frac{1+g}{1+r_e} + \frac{(1+g)^2}{(1+r_e)^2} + \frac{(1+g)^3}{(1+r_e)^3} + \ldots\ldots + \frac{(1+g)^n}{(1+r_e)^n}\right] \tag{4}$$

Multiply both sides by $(1+r_e)/(1+g)$

$$P_0\frac{(1+r_e)}{(1+g)} = D_0\left[1 + \frac{1+g}{1+r_e} + \frac{(1+g)^2}{(1+r_e)^2} + \frac{(1+g)^3}{(1+r_e)^3} + \ldots\ldots + \frac{(1+g)^{n-1}}{(1+r_e)^{n-1}}\right] \tag{5}$$

Subtract Equation 4 from Equation 5:

$$P_0\left[\frac{1+r_e}{(1+g)} - 1\right] = D_0\left[1 - \frac{(1+g)^n}{(1+r_e)^n}\right] \tag{6}$$

Assuming $r_e > g$ and n approaches infinity, then the term in brackets on the right-hand side of the Equation 6 approaches unity. Therefore:

$$P_0\left[\frac{(1+r_e)-(1+g)}{(1+g)}\right] = D_0$$

and $(r_e - g)\, P_0 = D_0(1+g) = D_1$.

Therefore, $P_0 = \dfrac{D_1}{(r_e - g)}$

The Efficient Capital Markets Hypothesis

CHAPTER 3

It is often said (but usually only by economists) that whilst individuals may not act rationally some of the time, most people do most of the time. If we wished to forecast what most people would do in a situation, it would simply be a matter of establishing what a rational person would do. Hence, the market price which represents the collective view of investors, and in particular experts, is said to be 'rational' and what is known as the Efficient Capital Markets Hypothesis (ECMH), the subject of this chapter, is a part of 'rational economics'. See the Appendix in this chapter for a mathematical definition of the ECMH.

The theory

The idea that the stock market is informationally efficient and that this leads to allocative efficiency is probably an old one. However, it was not until the early 1960s that the full implications of stock market efficiency were studied. These were brought together in 1970 by Eugene Fama who defined the hypothesis that 'security prices fully reflect all available information' (1970, p. 383) together with a number of subhypotheses. Fama said that there were three forms of stock market efficiency: weak, semi-strong and strong.

THE WEAK FORM

This states that as all new information about the company is immediately and fully reflected in and by a new price movement. As we are unable to forecast new news, and past news is fully impounded in an existing share price, it follows it is not possible to predict new share movements from old share price movements. It also follows that the movement in a share price on one day is not correlated with the share price change the following day. This is often referred to as a 'random walk'. The principal implication of this is that an investor cannot use past share price movements to predict new price movements in an attempt to earn 'abnormal returns'. (Abnormal returns are defined as the earning of a higher return on a stock or portfolio than that which is on average earned by the market as a whole. Here and elsewhere, 'return' includes both the dividends received during the period plus the increase in the share price as defined in Chapter 2.) It also follows that information about recent trends in stock prices would be of no use in selecting stocks and studying patterns in the movement in a company's shares in order to earn abnormal returns is futile.

There have been many empirical studies of the weak form. They have almost unanimously concluded that there is no correlation between one day's share price change and the next. For a contemporary review see Brearley (1969). Economists have usually concluded that this supports the ECMH. However, it should be noted that this also supports an alternative hypothesis – that share price movements are totally unrelated to the provision of new information and, as a result, move randomly. We will examine some alternative theories to the ECMH that are more or less consistent with that proposition in Chapter 4.

THE SEMI-STRONG FORM

This states that share prices adjust immediately and once and for all to new information as it becomes publicly available. There have been many studies that have tested this.

It follows that as current market prices reflect all publicly available information, no one can consistently outperform the stock market and earn abnormal returns. There is, therefore, no point in attempting to do so. To quote the authoritative textbook, Brearley and Myers 'If capital markets are efficient, then purchase or sale of any security at the prevailing market price is never a positive NPV (net present value) transaction' (2006, p. 289). The important point about the semi-strong form is that it refers only to publicly available information and recognizes the existence of inside information and that those in possession of it can outperform the stock market.

Most of the early studies of the semi-strong form were 'event studies'. These studied the stock market reaction to the announcement of a new piece of information both during the days prior to, and after, the event. They compared the 'expected' normal return (based on the market as a whole for the same period) for a sample of shares that had experienced such an event over the period surrounding the event with their actual returns. The difference between the two (expected and actual returns) is referred to as the abnormal return and interpreted as the change in the share price in excess of the market caused by the event or new piece of information. Most studies have used what is known as the Market Model (see the Appendix in this chapter for a mathematical specification of this). If the abnormal returns were statistically significant and occurred prior to, or immediately after, the event or release of new information, they would be regarded as evidence to support the ECMH. Invariably, the evidence from these short-window event studies was consistent with market efficiency.

THE STRONG FORM

This states that current market prices reflect all relevant information, whether publicly available or privately held. It is generally believed that all large stock markets are efficient in the weak and semi-strong forms but they are not efficient in the strong form and that insiders and others who profit from inside information exist on a fairly large scale. Whilst academics have had access to the necessary information to test the other forms of the ECMH, they are usually unable to test the strong form because of the secrecy of inside traders. They have usually only been able to go so far as to infer from observed market reactions prior to the announcement of an important piece of news that insider dealing has occurred and on such a large scale as to cause share prices to change (Barnes 1996). These studies are reviewed in Chapter 9.

Problems with the ECMH

For many years, there was general agreement between academics about the ECMH and that in the words of Fama (1970) 'the evidence in support of the efficient markets model is extensive and (somewhat uniquely in economics) contradictory evidence is sparse' (p. 416). However, stock market crises and closer examination of share price behaviour have suggested a degree of inefficiency. We will look at the implications of the crises later but, more recently, the view has emerged that whilst share prices undoubtedly do adjust to new information, they do not necessarily do this instantaneously and, more importantly, they tend to overreact and may not discriminate between differences in the quality of information (Kothari 2001). Frankel and Lee (1998) write 'Price convergence to value is a much slower process than prior evidence suggests.' Almost all of the evidence is from the US, but it is reasonable to presume that the situation is similar in the UK. Certainly, there is no reason to suppose the UK markets are more efficient than those in the US.

Regarding overreaction, there have been many US studies comparing the immediate share price reaction to the release of new information with the longer-term behaviour, say, over the next five years. For a summary of these see Kothari (2001). However, the evidence provided by these longer-term studies should not necessarily be accepted. There are significant empirical estimating problems in drawing inferences from longer time periods. For example, the event studies assume for the short window examined that other factors affecting the share price are either negligible or, if not, cancel one another out as they are equally likely to be good as bad news. In the case of longer-term studies, such an assumption cannot so easily be justified.[1]

I have conducted most of the few studies in the UK of this phenomenon. In the first, I examined the share price reactions of bidding firms at the time of a merger announcement (Barnes 1978). It is obvious that the share price of a target firm will increase because of the premium offered to the target's shareholders. It is less obvious what should happen to the shares of the bidder. They should increase if the expected present value of the benefits from merger (usually referred to as 'synergy') exceed the premium paid to the target's shareholders. Given the large premium that is usually offered, it is not certain that this will be so. (These issues are discussed in full in Chapter 5.) I found that, whilst the bidder's share prices at the time of the announcement of the bid did, on average, marginally increase, after a longer time period they actually fell.

During the 25-month period following the announcement, bidders' share prices fell by 11.25 per cent, although by month 60 (5 years after the bid) this had recovered to minus 6.3 per cent (Barnes 1984). Whilst this evidence supports the general hypothesis of overreaction, it is also consistent with the view that management overstate the benefits from merger at the time of the bid and the market is unable to recognize these exaggerations.

The reaction of share prices to earnings announcements

The US evidence also suggests that the relationship between market prices and reported profits or earnings (these two terms are used interchangeably) is complex. Clearly, future earnings are a fundamental (probably the most important) component of the calculation of the value of a share. However,

1 Over a longer period, whilst there are likely to be many events to cancel one another out, it is also likely that there will also be major events that cannot be ignored. For example, say the event being examined is a merger announcement. If the merger is successful, it is likely that the company will embark on another. This will be such a major event with implications for the company's share price that it cannot be ignored and assumed to be cancelled by some other event. This raises problems for the researcher, who can either attempt to adjust the measure of share price performance over that longer period in some way or he can restrict his sample, in this case of companies involved in mergers, to only those companies involved in only one merger. If the researcher chooses the second, the sample will be biased against companies that had experienced a good merger and embarked on another.

information affecting expected earnings is diverse, subjective, possibly biased and untimely. At first glance, the annual earnings announced at, or just before, a company's annual general meeting are likely to be most important. However, these are historical with very limited relevance to future returns although they may be compared with what the market was expecting. They may also contain new information from which analysts may improve their estimates of future earnings. In other words, the amount of new information being provided in the publication of the annual financial statements may be quite small and mainly inferential.

The most famous academic study to confirm such a role for annual financial statements is still Ball and Brown (1968) who found that companies' share price movements anticipated their earnings results and that there was virtually no abnormal share price movement immediately after the announcement. Ball and Brown estimated whether a company had exceptionally good or bad earnings (that is significantly above or below those expected) relative to other similar firms.[2] They then measured the share price behaviour of those firms over the period 12 months prior to the earnings announcement to 6 months afterwards. They found that firms whose results were better than expected earned above-average stock market returns and firms whose results were worse than expected earned below-average stock market returns. More importantly, Ball and Brown found that only about 10 to 15 per cent of the total price adjustment over the entire period took place in the month in which the final earnings announcement was made and that the remaining 85 to 90 per cent of the adjustment occurred earlier (see Figure 3.1).

The other seminal work, also at that time and also in the US, is Beaver (1968). Beaver avoided the problem of specifying an earnings model in the way that Ball and Brown found necessary and simply examined the variability of share returns and the volume of trading at the time of the earnings announcement compared with other periods. He found that the volume of trading was 33 per cent higher in that week compared with other weeks (see Figure 3.2).

2 The model used to forecast under- or over-performance is similar to the market model described in the Appendix. Here:

$$\Delta I_j = \alpha + \beta \Delta R_m + e_j$$

where ΔI_j represents the change in the earning for company j in comparison with those for the previous year, ΔR_m represents the change in the earning for all companies in comparison with their earnings for the previous year and the error term, e_j, represents the abnormal performance of company j, α is the intercept term and β the regression coefficient. β and α are estimated by means of simple regression analysis in which e has an expected value of zero. From this model we can derive the expected change in earnings for firm j by substituting in the value ΔR_m and comparing with it the actual change in j's earnings. The difference will show whether the firm under- or over-performed compared with expectations.

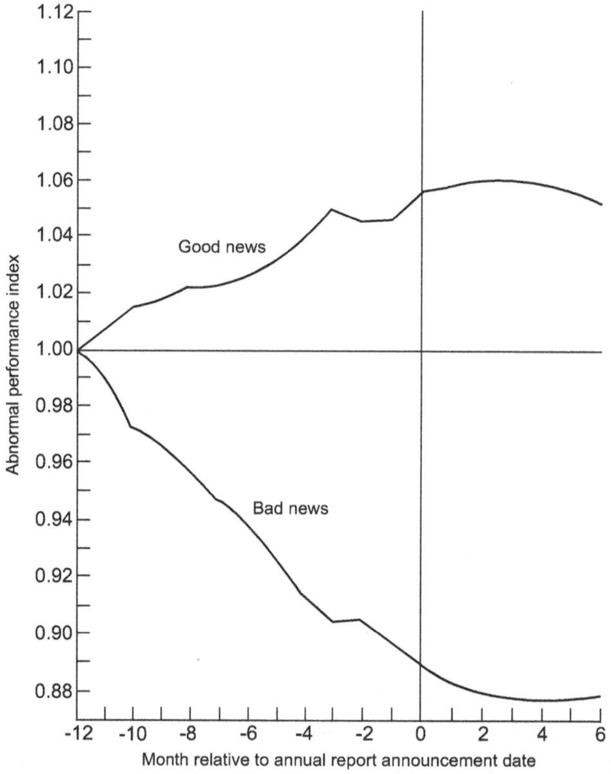

Figure 3.1 Monthly stock returns in anticipation of earnings announcements (Ball and Brown 1968)

Beaver saw this as evidence of increased information for investors at the time of the earnings announcement in which the earnings announcement resolves uncertainty and narrows the homogeneity of beliefs causing trading between those with different beliefs.

The interesting thing about these two very influential studies is that they are both taken as providing evidence for the ECMH even though they may be seen as both contradictory to one another and the ECMH. The Ball and Brown study showed that the market anticipates published earnings and that the actual announcement is something of an anticlimax in that the share price reaction is limited to an adjustment between what was expected and what actually occurred. On the other hand, the study by Beaver found that the earnings announcement, rather than being an anticlimax, caused an increase in the volume of trading. It is interesting also to speculate whether different findings would contradict the ECMH. Say that Ball and Brown had found

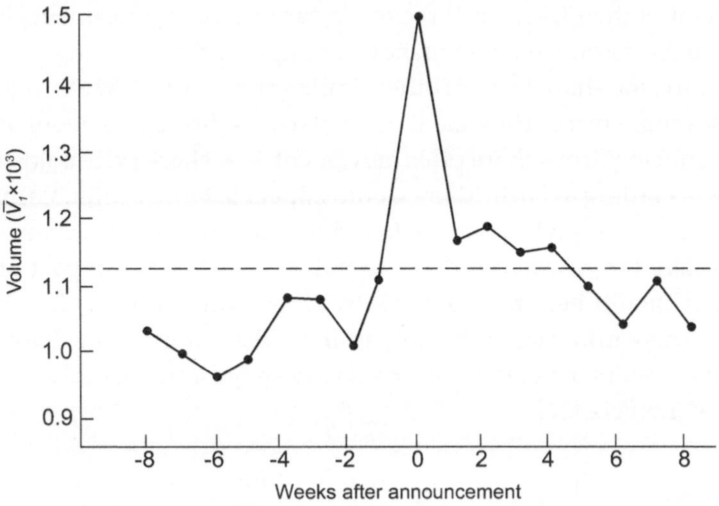

Figure 3.2 Volume of trading in company securities around the earnings announcement (Beaver 1968)

large share price changes at the time of the earnings announcement. Surely this suggests that the market is adjusting to new information, confirming the ECMH? In the same way, say Beaver had found reduced trading at the time of the announcement. Surely this was evidence of the market having already estimated earnings accurately, thereby confirming the ECMH? In both cases, completely opposite results could be interpreted as being consistent with the ECMH. It also follows that, whatever the results, both of these studies could be interpreted as being *inconsistent* with the ECMH. Ball and Brown's actual results could be seen as evidence that the market does not act on earnings news and Beaver's actual results could be seen as providing equivocation in the market and, therefore, heterogeneous expectations leading to increased trading. It is also interesting that the actual Ball and Brown evidence suggests that if an investor knew that a firm was going to under- or over-perform other firms, then they could earn large abnormal returns. This is, of course, contrary to the ECMH which suggests that this is not possible.

Another example of how we may differently interpret what is at first glance evidence supporting the ECMH is the evidence relating to the weak form. Whilst uncorrelated returns for successive days and the random walk of share prices may suggest that share prices instantaneously adjust to new information, they could equally be seen as evidence that share prices do not adjust to information at all (new or old) but simply move in a totally unpredictable and random way, for example purely in accordance with supply and demand.

A variant of the ECMH as it relates to earnings announcements is that one firm's earnings announcement will have an impact on the earnings expectations and, therefore, the share price of other similar firms. Firth (1976a) found that on average the share price adjustment of similar-type firms was about 54 per cent of the announcing firm's share price movement. The share price adjustment was quick and, according to Firth, 'there would appear to be no profitable mechanical investment strategies which can be based on earnings announcements' (1976a, p. 304). Again, the research did not hypothesize what the impact of the new information should be. Therefore, whilst at face value this evidence supports the ECMH (new information having an immediate impact on share prices), a more precise model using the same data may suggest the partial adjustment as evidence of inefficiency.

The suggestion that the market may not fully adjust to reported financial information raises a number of fundamental questions. Does the market adjust for differences in accounting methods between companies when one reporting method is likely to show the company in a better light than another and does the market 'see through' management bias in reported earnings and estimates? If it does not, then clearly it is not efficient.

The general view is that, in respect of the simplest changes, to the extent that they are able, investors and financial analysts are sufficiently astute to see through these and the raising of reported earnings by altering accounting procedures will not necessarily result, even in the short run, in higher stock prices (Firth 1976b). However, more recently, the view certainly in the US is that the market does not fully adjust for such changes and that 'Wall Street rewards reported earnings'. That is, the market does not fully adjust shares prices for differences in reported earnings (or, to be more precise, capitalized future earnings) that are purely due to the ways by which they are measured. However, these researchers did not discover large differences in the prices of firms employing different accounting methods (Kothari 2001).

Whilst some investors may be able to see through an accounting change, others may not and it may not even be possible. A number of the early ECMH event studies examined whether share prices changed as a result of a change in the way in which certain items in the financial statements were measured, for example depreciation and inventory, thereby affecting reported profits. The researchers hypothesized that as there was no economic change, that is the company's profitability had not changed but merely the way it was measured, there should be no effect on share prices. The studies supported the hypothesis. For an authoritative, although old review see American Accounting Association

(1977). However, in many cases, there was an economic effect. For example, tax payable on the reported profits may be affected and when it becomes due. Unfortunately, investors may not be sufficiently informed of the effect on the reported profits of the change, and would, therefore, be unable to change their assessment of the value of the company's shares accurately.

Additionally, some investors, possibly enough to affect the share price, may be affected by what is known as 'functional fixation'. Functional fixation relates to the inability of decision-makers to change their decision-making processes in response to a change in the accounting process that provided them with the data. The failure of investors to change their decision-making processes to a change in accounting method is attributable to this phenomenon. Ijiri, Jaedicke and Knight (1966) were the first to 'borrow' the concept from psychologists who usually used it in relation to objects, for example boxes, pliers and paper clips, to investigate how individuals' problem solving was impaired or inhibited by their prior use, and apply it to data processing.[3] There have been many empirical studies in accounting, usually supporting the hypothesis (for a summary see Riahi-Belkaoui 2004). Consider the input–output process of an investor's decision-making process in which the input is annual earnings and the output is the intrinsic value of the stock. The process, in its simplest form may be the use of a multiple, for example the P/E ratio (see Chapter 2). A change in the accounting method implies that the investor should slightly change the value of the multiple. The functional fixation hypothesis suggests that they may not do so because they have been conditioned to do it in a certain way, or use a certain multiple and they are unable (for whatever reason) to revise the multiple as they should. The literature suggests that whilst some investors may act in this way, other abler, 'sophisticated', investors may not. It is separate empirical question as to whether there is a sufficient number of 'sophisticated' investors at the margin to affect the share price. The possibility of this occurring is referred to as the 'extended functional fixation hypothesis' (Riahi-Belkaoui 2004).

The issue of the manipulation of accounting data by means of a change in accounting method is left to Chapter 8 to be examined in a UK context. However, it must be said that this is not an unexpected result. Companies do change accounting methods in order to improve their reported earnings, and they would not do this if they did not believe that it had no effect.

3 For a discussion of how the hypothesis has been changed by accounting researchers and how it is different in the two disciplines see Barnes and Webb (1986).

Reconsideration of the ECMH has led recent studies of the reaction of share prices to earnings announcements to suggest 'post-earnings announcement drift'. Even after earnings are announced, abnormal returns have been found to persist and a tendency for abnormal returns to be predictable on the basis of past earnings announcements. For 'good news' firms, the drift is upwards (that is, prices increase), whereas for 'bad news' firms share prices continue to fall. Hew *et al.* (1996) found post-earnings announcement drift for both interim and final announcements in the UK for the smallest two-thirds of LSE companies but not for the largest one-third. One interpretation is that share prices fully react to earnings news but only after a considerable lag. Whilst markets do react to the earnings announcement, it takes up to 60 days for the full effect to be impounded in the share price (Bernard and Thomas 1989). In other words, investors under-react to very fundamental signals leading to forecast errors and incomplete share price adjustments. There may be other explanations. For example, share prices reacted correctly in the first place, but the 'good' or 'bad' news affected analysts' subsequent perceptions and judgments.

Suggestions that share prices underreact or overreact to new information, or even that investors are misled by data relating to future earnings and dividends per share, have led to a belief by academics that share prices may be mispriced and the formation of the 'incomplete revelation hypothesis' (Bloomfield 2002). This hypothesis, which is best seen as a qualification to the ECMH, suggests that some accounting numbers are more difficult or costly to uncover or understand and as a result their effect may not be fully reflected in share prices. In other words, data or estimates that are more costly or more difficult to derive from publicly available data are less completely revealed by market prices than those that are cheaper and more easily obtained. Therefore, difficult and costly data derive less interest from investors than easily derived data. For example, critical information that may be hidden in footnotes will have less impact on a share price than if it were presented in the main body of the financial statements.

Other influences contributing to market efficiency and inefficiency

In Chapter 1, it was suggested that, nowadays, there are other parties involved in the information evaluation process contributing to market efficiency who, possibly because of their lack of independence, contribute bias.

In addition to the historical financial statements, management inform shareholders of their expectations and possibly provide forecasts. Management forecasts affect investors' beliefs and expectations. Investors are likely to regard these as superior to general market expectations because management are more familiar with the company than both them and analysts. However, empirical evidence suggests that management forecasts are no more accurate than outside experts' forecasts and the general view (certainly in the US) is that the market fails to recognize their optimistic bias (Kothari 2001). Management are reluctant to release bad news and revise expectations downwards (even though they have an obligation to do so) whereas they are eager to revise expectations upwards.[4]

Financial analysts collect information from public and private sources, use their expertise to evaluate the current performance of a company, make forecasts about its future prospects, and make recommendations to investors whether to buy, hold or sell its shares. Their actions, therefore, affect the efficiency of the stock market. The share prices of companies with higher analyst interest adjust to the release of new information more quickly than those with less analyst interest (Barth and Hutton 2004). Overall, academic studies indicate that financial analysts add value by reducing investor risk. (For a review of the extensive evidence see Healy and Palepu 2001.) Their earnings estimates are more accurate than those generated by statistical models using publicly available data. Most importantly, their reports are likely to influence stock market prices and become self-fulfilling, because not only do small investors act on their public recommendations but so do financial institutions with huge holdings.[5] It is also necessary to distinguish between the incentives of differently employed analysts. An analyst may have an incentive for independent, objective and accurate estimates and recommendations or, on the other hand, may be rewarded for providing information that generates trading volume and investment banking fees for the client brokerage houses. In which case, the analyst may have an incentive to make optimistic forecasts and recommendations. This conflict may be particularly acute if there were no regulations or in-house rules (such as Chinese walls) when an analyst's own brokerage house has been hired to underwrite or is being considered to underwrite a new issue.

Auditors also contribute to efficiency by providing investors with an independent assurance that the company's financial statements are true and fair. The fact that share prices react to earnings announcements demonstrates

4 The buying and selling of company shares by insiders prior to management forecasts, is of course insider dealing and unlawful. Such cases as exist in the UK are described in Chapter 8, For the USA, see Noe (1999).

5 In the US, this has led to insider dealing.

that investors regard accounting information as credible. As companies whose shares are traded on the LSE (or for that matter, most other exchanges) are required to have their financial statements audited, it is not possible to know whether their credibility derives from this or the legal liability of management if they provide misleading information. Nevertheless, there is clear evidence that if the credibility of the auditing firm is undermined, this does affect the market's confidence in its clients' financial statements resulting in a fall in their share prices. Chaney and Philipich's (2002) event study of the impact on the share price of Andersen's clients at the time of the Enron scandal and Barton's (2005) study of how those clients visible in the capital markets quickly replaced it with other auditing firms with an untarnished reputation illustrate this.[6] Any suggestion, or perception, in the market that an auditor is prepared to accept lower standards are simply deadly to the reliability of a company's earnings.

Although we can assume that a clean audit report does add credibility to the financial statements (and, therefore, adds value to the company), research into their effect suggests there is no stock market reaction to their issue. This is primarily because an unqualified report provides no new information to investors. Unless there are indications to the contrary, the market will expect and assume an unqualified report (Healy and Palepu 2001). The first UK study of these issues was Firth (1978) who found that a qualified report did affect a company's share price, although the extent depended on the type of the report. (The significance of a qualified audit report can range from being innocuous, for example the auditor being unable to conduct certain tests, to threatening the future viability of the company, for example a going concern qualification. See Chapter 7.) A more recent study by Taffler, Lu, and Kausar (2004) updated this. They found that shares of companies with going concern qualifications underperformed the stock market by between 24 per cent and 31 per cent depending on the benchmark used. The issue of auditor independence will be taken up in Chapter 7.

Other signals in an efficient market

The important point about the ECMH and related empirical studies is that it is only in very rare instances that it is possible to know precisely how much a share price should move in response to new information and, even then, the actual change includes an adjustment for the signal inferred. For example, even

6 Krishnamurthy *et al.* (2006) also show that when firms quickly dismissed Arthur Andersen, the abnormal returns at the time of the announcement were significantly higher when firms switched to a Big 4 auditor than when they switched to a non-Big 4 auditor or did not announce its identity.

when shareholders in a target company are offered a specific amount of cash for their shares, the share price does not usually change to that figure but to a higher price than that offered. It will take into account the likelihood and value of an improved offer the original offer has prompted.

There are other examples of the share price adjusting to signals inferred by investors relating to other matters. For example, if a company issues new shares instead of cash when making a dividend, the market will usually react badly because this is a signal that the company has cash difficulties (Bechmann and Raaballe 2007). (On the other hand, it could suggest that it is planning to invest this money in a particularly profitable project and the share price will rise.) Another example is the form of consideration in a takeover bid. Offering shares, suggests that management believe the shares are currently overvalued (or, at least, not undervalued). The share price will fall in response to this signal. Similarly, offering cash as consideration suggests that the company is not prepared to offer shares because it considers the current price to understate their real value. This is a good signal and will push the share price upwards (Travlos 1987). In the case of a scrip issue, it is possible to calculate what the price should be.[7] Nevertheless, it may not change to that. The naive investor may think they are being given something they do not already own. The

7 A scrip issue is little more than an accounting adjustment. When a company has retained profits, these appear on its balance sheet as 'reserves'. These may be considerable if the company has been trading profitably for some time and may outweigh its ordinary shares as a proportion of total shareholders' funds. Say a company had shareholders' funds of:

- Ordinary shares capital (10p par value × 500 million shares in issue) = £50m.
- Profit and loss account reserves = £250m.

Also suppose that the share price was 900p. The directors of the company may decide that the shares would be more marketable if the share price was lower. One way to achieve this is to have a scrip issue and convert some of the reserves (which the shareholders already own as they own the company) into new share capital. Say the company decided to convert £50 million of reserves into new shares in the following way:

- Create 500 million new shares at 10p par value.
- Use £50 million from the reserve account to make them 'fully paid'.
- Give the new shares to existing shareholders pro rata to their existing holding; that is one new share for every share they already hold.

After the scrip issue shareholders' funds would appear on the balance sheet as:

- Ordinary share capital £100 million.
- Profit and loss account reserves = £200 million.

Shareholders now have twice as many shares as they had before but total shareholders funds have not changed. They are still £300 million. The price of the shares will change to reflect the fact that there are now twice as many in issue. Instead of being 900p each, they will be 450p.

sophisticated investor, knowing that they already own the reserves being conferred on them, would not adjust their judgement of their intrinsic value. Instead, they may infer from the announcement that the company is short of good news and is attempting to provide some. As a result they may adjust their valuation downwards – especially if they were expecting some good news and this was the best the company could do! (Myers and Majluf 1984).

On the one hand, therefore we see the market as very efficient and very sophisticated in revising its judgements affecting investors' intrinsic values. On the other hand, we have seen evidence that the market is not as sophisticated as we would expect in relation to, say, accounting data. We may reconcile these views by remembering that sufficient investors need to act in order for a price to change.

Final remarks

I have attempted in this chapter to review the evidence relating to the efficiency of the market. Despite the overwhelming expectation that it could hardly be anything other than efficient, the empirical evidence is not as convincing as may be expected – or was believed to be so in 1970 by Fama. In some respects the market is very efficient with sophisticated investors looking for subtle inferences from new pieces of information. In other respects it is not, for example where the market appears to be easily misled by accounting data. The most important aspect, however, is how investors turn news and information into judgements. It is here the ECMH fails us. It is a 'black box' and says very little about the process. We should, therefore, look to other theories to explain how as a result of negligible new information the market can alter its judgements radically at times. These are examined in the next chapter.

References

American Accounting Association, Committee on Concepts and Standards for External Financial Reports (1977) *Statement on Accounting Theory and Theory Acceptance*, (SOATATA), Sarasota, FL, American Accounting Association.

Ball, R. and P. Brown (1968) 'An Empirical Evaluation of Accounting Numbers', *Journal of Accounting Research*, 6: 159–177.

Barnes, P.A. (1978) 'The Effect of a Merger of the Share Price of the Attacker', *Accounting and Business Research*, 9: 162–168.

Barnes, P.A. (1984) 'The Effect of a Merger on the Share Price of the Attacker Revisited', *Accounting and Business Research*, 15: 45–49.

Barnes, P.A. (1996) 'The Regulation of Insider Dealing in the UK. Some Empirical Evidence Concerning Share Prices, Merger Bids and Bidders' Advising Merchant Banks', *Applied Financial Economics,* 6: 383–391.

Barnes, P.A. and J. Webb (1986) 'Management Information Changes and Functional Fixation: Some Evidence from the Public Sector', *Accounting, Organizations and Society,* 1–18.

Barth, M.E. and A.P. Hutton (2004) 'Analyst Earnings Forecast Revisions and the Pricing of Accruals', *Review of Accounting Studies,* 9(1): 59–96.

Barton, J. (2005) 'Who Cares About Auditor Reputation?', *Contemporary Accounting Research,* 22(3): 549–586.

Beaver, W. (1968) 'The Information Content of Annual Earnings Announcements', *Journal of Accounting Research,* 6 (Supplement): 67–92.

Bechmann, K.L. and J. Raaballe (2007) 'The Differences between Stock Splits and Stock Dividends: Evidence on the Retained Earnings Hypothesis', *Journal of Business Finance and Accounting,* 34(3–4): 574–604.

Bernard, V. and J. Thomas (1989) 'Post-earnings Announcement Drift: Delayed Price Response or Risk Premium?', *Journal of Accounting Research,* 27: 1–48.

Bloomfield, R.J. (2002) 'The "Incomplete Revelation Hypothesis" and Financial Reporting', *Accounting Horizons,* 21: 233–243.

Brearley, R.A. (1969) *An Introduction to Risk and Return from Common Stocks,* Cambridge, MTMA, MIT Press.

Brearley, R.A. and S.C. Myers (2006) *Principles of Corporate Finance,* London, McGraw-Hill.

Chaney, P.K. and K.L. Philipich (2002) 'Shredded Reputation: The Cost of Audit Failure', *Journal of Accounting Research,* 40: 1221–1246.

Fama, E. (1970) 'Efficient Capital Markets: A Review of Theory and Empirical Work', *Journal of Finance,* 25: 383–417.

Firth, M. (1976a) 'The Impact of Earnings Announcements on the Share Price Behaviour of Similar Type Firms', *The Economic Journal,* 86(342): 296–306.

Firth, M. (1976b) *Share Prices and Mergers,* Farnborough, Saxon House.

Firth, M. (1978) 'Qualified Audit Reports: Their Impact on Investor Decisions', *The Accounting Review,* 53(3): 642–651.

Frankel, R. and C.M.C. Lee (1998) 'Accounting Valuation, Market Expectation, and Cross-xsectional Stock Returns', *Journal of Accounting and Economics,* 9: 195–228.

Healy, P.M. and K.G. Palepu (2001) 'Information Asymmetry, Corporate Disclosure, and the Capital Markets: A Review of the Empirical Disclosure Literature', *Journal of Accounting and Economics,* 31(1–3): 405–440.

Hew, D.L.L. Skerrat, N. Strong and M. Walker (1996) 'Post Earnings-Announcement Drift: Some Preliminary Evidence for the UK', *Accounting and Business Research,* 27: 283–293.

Ijiri, Y., R.K. Jaedicke and K.E. Knight (1966) 'The Effects of Accounting Alternatives of Management Decisions', in R.K. Jaedicke, Y. Ijiri, and O. Neilson (eds) *Research in Accounting Measurement,* pp. 186–199. New York, American Accounting Association.

Kothari, S.P. (2001) 'Capital Markets Research in Accounting', *Journal of Accounting and Economics,* 31(1–3): 105–231.

Krishnamurthy, S., J. Zhou and N. Zhou (2006) 'Auditor Reputation, Auditor Independence, and the Stock Market Impact of Andersen's Indictment on Its Client Firms', *Contemporary Accounting Research,* 23(2): 465–490.

Myers, S.C.and N.S. Majluf (1984) 'Corporate Financing and Investment Decisions when Firms have Information that Investors do not have', *Journal of Financial Economics,* 13: 187–222.

Noe, C. (1999) 'Voluntary Disclosures and Insider Transactions', *Journal of Accounting and Economics,* 27: 305–326.

Riahi-Belkaoui, (2004) *Accounting Theory,* London, Thompson Learning.

Taffler, R.J., J. Lu and J. Kausar (2004) 'In Denial? Stock Market Under-Reaction to Going-Concern Audit Report Disclosures', *Journal of Accounting and Economics,* 38: 263–296.

Travlos, N. (1987) 'Corporate Takeover Bids, Means of Payment and Bidding Firms' Stock Returns', *Journal of Finance,* 42: 943–964.

Appendix
A Mathematical Statement of the ECMH

Fama provides a mathematical definition of the hypothesis:

$$E(p_{j,t+1} \mid \Phi_t) = [1 + E(r_{j,t+1} \mid \Phi)]p_{j,t}$$

where E is the expected value operator, $p_{j,t}$ is the price of a share in company j at time t; $p_{j,t+1}$ is its price at t + 1; $r_{j,t+1}$ is the return on an ordinary share in j during the period t to t + 1,that is $[(p_{j,t+1} - p_{j,t})/ p_{j,t}]$; Φ_t is a general symbol for whatever set of information is assumed to be 'fully reflected' in the price at t. Fama's definition simply states that the share price at t + 1 (tomorrow) is determined by the expected return for that period conditional on information at t (Φ_t) which is fully reflected in the share price at t. The one period return $E(r_{j,t+1}) = [E(p_{j,t+1}) - p_{j,t}]/ p_{j,t}$ simplifies to $E(r_{j,t+1}) = [E(p_{j,t+1})/p_{j,t}] -1$. This may be rearranged as $E(p_{j,t+1}) = [1 + E(r_{j,t+1})]p_{j,t}$.

Although at first glance this equation appears to be very precise and 'scientific', this is, in fact not the case. On the contrary, it is little more than a 'black box' in which the inputs – what is known at t: $p_{j,t}$ and expected at that time $E(r_{j,t+1} \mid \Phi_t)$ – and outputs – $E(p_{j,t+1} \mid \Phi_t)$ relating to t +1 but as expected at t based on information at that time – are defined and identified but the process (that is, what is happening in the box) is not specified. (A black box is a theory relating to inputs and outputs where nothing is known, or at least nothing is defined or specified, about the transformation process of the inputs into outputs.) This is an important point because it allows for irrationality, changing moods and sentiment in the market both generally and about the company concerned. The model implies that a change in the information, that is new information, causes a revision of the share price. However, a change in the share price may occur where there is no new information but just a change in market mood or sentiment, that is there has been a change in the transformation process. This is taken up in Chapter 4. The model also, of course, implies that as new information changes share prices so may changes in the way information is measured and presented. This is taken up in Chapter 7.

A mathematical statement of the market model

The market model is:

$$R_{j,t} = \alpha_{j,t} + \beta_{j,t} R_{M,t} + e_{j,t}$$

where $R_{j,t}$ represents the return for shares in company j during period t, $R_{m,t}$ represents the return for the market as a whole for that period and the error term, $e_{j,t}$, represents the abnormal performance of the shares in company j during period t. $\alpha_{j,t}$, the intercept term, and $\beta_{j,t}$, the regression coefficient, are parameters that vary between shares. β and α are estimated by means of simple regression analysis in which e has an expected value of zero.

The return, R, on a share for period t is calculated as:

$$R_t = (D_t + P_{t1} - P_{t0}) / P_{t0}$$

which simplifies to $[(D_t + P_{t1})/ P_{t0}] -1$ where P_{t0} represents the share price at the beginning of the period, P_{t1} represents the share price at the end of the period and D_t represents the dividend per share received during the period.

The error terms are collected for the firms in the sample and averaged to produce 'average residuals' as a measure of abnormal performance associated with the event or news at that point in time, for example that day. These averages may also be aggregated to produce 'cumulative average residuals' up to a specified point in time as an indication of the speed of adjustment of the share price to the news so far.

Market Irrationality: Bubbles, Manias, Panics, and Crashes

CHAPTER

4

I can calculate the movement of the stars, but not the madness of men.

Sir Isaac Newton

Introduction

It was argued in the previous chapter that whilst the ECMH is seen as part of rational economics, it does not specify in any precise way how rational people should or will act. It was also shown that whilst it may be a useful model of the workings of the market as a whole, it does not represent the behaviour of individual investors, nor does it represent the workings of the market the whole of the time. Indeed, the theory asserts that efficiency comes about by participants acting in ways other than it predicts. That is to say, transactions occur between individuals because they have different views of the value of a share than each other and the market as a whole.

Whilst the ECMH provides a basis for understanding the normal working of the markets, the market as a whole or the price of an individual stock may act unusually or irrationally from time to time. A 'bubble or 'speculative bubble' occurs when the market price of a share begins to depart from its intrinsic value, as in Figure 4.1. This may occur gradually or quite quickly but the 'bursting' of the bubble usually does occur rapidly as a stock's market price reverts back to, or even below, its intrinsic value. There is no reason why the bubble should be limited to market prices exceeding fundamental values. In the same way that excessive optimism may cause prices to exceed intrinsic value, pessimism may cause prices to fall below it.

Such behaviour is well-known and the term well-used, but the reasons for the occurrence are less clear. In fact, whilst the market as a whole has become more efficient – because of the rapid and free transmission of information – instances of irrationality have actually become more common, or at least appear to be.

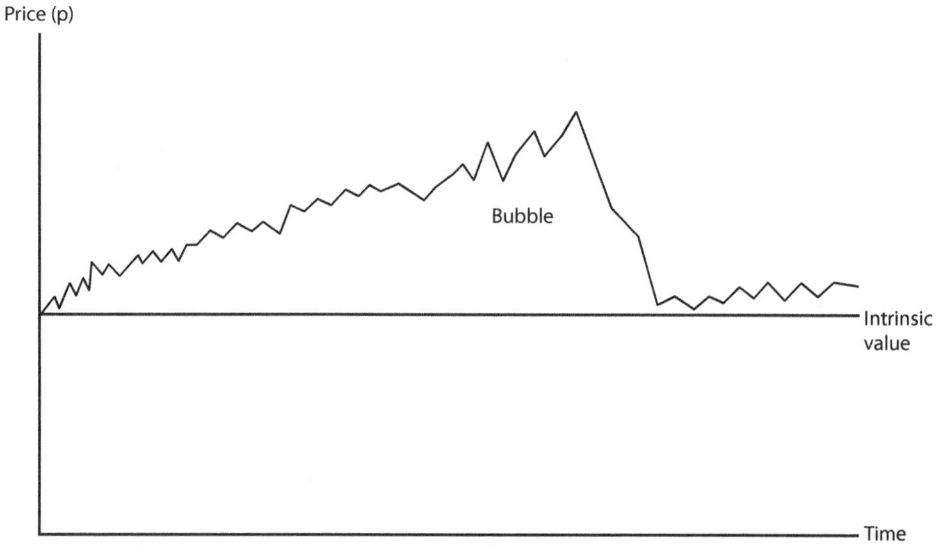

Figure 4.1 A stock market bubble

The ECMH suggests that in the absence of new information, a share should remain unchanged, fluctuating slightly as market makers attempt to balance their supply and demand, but asset prices do change as people's tastes and fashion change. Crazes may come, causing prices to rocket, and just as quickly go, causing prices to crash. In the case of financial assets, this may be dramatic. It is the purpose of this chapter to look at some of the best-known instances of those together with theories that attempt to explain such irrationality. I will first look at these theories that relate to markets more generally. I will then look at some of the famous cases involving stocks and shares. Finally, I will revisit these theories in the context of these.

Manias, panics and crashes

Large price rises followed by collapse, and the general irrationality of financial and other economic markets, have long been recognized. Kindleberger (2002) is regarded as the best-known modern authority on the phenomenon and has documented numerous crises across the world from 1618 to the early twenty-first century. According to him, the phenomenon was first recognized by Charles Mackay in 1841 (1841/1980). Mackay cited various examples but probably the most famous case was 'tulipmania' in Holland.

The story of tulipmania begins in 1559 when Conrad Guestner brought the first tulip bulbs from Constantinople to Holland and Germany, and people fell in love with them. Soon tulip bulbs became a status symbol for the wealthy, because they were beautiful and hard to get. Although early buyers were people who truly prized the lovely flowers, later buyers primarily considered them an investment. Soon speculators became involved and they began to be traded on the local market exchanges. By 1634, the craze of owning tulips had spread to the Dutch middle classes and merchants and shopkeepers vied with one another for single tulip bulbs. At the height of tulip mania in 1635, a single tulip bulb was worth almost £20 000 in today's prices and they were traded on the Amsterdam Stock Exchange and other exchanges in Holland and elsewhere in Europe. Trade grew so rapidly that tulip notaries and clerks were appointed to record transactions, and public laws and regulations were developed to control the tulip craze.

However, in 1636, some people began to sell their tulip holdings. The price of tulip bulbs began to weaken, slowly at first, and then rapidly. Confidence was soon destroyed, and panic seized the market. Within six weeks, prices had fallen by 90 per cent. Defaults on contracts and liens on owners were widespread. At first the Dutch government refused to interfere. It simply advised owners of tulip bulbs to agree among themselves on some plan to stabilize prices and restore public confidence. These plans failed and it was forced to act. All contracts prior to November 1636 were declared null and void. Contracts made after that date were settled if buyers merely paid 10 per cent of the prices to which they had earlier agreed. Prices continued to fall. The provincial council in The Hague was then asked to invent some measure to stabilize the price of tulip bulbs and public credit. Those efforts failed. Tulip prices fell even lower. In Amsterdam, judges unanimously refused to uphold tulip contracts and treated them as gambling activities. No court in Holland could, or would, enforce payment. The price of tulip bulbs eventually fell to, in real terms, less than their price today.

Keynes's 'biggest fool' theory

Probably the most insightful theory to explain this phenomenon with obvious relevance to share prices is Keynes (1936) and his 'biggest fool' theory. Whilst Keynes used the theory to explain the role of interest rate movements in the economy, his understanding also derives from his own dealings on the stock market on behalf of his university college which were very successful and earned it millions of pounds. Keynes suggested a completely different, but nevertheless rational, strategy for choosing those shares whose price was most likely to rise the most. He argued that investors do not estimate a company's intrinsic value as suggested in Chapter 2 and then compare it with the market price. Instead, he said, investors were more interested in whether other investors thought a share would rise in price. In short, a company's intrinsic value is irrelevant.

Keynes used the analogy of attempting to forecast the winner of a beauty contest. At that time it was common for London newspapers to run competitions requiring their readers to choose a set of 6 faces from 100 photographs of women that were the 'most beautiful'. Anyone who picked the most popular face was then entered into a raffle for a prize. The most obvious strategy would be to choose the six faces that, in the opinion of the reader, are the most beautiful. Keynes said that a more successful approach would be to attempt to identify the six faces most likely to be chosen by the public. This could be carried one step further to take into account the fact that other entrants would also be making their decision based on knowledge of public perceptions. Thus the strategy can be extended to the next order, the next, and so on, at each level attempting to predict the eventual outcome of the process based on the reasoning of others:

> *It is not a case of choosing those [faces] which, to the best of one's judgment, are really the prettiest, nor even those which average opinion genuinely thinks the prettiest. We have reached the third degree where we devote our intelligences to anticipating what average opinion expects the average opinion to be. And there are some, I believe, who practise the fourth, fifth and higher degrees.*
>
> Keynes (1936, p. 147)

Keynes believed that the stock market behaved in a similar way. People priced shares not on what they thought their fundamental value was, but rather on what they thought everyone else thought their value was, or what everybody else would predict the average assessment of value to be (see Figure 4.2). If an investor thought that the price of a share price would rise and that other investors would buy it, he would buy it, not because he thought it was undervalued but because others thought it was. This would increase the demand for the stock and force its price up. This would continue whilst investors continue to think that other investors thought the share price would rise and that they should buy the stock. Eventually, the price will be so far removed from reality that investors realize this and stop buying. When they realize that it is unlikely to rise any further, they then start selling. The process will then go into reverse in which people think the share price will fall further and decide to sell. The person who bought at the top of the market was described by Keynes as the biggest fool.

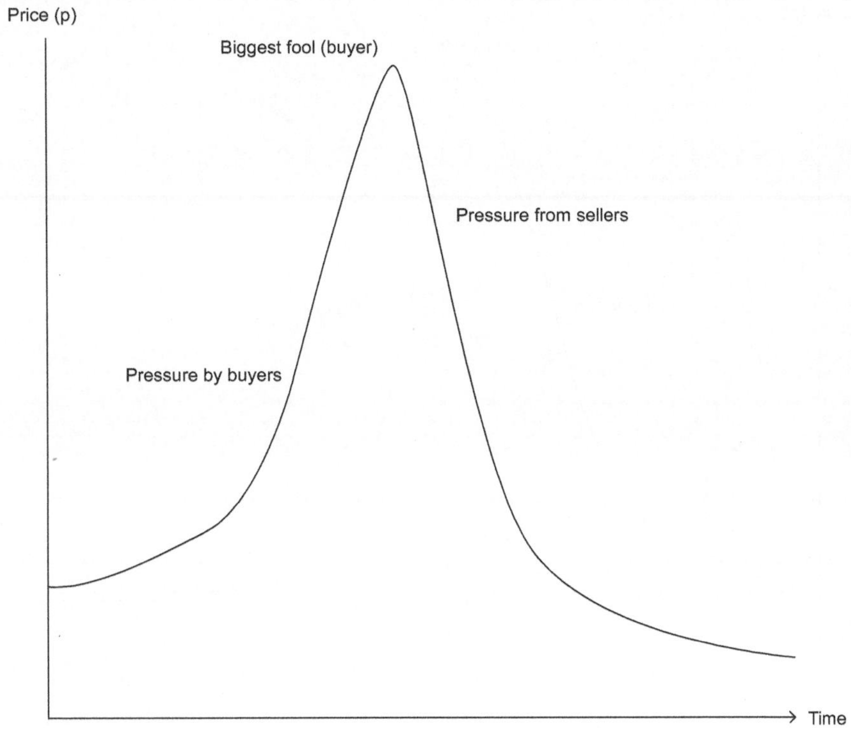

Figure 4.2 Keynes' biggest fool theory

Minsky's financial instability hypothesis

Kindleberger (2002) argues and presents countless examples to show that financially fueled boom-and-bust cycles frequently occur. They extend from the simple irrationality of financial and other markets to whole economies and economic sectors. He cites Minsky's Financial Instability Hypothesis (FIH) (Minsky 1964, 1969, 1975, 1977, 1982, 1989) as the principal theory to underpin his observations. The FIH attempts to explain the irrationality of financial markets during periods of extreme boom and bust which may lead to a financial crisis. According to Minsky the cycle takes the following form: boom – overestimation of expected returns – euphoria and bandwagon effect – profit-taking and the recognition that earlier expectations were unjustified. In the final stage, as losses occur, panic sets in (the irrational herding instinct) together with revulsion and the overall discrediting of the subject of the boom in the first place (see Figure 4.3).

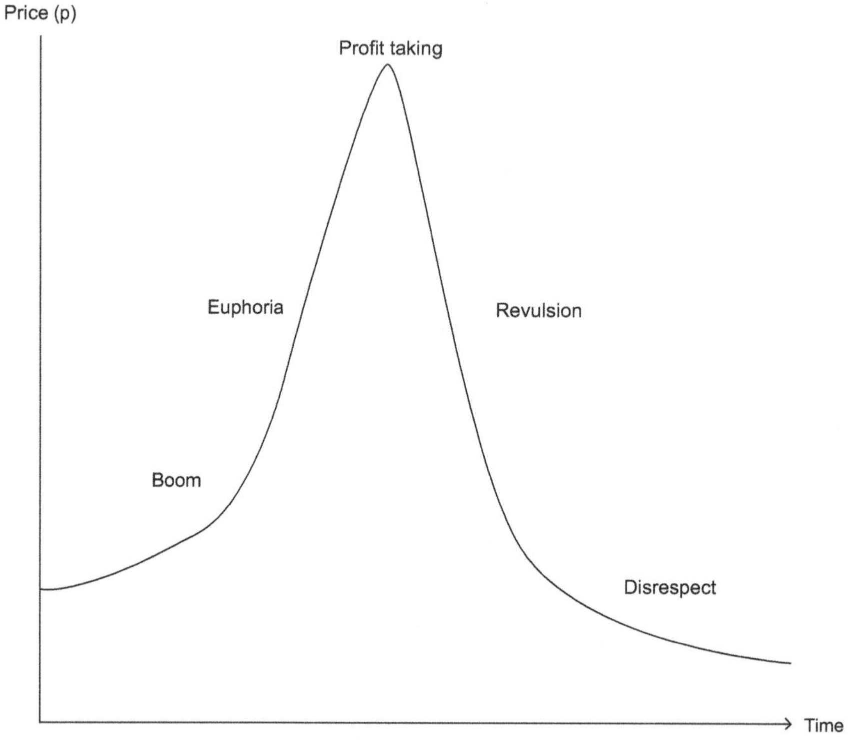

Figure 4.3 Minsky's financial instability hypothesis

The theory, which may apply to any good including stocks and shares, is set in the context of an expanding economy. As expansion develops, optimism increases and beliefs about the proper level of debt and risk change. Prices of financial assets rise and the general level of speculation increases. Here, 'speculation' refers to attempts by investors to bet on the future direction and psychology of the market (Minsky 1975, pp. 120–123).

The early stages of the process involve changing attitudes about risk. As these and liability structures change, the financial system becomes increasingly fragile. In such a vulnerable situation, a 'not unusual' event is capable of initiating a financial crisis. The fragility of the system and the pressures building within it actually make the occurrence of such an event more likely. If such an event, say the failure of a large company or bank, suddenly occurs, the optimistic expectations that had developed during the boom are subject to significant revision. In Minsky's view, the resulting financial crisis leads to an increased unwillingness to finance investment and an increase in the required rate of return to cover the increased perceived risk. A fall in the value of financial assets and company profits are the result, leading to corporate failures and a depression.

At the heart of the theory is a micro-structural concept of individual firms' financial fragility where all economic units are viewed in terms of their balance sheets and the management of these in the face of uncertainty. Firms are characterized as having one of three types of financial structure:

1. robust structures, which Minsky calls 'hedge firms', firms that can meet their financing obligations and have positive net cash flows even if their realized returns are disastrous;
2. fragile structures, which he calls 'speculative firms', whose expected net cash flows are positive but their realized net cash flows and expected cash flows in the short term may be negative; and
3. 'Ponzi structures', whose expected net cash flows are negative but are compensated by high returns in later years.

Clearly, (1) will have a positive net present value, (2) may not, depending upon how disastrous the returns are, and (3) also may not, depending on the magnitude of the later returns. They are all sensitive to interest rate changes. It is, of course, possible for firms to move from one classification to another as the result of an interest rate change. It is more likely, however, for them to move classifications because of a financing decision relating to the amount of leverage.

Changing to a higher risk classification will raise the required rate of return required by investors as the relative strength of the firm's balance sheet will be perceived to be lower. Its value will, therefore, be lower. Firms may also be affected not only by the attempts of their owners to manage their balance sheets but also by the attitude of financiers and banks. During optimistic periods, banks may be prepared to lend on more speculative projects and balance sheets. In more pessimistic times they may not. During a pessimistic period, banks may also attempt to reign in their lending. Minsky (1989) writes:

> *Over a period of good times liability structures change so that the weight of hedge financing units decreases and the weight of speculative and Ponzi financing units increases. Note that any change toward a conservative view of what constitutes an apt liability structure for holding capital assets will put pressure on firms that are in speculative and Ponzi financing structures to use their cash flows to clean up their*

> *balance sheets: to use retained earnings to retire debt rather than as the basis for leveraged investment. In addition speculative and Ponzi debtors may be constrained to sell assets to improve their balance sheets … (this) can well lead to a fall in the price of assets being offered. As a result a smaller amount of cash than the books indicated will be generated … This can lead to a broad erosion of mark-to-market net worths and to a decline in the ability to finance investment. As a result investment falls and so will aggregate business profits.*
>
> (1989, p. 180)

This quotation demonstrates how, according to Minsky, market mechanics and the decisions of owners may bring about a financial crisis and a recession. There, financial information, investors (as opposed to bankers) and changes in their expectations apparently have no part to play. Minsky does not consider the possibility that information may be manipulated, either legally or illegally, and that there may be a strong incentive to do this for both owners (who may wish to mislead bankers and other investors) and managers (who may wish to mislead bankers, other investors and owners). Minsky may also be criticised for focusing on this behaviour in terms of business units, although at the time of writing he may have been correct. Nowadays, with the use of credit cards and the general ease by which individuals may now borrow and manage (or, to be more precise, mismanage) their finances, the asset structures he refers to may be seen to apply at individual level. These extensions to Minsky's analysis do not undermine his results and predictions. On the contrary, they represent two other important factors and introduce more instability into the financial system.

Irrational exuberance

The term 'irrational exuberance' was used on 5 December 1996 by Alan Greenspan, chairman of the US Federal Reserve Board, to describe the behaviour of investors in the US and the mood behind the rise in stock market prices at that time. It became his most famous quotation. Immediately following his speech, the Nikkei index dropped 3.2 per cent, the Dow Jones Industrial Index dropped 2.3 per cent and the FTSE 100 index fell 4 per cent. Shiller (2005) has argued that reasons for the rise relative to the level of corporate earnings which began in 1982 include the Internet boom, the rise of online trading, the Republican Congress and the proposed capital gains tax cut. Other factors such as the rise of defined contribution pension plans, the growth of mutual funds, the decline in inflation and the expansion of the volume of trade in stocks were clearly associated with events that occurred from 1982 onwards.

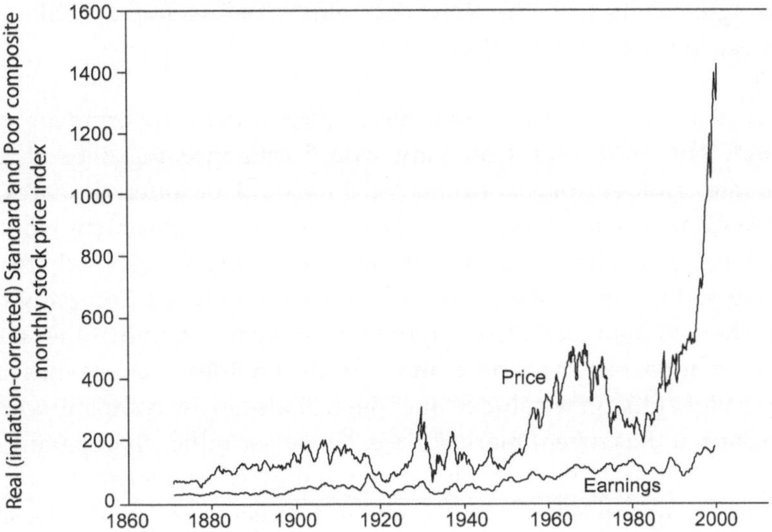

Figure 4.4 Stock prices and earnings 1871–2000 (Shiller, 2005)

Although the term represents a contemporary recognition of the phenomenon, it does not represent a new theory or offer new insights into the reasons for its occurrence. The theories of Minsky and Keynes continue to underpin modern understanding.

Famous instances of stock market bubbles, manias, panics and crashes

THE SOUTH SEA BUBBLE, 1711–1720

The South Sea Bubble involved the ramping of shares. The South Sea Company was formed in 1711 by the British Lord Treasurer and a group of merchants and given exclusive trading rights on British trade with the South Seas, that is Spanish South America, in exchange for taking over some of the British government debt. The British government needed to provide a mechanism for funding its debt incurred in the War of Spanish Succession. It could not establish a bank because the charter of the Bank of England made it the only joint stock bank. It therefore established what was, on the face of it, a trading company, though its main activity was in fact the raising of funds to pay off government debt. A problem for the company was that Spain was unwilling to allow much British trade. Actual trade with the South Seas was limited, although rumours of trade agreements with the King of Spain helped to fuel speculation. The 'bubble' related to the financial aspects.

In 1719 it was proposed that the entire British government debt be privatized. The South Sea Company would refinance the debt at a lower interest rate. Holders of government debt would be offered shares in the South Sea Company in exchange for their loans. The government would have lower interest payments, and the debt holders would be given shares which they could sell if they wished. Not only did the South Sea Company hope to profit as the middleman, it also sought to improve its profit by other means. It attempted to inflate its share price and offer debt holders shares whose market value was higher than the value of their debt. Shares in the company were 'sold' to politicians at the current market price. However, rather than paying for the shares, they simply held on to those shares they were allocated, 'sold' them back to the company when they chose, and received as 'profit' the increase in market price. This method, while winning over the heads of government, the King's mistress etc., also cemented their commitment to the South Sea Company and helped to drive up the share price further. Also, by publicising the names of their most famous shareholders, the South Sea Company was able to appear legitimate and attract further investors. It also helped shareholders buy its shares – they were offered for sale requiring 20 per cent deposit. The money gained from this was then lent to existing shareholders to buy more.

The company talked up the share price with 'the most extravagant rumours' concerning the value of its potential trade in the New World. The share price rose from £128 in January 1720, the time the scheme was proposed, to £175 in February, £330 in March and, following the scheme's acceptance, £550 at the end of May and £1000 on 1 August. Its success caused a country-wide speculating frenzy. All classes of people, from peasants to lords, developed a feverish interest in investing; in the South Sea Company primarily, but in shares generally. Many new companies were formed, some more legitimate than others. Amongst those to go public in 1720 was one that famously advertised itself as 'a company for carrying out an undertaking of great advantage, but nobody to know what it is' (Mackay 1841/1980, p. 55).

After reaching £1000 in August, the number of shares in the South Sea Company being sold caused the price to fall, dropping back to £100 per share before the end of the year. It was then discovered that the directors of the South Sea Company had sold their own shares. This caused further selling. Short selling started to occur, causing the price to fall further. Investors were left stranded. Panic selling immediately ensued. The collapse of shares in the

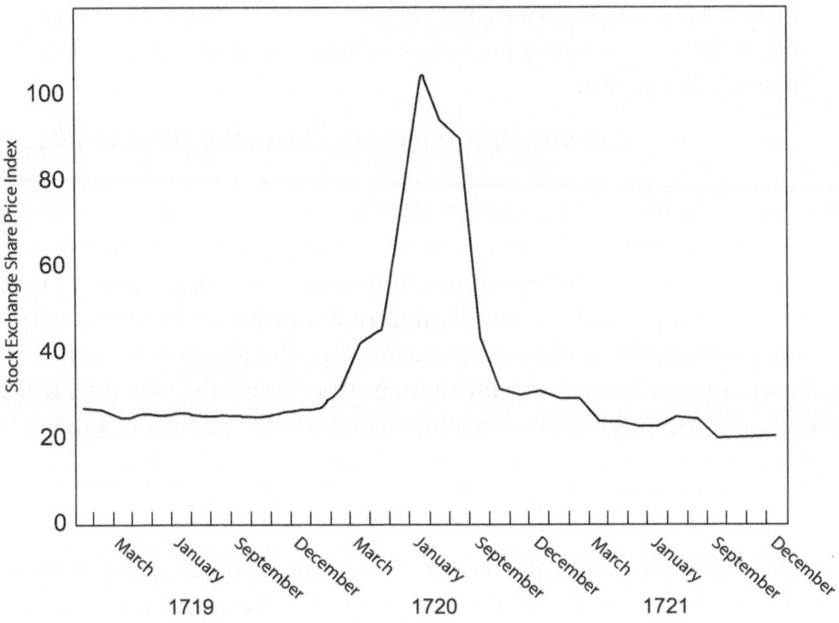

Figure 4.5 UK share prices 1719–1721

South Sea Company spread to others and the stock market crashed. By the end of September, thousands of individuals were ruined, including many members of the aristocracy. Jonathan Swift and Sir Isaac Newton were just two of those who lost large amounts. Newton remarked 'I can calculate the movement of the stars, but not the madness of men' after losing £20 000 in the bubble, equivalent to over £2 million today. With investors outraged, Parliament was recalled in December and an investigation began. Reporting in 1721, it revealed widespread fraud amongst the company directors.

RAILWAY MANIA, 1841–1847

The creation of the railways in the UK represented not only a huge technological revolution but also a change in the way people and goods travelled. This fuelled the Industrial Revolution enormously. Although there was excitement about the opening of the first railway, the Stockton and Darlington Railway, in 1825, it was not until the early1840s that others began opening. They required investment on a massive scale. This followed the same pattern as the South Sea Bubble. As the price of railway shares increased, speculators invested more and more. The boom reached its peak in 1846 when 272 Acts of Parliament were passed to set up new railway companies. A crash was inevitable. The following letter to *The Times* sums up the feeling at the time:

> *There is not a single dabbler in scrip who does not steadfastly believe – first, that a crash sooner or later, is inevitable; and, secondly, that he himself will escape it.*
>
> 12 July 1845, quoted in Chancellor (1999, p. 136)

Investment in railway companies was discredited by dubious and illegal practices. These included deliberately misleading prospectuses, paying dividends out of capital, inadequate accounts and audit, rigged board meetings and unscrupulous promoters who floated new railway companies, talked up their share price and then sold out before they had got under way (Kellett 1979). The railway companies were financed mainly by small shareholders from the middle classes. Although they were able to make their annoyance known, they were powerless in preventing their investments more than halving in value during 1846 and 1847 (see Figure 4.6).

By way of postscript, the disgrace of railway shares made it very difficult for entrepreneurs in other industries to set up limited companies. The sentiment lasted until the early 1860s when new legislation was passed and made it easy. Limited liability companies again became popular, only for them to fall into disgrace again with the collapse of Overend Gurney Ltd in 1866. It then took them until the 1890s be accepted again (Barnes and Firman 2002).

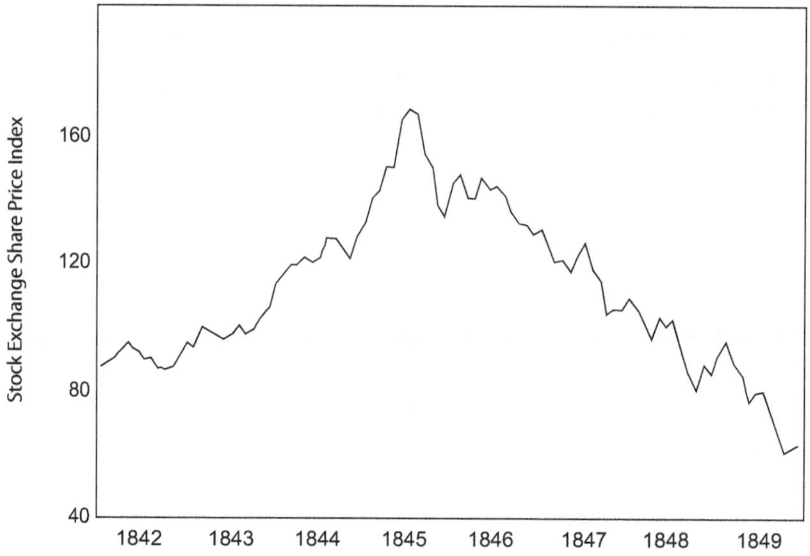

Figure 4.6 UK railway share prices 1841–1850 (Simon 2003)

THE NEW ISSUE (OR INITIAL PUBLIC OFFERING) AND 'TRONICS' BOOM, 1959–1962

The tronics boom of the early 1960s centred on the USA but extended to the UK. According to Malkiel (1981), more new shares were offered in the 1959–62 period than at any other time in history. It rivalled the South Sea Bubble both in intensity and in the fraudulent practices that were revealed. It was called the 'tronics boom' because the new companies' names invariably included the word 'electronics' in their title even if they had nothing to do with the electronics industry. Buyers of these new issues did not really care, of course, what the company made so long as 'tron' or 'onic' was in the title. Names included trons such as Astron, Dutron, Vulcatron, and Transitron, and 'onics' such as Circuitronics, Supronics, Videotronics. There were also several 'Electrosonics' companies and even a Powertron Ultrasonics. The bubble burst in 1962. Many stocks later sold for less than 10 per cent of their peak price.

There were two aspects to the boom – the excitement by investors of a new industry that could make them rich and the ease with which investors could buy into such companies at their outset by means of the new issue market, as it was known then, or the initial public offering (IPO) market, as it is known today. Typically, when a company offers new shares it is forced to offer them at a substantial discount, say 30 per cent relative to the price they will be trading once a proper market in them exists.[1] Over a short period of time, the company will become accepted and a proper market in its shares will be established. Investors (referred to as 'stags') stand to profit, not only from the rise of the company but also from the discount offered to initial subscribers.

POSEIDON, 1969–1970

Poseidon NL (no liability) was an Australian mining exploration company whose shares were traded on the Australian and London exchanges. It shares had been languishing for many years but in 1968 it acquired some exploration leases and hired a prospector. Although the exploration leases did not turn into a mine, it did find a promising site in Windarra, Western Australia and in 1969 it made a major nickel discovery.

Poseidon's share price started rising around 25 September 1969 when results from drilling at Windarra became known to some insiders. Shares had been trading at around AUS$ 0.80 earlier that month but rose to AUS$1.85 on Friday 26 September. The following Monday, Poseidon made a preliminary announcement that it had found nickel. This pushed the share price up to

1 This does not mean that the shares will be issued at a discount relative to their par value.

AUS$5.60. On 1 October, Poseidon made a more detailed announcement stating it had made a major nickel find. The share price jumped that day from AUS$6.60 to AUS$12.30 and kept rising.

From that point onwards, other mining shares began to rise as speculators bought nickel stocks, in companies with leases near Windarra. From October to December 1969, the Australian Stock Exchange All Mining Index rose 44 per cent from 438 to 632. The volume of trading also rose substantially, reaching 37.9 millon shares on 3 November compared with a pre-bubble record of less than 20 million. This only served to further fuel excitement.

From October onwards, there was little new information about Poseidon and its shares continued to trade around AUS$50, although the price did rise around the company's AGM on 19 December. The share price rose to AUS$110 the day before the AGM and to AUS$175 the following Monday. The Australian Stock Exchange All Mining Index peaked in January 1970 and Poseidon the following month. Both fell quickly. It is unclear what prompted this but as the price of mining shares grew, many new companies were listed by promoters looking to cash in. Some of these new listings did not even have any mining leases, let alone viable mines. Many investors lost money on these shady listings, and this attracted substantial negative press, forcing prices down further.

At least the rise in Poseidon's share price was based on a real discovery. A number of other companies were floated with 'empty' prospectuses containing no details of their prospects. Clearly, insiders managed to extract huge sums from the boom. The *Australian Financial Review* examined the profits of one group of promoters in an article on 3 October 1969 entitled 'How to turn $1 into $12m'. A good example is Tasminex NL, an exploration company. In January 1970, it was investigating some leases at Mount Venn in Western Australia. On Friday 23 January, one of its directors panned some drill samples and identified some heavy metals in it. A rumour that they had discovered nickel immediately ensued. Tasminex's share price rose that day from AUS$2.80 to AUS$3.30. The next trading day, Tuesday, it soared to AUS$16.80. Following the publication of an interview with the company's chairman the share price rose as high as AUS$75 and AUS$96 in overnight trading in London. The chairman then sold most of his shares and the share price gradually fell back. No discovery was ever made at Mount Venn.

What happened to Poseidon? By the time it actually started producing nickel, the price of nickel had fallen. Also, the ore was of a lower grade than originally thought, so extraction costs were higher. Profits from the mine were

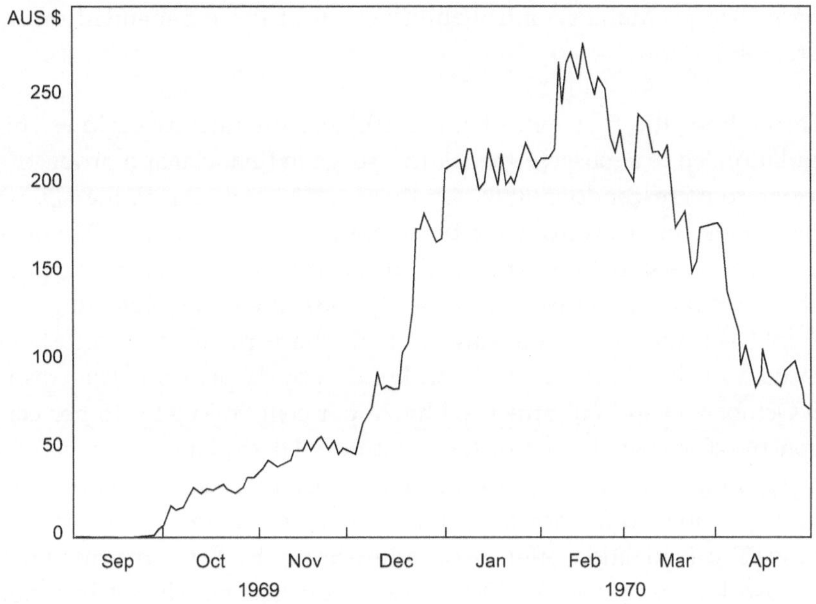

Figure 4.7 Poseidon's share price 1969–70 (Simon 2003)

not sufficient to keep Poseidon afloat, and in 1976 it delisted. Western Mining then took over the mine, operating it until 1991.

THE STOCK MARKET BOOM OF THE 1980S AND THE CRASH OF 1987

A fundamental change occurred in the 1980s in both the USA and the UK. This involved the deregulation and liberalization of the financial markets and institutions by the Reagan and Thatcher governments. The objective in the UK was to break down a number of powerful monopolies and create what Margaret Thatcher called a 'shareholder democracy' in which everyone had an opportunity to invest in companies and to understand, and share in, their risks. One of the ways of encouraging this was the sell-off of nationalized industries to private companies – or to new companies formed for the purpose and financed by public subscription for new issues.[2] Whist deregulation changed the way in which financial institutions worked, it also created new forms of financial instruments (for example junk bonds, high-yield bonds because of their high risk) new forms of financial reconstruction (for example leveraged buy-outs) and the way in which they were financed (for example the involvement of banks). The essence of these new forms of finance was leverage – large scale borrowing at a rate of interest significantly lower than that earned by the

2 Probably the most famous example is the flotation of British Telecom in 1986.

business. The profitability and viability of all of these depended on interest rates remaining low.

Throughout the first half of the 1980s interest rates were low. This and deregulation led to a massive speculative surge in financial and property assets that came to a crescendo in 1986. By then, whilst inflation in the UK was 2.4 per cent, house prices were rising by 16 per cent nationally and 24 per cent in London. The stock market continued to rise (up 23.5 per cent over the year) and the takeover market was buoyant. By 1987, the boom was out of control. Between December 1986 and August 1987 share prices on Wall Street had increased a further 43 per cent and in London by 45 per cent. The crash came on 19 October when Wall Street fell by 23 per cent, Tokyo by 15 per cent and London by 20 per cent. One of the most popular explanations given for this was the gradual withdrawal of funds from the US market by Japanese investors during September to finance their applications for shares in the second stage of the NTT privatization offer. Soon afterwards, the UK Government began to increase interest rates. By 1989, a recession had clearly set in where the combination of rising interest rates and falling revenues had a huge impact on company profits. A number of large-scale corporate collapses soon followed.

In many cases, the failure of these companies was directly attributable to their expansion plans during the mid-1980s when they were able to borrow cheaply. Smith and Sterne (1994) have shown that whilst leverage increased overall during the 1980s in the UK, there was a growing variation in leverage between firms. Hunter and Isachenkova (2003) have shown how the sharp rise in interest rates from 1988 onwards increased companies' cost of debt which contributed to the higher propensity of highly leveraged UK listed companies to fail.[3] During the 1989–93 recession an unprecedented number of publicly listed companies were liquidated or went into administration or receivership. Between 1990 and 1992 alone, 49 listed companies failed. Many others were rescued by takeover or reconstruction (Bhattacharjee *et al.* 2002).

Most of these companies had one thing in common. They were the subject of earnings exaggeration that occurred at a relatively early stage of the boom–bust cycle during the 1980s as they attempted to maintain the impression (or illusion) of growth. These manipulations later turned into attempts to hide losses. Smith (1992), a leading practicing financial analyst at that time, provides

3 This result is consistent with empirical studies for earlier periods in the UK and elsewhere which identify leverage as positively correlated with the probability of failure (see Morris 1997).

an excellent record of this.[4] A good example of the way in which companies could exploit permitted accounting methods and maintain the impression of growth in profitability is 'merger accounting', an accounting procedure similar to 'pooling of interests' accounting in the US. The effect was to greatly exaggerate reported profits and, therefore, the benefits from merger.[5] Coloroll plc and Mirror Group Newspapers plc were two very large publicly listed companies that used this to overstate profits before failing, and this was just when it was so necessary for investors to know the real effect of the decision. It is ironic that, instead of company reports helping to reveal the non-existence of financial benefits from proposed mergers, they were used to support it. The fact that this largely went unnoticed was, no doubt, a result of the merger mania and euphoria at the time.

Many publicly listed companies that later collapsed attempted to manipulate their financial results in other areas. Good examples are the treatment of exceptional and extraordinary items by Arley plc, Bestwood plc, Goldberg and Sons plc and Reliant Group plc; the capitalization of patent and development expenditure by Rockwood Holdings plc; the capitalization of interest payments by Rush and Tomkins plc and the Kentish Property Group plc; and off-balance sheet finance by Rush and Tomkins Group plc. Although some of the accounting manipulations were within the parameters set by accounting standards, others were not. It would appear that many audit firms were complicit in this and were later sued for negligence either by their shareholders or their lenders. This included some of the large auditing firms, some of whose partners were investigated and/or censured by the Chartered Accountants' Professional Conduct Committee. Some previously highly reputable auditing firms even had to be taken over in order to avoid failure (Lennox 1999).

In some very large publicly listed companies, the manipulation of published accounting information was combined with theft and fraud. When companies encountered difficulties so severe as to threaten survival, in some instances (if ownership was not so dispersed that they were unable to act as a group)

4 Smith (1992) is not a balanced academic discussion but actually a description of 'worst practice' and its 'practitioners'. The extent to which individual listed companies used these creative accounting techniques was scored by means of 'blobs' (one for each creative accounting technique adopted) and the book became known as the 'blob guide'. It attracted considerable criticism and debate at the time and, no doubt, played a significant part in exposing the use of creative accounting.

5 There is considerable empirical evidence in the form of share prices (which fell after a merger) compared with accounting rates of return (which rose after a merger) to support the proposition that the financial statements were misleading. For a direct comparison of these see Chatterjee and Meeks (1996). See Meeks and Buckland (2001) for a demonstration of the applications of the various methods and how merger accounting was misleading.

their effective owners decided to salvage what they could (see Table 4.1). The case of Jim Raper and Milbury plc was typical. Milbury was a house building company listed on the LSE but effectively controlled by a single person, Jim Raper, through nominees. When it was floated on the LSE, Milbury issued a prospectus, later shown to be intentionally misleading. Milbury's subsequent financial reports were also shown to significantly overstate profits (DTI 1988). When it became clear that Milbury was losing money, Jim Raper decided to transfer the profitable business and valuable assets which were located in one of its subsidiaries, Westminster Property Group Ltd, to another company he owned. It then sold them on to a third party abroad. The remaining shareholders in Milbury were left with the group's debts and its loss-making business. Because Jim Raper was resident abroad and the funds had also been transferred outside the UK, the courts could not revoke the transactions and recover the lost money.

A similar case to occur at that time was the failure of the conglomerate Polly Peck plc, one of the largest companies to be listed on the LSE. Corporate funds were siphoned into offshore companies owned by the CEO and founder, Asil Nadir. His subsequent escape from Britain to Turkish-held Cyprus whilst

Table 4.1 The largest failures of UK publicly listed companies (excluding banks) during the early 1990s involving impropriety

Name	Impropriety	Principal accounting failure
Polly Peck	Business failure, attempted cover-up and subsequent looting of its funds by its 'owners'	Foreign currency accounting/mismatching and falsification of accounts
British and Commonwealth	Business failure, attempted cover-up and subsequent looting of its funds by their 'owners'	Merger accounting Accounting for contingent liabilities
Milbury	Business failure, attempted cover-up and subsequent looting of its funds by its 'owners'	Merger accounting Fraudulent prospectus
Mirror Group Newspapers, Maxwell Communications	Business failure, attempted cover-up and subsequent looting (including employees' pension fund) of their funds by their 'owners'	Numerous, including falsification of accounts

on bail was a major embarrassment both to the British Government and to the prosecuting authorities. British and Commonwealth was also one of the largest companies to be listed on the LSE when it collapsed. It began a series of large acquisitions when John Gunn, its main driving force, joined as an executive director in 1985. British and Commonwealth's downfall is largely attributable to one subsidiary, Atlantic Computers, which made massive losses. These were largely covered up and its contingent liabilities not disclosed (Smith 1992, pp. 213–220). However, the most notorious case involved the collapse of Maxwell Communications and Mirror Group Newspapers, two large corporations, the latter listed on the LSE, and the theft of over £5 million in employee pension funds by their chairman and chief executive, Robert Maxwell, to support his ailing business empire (DTI 2001).

Milbury plc, Polly Peck plc, British and Commonwealth plc, Mirror Group Newspapers plc were publicly listed companies with a wide share ownership but controlled by a single individual or small group. They were in a sufficiently strong position to control their company's decision-making and loot it when it ceased to be profitable. There were failures of other large listed companies but these did not involve looting because their share ownership was dispersed, e.g Coloroll plc, which had expanded rapidly during the 1980s through acquisitions financed by debt.[6]

There were other large-scale frauds at this time that raised the level of public distrust of financial advisers and auditors and scepticism about their independence. Blue Arrow plc was an employment agency, and, at that time, the biggest ever rights issue launched on the LSE. This scandal involved the manipulation of the market in its shares by its financial advisers when they were caught out by the 1987 stock market crash. The details of this scandal are described in Chapter 8. Around this time, the spectacular collapse of the Bank of Credit and Commerce International (BCCI) also occurred. Although it was not a publicly listed company, BCCI raised concerns over the role of auditors and their affirmation that a company is a going concern. Shortly before it collapsed, it had issued its latest annual report. In it there was no indication of impending bankruptcy and, as with the other failures, no going-concern qualification or any mention of fraud within BCCI.

6 As an aside, it is interesting that many of the listed companies that failed in the 1989–91 were property companies because they were financed by debt. Smith (1992, pp. 105–106) shows how these companies' capitalized interest was a high proportion of operating profit. The effect was not revealed in their annual accounts because the capitalization of interest payments was an acceptable accounting treatment at the time and they were not charged to current revenue.

We saw earlier how according to Minsky, interest rates affect the value of the firm and its ability to continue. During the early 1980s rising profitability occurred as a result of low interest rates and increasing leverage. The fact that interest rates rose and profitability and growth ceased so abruptly were enough to bring down hitherto financially sound companies. Pressures on directors and top management to report continued growth in the first place and then later to conceal financial difficulties were so great that they resorted to exploiting informational asymmetry and manipulating their accounts. In some cases this involved the complicity of their auditors. It also involved the actions of owner-managers of very large companies to salvage their own investments and leave both creditors and other shareholders with nothing. Long firm fraud by the directors and owners of small private companies had always been common. ('Long firm fraud' is an expression referring to the formation by fraudsters of a limited company designed to obtain credit from banks and suppliers which then fails or disappears with the cash.) However, this was the first time that it had occurred in large publicly listed companies where the principal shareholders were able to control the decision-making and make the necessary transfers.

THE INTERNET BUBBLE, 1995–2001

The rise and fall of dot coms is a more recent instance. The rise of Internet-related stocks started gradually in 1995 and extended across most stock markets in the developed world, but notably the US and UK. Again, it was stimulated by an amazing belief in the potential for profit from the Internet, both by ordinary people and professional investors. The simple addition of 'dot com' to a company's name was sufficient for it to become the object of speculation (Cooper, Dimitrov and Rau 2001). The rise in tech shares was frequently justified by claims that the old rules of business no longer applied to these firms (see Box 4.1). As Simon (2003) remarks: 'a surprisingly familiar refrain'. Of course, while there were some genuinely innovative start-ups that could only benefit users via the Internet, many were mere hype. Those that did have something new to offer can now probably be identified, having survived the subsequent fallout. There were other Web-based businesses founded on ideas that were not so marvellous and only offered fairly unlikely or negligible benefits. They were only seen as credible investment opportunities during a period when everyone wanted to invest in IT stocks and did not look too closely at what they were buying and what the company was doing.

It was not surprising that the bubble burst and the realities of business ultimately prevailed. During the early months of 2000, business commentators in the UK and the USA were openly wondering whether high tech stocks were overvalued. The comment from probably the UK's most respected financial

Box 4.1

Shares in a small listed company, Pacific Media, rose from 2.32p on 23 November 1999 to 8.7p on 30 November 1999, a rise of 375 per cent, simply based on expectations of a deal involving the reversal of Asian Internet assets into the shell company.

Little more than a suggestion that IT firm Viglen Technology planned to develop an e-commerce side to its business had the effect of more than doubling its share price from 181p on 17 January, 2000, to 366p the following day.

commentator, Hamish MacRae, is typical 'I know that the bubble in IT company stocks will burst. I just don't know when' (*The Independent*, 2 March, 2000). It started only a few days later in the US. The UK soon followed. The collapse was fairly rapid with no obvious real trigger. Many dot com and high tech stocks virtually collapsed. By the end of 2000, the reversal of popularity of high tech and dot com companies was more than complete but their unpopularity continued into 2001 and in some cases beyond.

Conclusions

The introduction to this chapter presented the theories of Keynes and Minsky as providing alternative explanations for stock market behaviour. Are they incompatible? It is often thought that they are and their advocates invariably present them as such. However, it is very difficult to see at one level how the stock market could be anything other than efficient, given the effort by investors to profit from inefficiencies and inconsistencies in the markets is so great and where information, and access to it, is so powerful. On the other hand, the behavioural theories that imply irrationality and the herding instinct are so intuitively appealing and recognizable.

The key to a reconciliation of the two models is contained within the ECMH's assumptions. The market adjusts to information and a market price reflects all known information relating to the stock – as it is interpreted by the market as a whole. The important point is that it reflects the market's opinion as to the effect of information on the future income to investors from owning the stock. If opinion changes, so does the value of the stock. Therefore, changes in the market's mood represented as bubbles and crises are quite compatible with the ECMH. Minsky provides an important insight into the way the mood of the financial markets change. Empirical tests of the ECMH relate to the receipt of new information and the hypothesized directional changes in the price of the stocks affected. Very rarely is the researcher able to hypothesize about the magnitude of the change. That is left to the judgment and, therefore, the mood of the market.

I have not mentioned in this chapter the efforts by mathematicians to go beyond random walk and model share price movements – most notably chaos theory (Peters 1991). Unfortunately, this does not present new economic or behavioural reasons for the occurrence of bubbles, manias, panics and crashes and we are left to financial economists to do this. Keynes, Minsky and Kindleberger provide most of these insights. I have also only mentioned the most significant crazes and crashes, attempting to avoid particular stocks. I have not mentioned the 1929 Wall Street Crash, mainly because it did not originate in the UK and was largely brought about by specific US factors there at that time. The Poseidon case was included because it is probably the best example of an individual stock and very dramatic, demonstrating how a sector, if not the whole of the market, may be drawn in. Mining is a sector that is particularly susceptible to this, regularly experiencing booms and slumps. Undoubtedly, Keynes' biggest fool theory provides an important insight into such behaviour.

The FIH provides not only insights into this but also into the origins of a recession more generally. The cases I have cited have usually been prompted by an event, in itself minor yet fundamentally changing the views of investors and the mood of the market. (At the time of writing, the collapse of the Northern Rock bank appears to have had such an impact.) However, the cases cited have usually contained an element of fraud and market abuse, whether this is in the form of an opportunist or corrupt promoter capitalizing on a craze in shares by setting up shell companies and selling their shares, or company directors manipulating their financial reports in an effort to maintain investor confidence. Kindleberger (2002) writes:

> *in a boom, fortunes are made, individuals wax greedy, and swindlers come forward to exploit that greed … sheep to be shorn abound, and need only the emergence of effective swindlers to offer themselves as sacrifices.*
>
> (2002, p. 76)

I criticised Minsky for ignoring this element. He assumed that the interests of the firms and their owners were the same and did not recognize the possibility of opportunists and fraudsters. He did not recognize the significance and implications of the asymmetry of information whereby management have access to information and knowledge that shareholders do not and they are able to exploit this. Clearly, fraud and market abuse – not only in the form of the manipulation of share prices but also accounting manipulation – were part of the stock market boom of the 1980s, the crash of 1987 and the succeeding recession. We will take up these themes in later chapters.

References

Barnes, P.A. and R. Firman (2002) 'The Loss of Popularity of Limited Liability Companies in Great Britain in 1866 and the Role of Financial Information: A Case Study', *Financial History Review,* 8(2): 143–161.

Bhattacharjee, A., C. Higson, S. Holly and P. Kattuman (2002) 'Macro Economic Instability and Business Exit: Determinants of Failures and Acquisitions of Large UK Firms', Cambridge Working Papers in Economics, Royal Economic Society Annual Conference 2002.

Chancellor, E. (1999) *Devil Take the Hindmost: A History of Financial Speculation,* New York, Farrar, Straus and Giroux.

Chatterjee, R. and G. Meeks (1996) 'The Financial Effects of Takeover: Accounting Rates of Return and Accounting Regulation', *Journal of Business Finance and Accounting,* 23(5 and 6): 851–868.

Cooper, M.J., O. Dimitrov and P.R. Rau (2001) 'A Rose.com by Any Other Name', *Journal of Finance,* 56(6): 2371–2388.

DTI (Department of Trade and Industry) (1988) *Milbury plc, Westminster Property Group Ltd: Investigations under Section 432(1) and Section 442 of the Companies Act 1985,* London, HMSO.

DTI (Department of Trade and Industry) (2001) *Mirror Group Newspapers plc: Investigations under Sections 432(2) and 442 of the Companies Act 1985,* London, HMSO.

Hunter, J., and N. Isachenkova (2003) 'Aggregate Economy Risk and Company Failure: An Examination of UK Quoted Firms in the Early 1990s'. Paper presented at the British Accounting Association Conference, Manchester, 2003.

Kellett, J.R. (1979) *Railways and Victorian Cities.* London: Routledge & Kegan Paul, Toronto: University of Toronto Press.

Keynes, J.M. (1936) *The General Theory of Employment, Interest and Money,* London, Macmillan Press.

Kindleberger, C.P. (2002) *Manias, Panics, and Crashes: A History of Financial Crises,* 4th edn, Basingstoke, John Wiley & Sons.

Lennox, C.S. (1999) 'Audit Quality and Auditor Size: An Evaluation of Reputation and Deep Pocket Hypotheses', *Journal of Business Finance and Accounting,* 26(7 and 8): 779–803.

Mackay, C. (1841/1980) *Memoirs of Extraordinary Popular Delusions and the Madness of Crowds*, London, Richard Bentley, reprinted, New York, Harmony Books, 1980.

Malkiel, B.G. (1981) *A Random Walk down Wall Street*, London, Norton and Co, London.

Meeks, G. and J.G. Buckland (2001) 'The Loser's Curse: Accounting for the Transaction Costs of Takeovers and the Distortion of Takeover Motives', *Abacus*, 37(3): 389–400.

Minsky, H.P. (1964) 'Longer Waves in Financial Relations: Financial Factors in the More Severe Recessions', *American Economic Review*, 54(2): 324–335.

Minsky, H.P. (1969) 'Private Sector Asset Management and the Effectiveness of Monetary Policy: Theory and Practice', *Journal of Finance*, 24(2): 223–238.

Minsky, H.P. (1975) *John Maynard Keynes*, New York, Columbia University Press.

Minsky, H.P. (1977) 'A Theory of Systemic Fragility', in E.I. Altman and A.W. Sametz, eds, *Financial Crises: Institutions and Markets in a Fragile Environment*, New York, John Wiley and Son.

Minsky, H.P. (1982) 'The Financial-Instability Hypothesis: Capitalist Processes and the Behavior of the Economy', in C.P. Kindleberger and J. Laffargue, eds, *Financial Crises: Theory, History, and Policy*, pp. 13–38. Cambridge, Cambridge University Press.

Minsky, H.P. (1989) 'Comment on "Economic Implications of Extraordinary Movements in Stock Prices" by B.M. Friedman and D.A. Laibson', *Brookings Papers on Economic Activity*, 2(3): 173–189.

Morris, R. (1997) *Early Warning Indicators of Corporate Failure: A Critical Review of Previous Research and Further Empirical Evidence*, London, Institute of Chartered Accountants of England and Wales.

Peters, E.E. (1991) *Chaos and Order in the Capital Markets*, London, John Wiley.

Roll, R. (1986) 'The Hubris Hypothesis of Corporate Mergers', *Journal of Business*, 59: 197–216.

Shiller, R.J. (2005) *Irrational Exuberance* Princeton, NJ, Princeton University Press.

Simon, J. (2003) 'Three Australian Asset Price Bubbles', in A. Richards and T. Robinson, eds, *Asset Prices and Monetary Policy*, pp. 8–41, Sydney, Reserve Bank of Australia.

Smith, J. and G. Sterne (1994) 'Personal and Corporate Sector Debt', *Bank of England Quarterly Bulletin*, 144–155.

Smith, T. (1992) *Accounting for Growth: Stripping the Camouflage from Company Accounts*, London, Century Business.

Outperforming the Market: The Case of Mergers and Takeovers

CHAPTER **5**

Introduction

The previous two chapters looked at the debate relating to the rationality, on the one hand, and the herding instinct, on the other, of the stock markets. This chapter looks at a section of the market in which the latter is likely to be particularly prevalent. Here we examine the issues surrounding one of the most important (if not the most important) event to affect companies listed on a stock exchange and investors: a takeover or merger bid.[1] The management of the target company faces enormous change – perhaps redundancy. To the management of the bidding company, the bid represents one of the largest investment decisions they are likely to be involved in and also major change. To the shareholders of the target company, it represents an immediate prospect to make a large profit and to the shareholders of the bidding company, although it is clearly a major event, it is unclear whether they stand to gain or lose. Is the market – or to be more precise, are its participants – able to act rationally and objectively when faced with this, or do they act subjectively and allow other factors to influence their decisions?

In most instances, the value of a good or other possession is unaffected by the identity of its owner. The value of a motor car is determined by its type, age and condition. It is largely irrelevant who previously owned it. It is just possible that the car may be worth slightly more if it had been owned by a famous person but this is not usually a factor. The same applies for most other possessions but not in the case of the ownership of a business and, therefore, shares in a business. The reason, of course, is that the value of a business is determined by its profitability, or more precisely, by its expected future profitability. Therefore, a change in ownership of a business is likely to affect its

1 'Merger' refers to a merger between two companies that are roughly equal size, whereas a takeover (or acquisition) refers to a situation in which the target company ('acquiree' or 'biddee') is significantly smaller than the 'attacker' ('acquirer' or 'bidder'). There is no precise measure which distinguishes between a merger and a takeover and in practice the terms are often used interchangeably – especially where it is politic to use the term merger rather than takeover or acquisition.

value. If it is thought that the new owners are likely to improve the profitability of the business, its value will rise; if the reverse is anticipated, its value will fall. This will affect the value of the shares in a business. A change in ownership of the business is likely to affect their value – but only if the change in ownership is likely to affect the control and day-to-day management of the business to the extent that its profitability is significantly affected. Of course, the mere buying and selling of a company's shares is unlikely to affect its value but a change in its management and control may do so.

The purpose of this chapter is threefold. First, we need to examine the opportunities for profits and losses – for both companies and investors. Second, as it offers so much scope for profit by investors, the prediction of takeovers and mergers is discussed. Third, the market for corporate control (that part of the stock market involving takeovers and mergers) is discussed, and in particular merger mania, the most recent craze occurring in the 1980s and early 1990s that helped to fuel the stock market boom and eventual collapse. It is with merger mania that we begin.

The reasons for takeovers and mergers: Merger mania

Whilst the stock market boom and subsequent crash may be understood in terms of the general theories relating to bubbles, an integral part of the 1980s boom was a phenomenal increase in the number and total value of mergers and acquisitions. The 'market for corporate control' as part of the stock market had its own reasons and motivating factors.

The last wave of merger activity began in the early 1980s and continued into the early 1990s. By 1987, it had turned into the largest wave of mergers ever known (Franks and Mayer 1996) and was commonly referred to as 'merger mania'. It continued until about 1994, when the number of bids a year gradually reverted to its normal level (see Figure 5.1). A feature of merger mania was the huge premiums that were being offered. Virtually all the expected benefits from a bid (and often more) were paid to the shareholders of the target company who were selling out.

It was argued in Chapter 1 that it is in the national interest that scarce resources are allocated where they are most needed and most productive. The market for corporate control is an important mechanism helping to achieve this. If a company is weak, inefficient and its resources are unproductive, this will be reflected in its share price. It will make the company vulnerable to a takeover

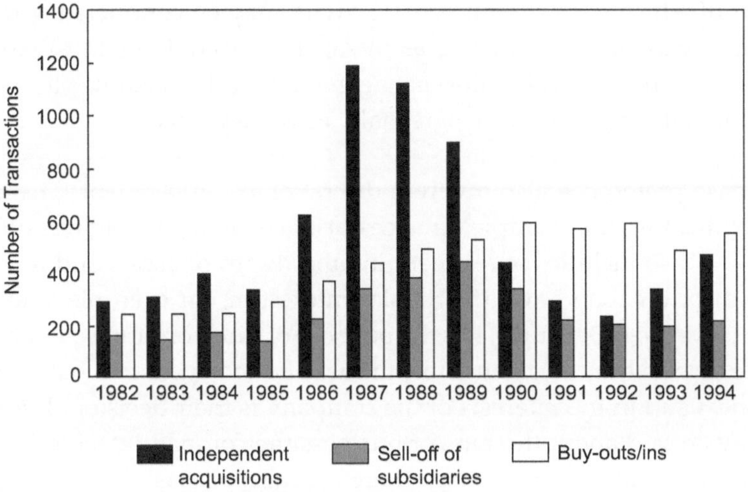

Figure 5.1 Merger mania. The UK market for corporate control, number of transactions 1982–1994

bid – probably by another more successful company that is able to manage the weak company's resources more efficiently. Because their careers may be at stake, senior managers and directors will do everything in their power to make the company successful and prosperous, thereby avoiding merger or takeover and possible redundancy (Marris 1964; Franks and Mayer 1996). It follows that the market for corporate control needs to work efficiently and that there are no unnecessary obstacles to merger activity.

That is the market approach: there is another view. This essentially recognizes that the decisions that organizations make – or the decisions that their managers and directors make for them – are not simply determined by the financial markets. Powerful company directors and senior managers are not slaves to the financial markets even if, at times, they pretend to be. They decide what is in their own best interests. In other words, directors and senior managers exercise their discretion. The importance of discretion by top management of large organizations has been widely recognized by academics since Berle and Means (1932). Probably the most famous exponent is Oliver Williamson (1963, 1964) with his notions of 'managerial discretion' and 'expense preference'. Williamson argues that the motives for managers principally include salary, security, prestige and power which may be seen through expense accounts, luxurious offices, company cars, the number of assistants and so on. In Williamson's world, profit merely acts as a fairly loose control on top management's activities. It needs to be earned so that there is sufficient slack out of which such discretionary activity may be conducted and funded. Profit also needs to be earned so as to satisfy shareholders but there is little incentive for directors and senior management to fully maximize it – especially if by minimizing costs they are personally adversely affected.

Expense preference also involves discretionary investment. This includes the investment in, for example, unnecessarily costly or prestigious offices and premises. It also includes investment in other types of assets and investments that the directors may have a particular interest in, for example a luxury flat, yacht or private jet. Of course, it is the purpose of directors and senior managers to decide corporate strategy and how this is to be achieved, so what is necessary for business and in the interests of the company is their decision. Precisely the same may be said about the type of business the company decides to enter or leave. Takeovers and mergers may, therefore, also be seen as part of directors' discretionary expenditure or activity. The decision to commit the company to a merger is theirs.[2] Whether it is really in the interests of shareholders to embark on a particular merger or takeover, and whether it is the most profitable and the wisest choice of all the available alternatives, may not be so clear.

Lying somewhere between these two extremities is another view. Directors may still overpay even if they are profit maximizing. They may quite genuinely overestimate the synergies (the gains from merger) available and the ease with which these may be achieved. They may convince themselves that their valuations are correct and, when it does not agree, that the stock market is wrong and does not reflect the full economic value of the combined firms. Rather than accept the fact that they should not pay the required premium to the target shareholders, because of pride and arrogance, they decide to raise their offer terms. This behaviour has been referred to as 'hubris' from the Greek meaning 'overbearing or excessive pride, over-belief in oneself, arrogance' (Roll 1986). It also involves stubbornness. In a takeover context, this relates to the directors of the bidding company being excessively determined to win at any cost. Roll suggests that directors of bidding firms convince themselves that their valuations are correct. They believe they will extract large synergistic benefits because they are such good managers. The simple truth is that they have offered too much but they are not prepared to accept that they are wrong. In this sense, hubris is another manifestation of managerial discretion.

2 Unless they are required to vote on the issue of new shares to fund the acquisition, it is quite likely that shareholders of the bidding company may not have the opportunity to vote on the proposed bid.

Roll finds an explanation for hubris in the 'Winner's Curse' hypothesis, deriving from auction theory in which the winner in a competitive bidding situation is to be the one who most overestimates the value of the subject of the auction.[3] By definition, the 'winner' is the person prepared to pay more than anyone else in the auction thinks the item is worth. In that sense, the amount by which his bid is higher those of others is therefore a measure of the curse.

An alternative to the winner's curse as an explanation of the hubris hypothesis relates to the convention in the market for corporate control of a 'minimum acceptable' premium. This is the amount that needs to be offered to the target's shareholders, which is largely insensitive to the amount of synergy the directors of the bidding company are expecting. During the merger mania period of the 1980s–1990s in the UK, a premium of less than 30 per cent would be rejected out of hand in the expectation that another bid of over 30 per cent would soon transpire (Greenfield 1992). That is, if the target's share price is currently 100p, a potential bidder would have to offer at least 130p to stand any chance of success. This percentage does fluctuate somewhat over time and market conditions, increasing to over 30 per cent during periods of high merger activity and falling to between 20 and 30 per cent during less active periods.[4] Between 1987 and 1993, the share price of targets in the UK on average increased by 31.5 per cent over the period surrounding a bid (Barnes 1998a). This reflected the price and premiums that were being offered. Barnes (1998a) has also calculated that the share price of bidders increased on average by only 1 per cent. This suggests that virtually all the expected benefits from the bid are paid to the shareholders of the target who are selling out. There was a large amount of dispersion around this figure[5] and many companies' share prices fell on the news that they were attempting a takeover.

Why is this? I have suggested hubris. There is another reason. There is no rigorous or independent check on management as to why they should embark on a particular merger/takeover or whether they are prepared to pay too much. Almost the only checks in practice are the comments or criticism by the financial press.[6] One of the methods by which mergers were accounted for allowed acquiring companies to effectively report improved profitability irrespective of the real economic effects (Chatterjee and Meeks 1996). It was eventually thrown

3 The hypothesis was originally developed to explain the behaviour of firms bidding for oil right tracts (Capen, Clapp and Campbell 1971).

4 It is interesting that Weston (1966) identified 20 per cent as a rule of thumb which had to be paid in the USA if the bidder was to stand a chance of winning.

5 The standard deviation for the 1 per cent for bidders is 34 per cent compared with 4 per cent for targets.

6 See Footnote 2 above.

out by the accountancy profession and only allowed to be used in certain very restrictive circumstances, but only after the scandal had been fully exposed.[7] It should not be thought that all the advantageous accounting treatment of a merger has been completely removed, however. Merging companies are still allowed to write down the value of assets and write off costs at the time of a merger, which has the effect of boosting post-merger profits.[8]

Synergy and the division of the gains to shareholders in the bidding and target companies

It is quite possible for the bidder to overpay without even shareholders and directors realizing until too late. The case of Ernest Saunders in the Guinness-Distillers scandal described in Chapter 7 is an example. It is the purpose of this short section to illustrate the financial dynamics involved.

Synergy refers to the '2 + 2 = 5' effect on the combined profits of the two merging firms. Synergy in the form of increased profits may be one-off items, for example the sale of one of the two firms' head offices and other unnecessary assets, or continuing benefits deriving from increased productive capacity and other efficiencies and economies of scale leading to increased yearly profits, for example increased factory size, merged R&D effort, greater buying power, merged advertising effort, better distribution facilities and so on.

Theoretically, the combined market price of two merging firms should increase to reflect the present value of the expected annual future additional earnings of the two firms arising from the merger's synergistic effects. Whether there is sufficient synergy to be made from a merger to justify and cover the necessary premium may be unimportant to the shareholders in the target firm if they are being offered cash. They should simply accept the offer, take the premium and run. Only if they are being offered shares in the bidding firm or think they stand to gain more if the company were allowed to continue independently, should they attempt to oppose the bid.

---

7 By the UK Financial Reporting Standard (FRS) 6, *Acquisitions and Mergers,* whose objective is to ensure that merger accounting is used only for those business combinations that are effectively mergers and that in all other cases acquisition accounting (which does not confer such benefits) is used.

8 Under FRS7 *Fair Values in Acquisition Accounting.* The writing off of assets and costs also has the effect of boosting the apparent post-merger growth and favourably affecting subsequent profit: capital employed financial ratios as the balance sheet value of net assets is reduced.

Consider the illustration in Table 5.1 involving a bid by Bidder plc for Target plc. Here £2m synergy is expected. This is sufficient for Bidder to offer a 30 per cent premium. If this were a cash offer with no alternative, this would cause Bidder's share price to rise from 260p to 270p as it is obtaining Target for £6.5m, Target is currently valued at £5m and the synergy arising from the merger is £2m. This is £13m + £5m + £2m = £20m. £20m – £6.5m = £13.5m. £13.5m/5m = 270p.Target's share price will rise from 100p to 130p irrespective of the amount of synergy because its shareholders are being offered this. If they are offered shares instead of cash (1 new share in Bidder for 2 in Target having the effect of offering a 30 per cent premium) this actually increases Target's share price to

Table 5.1 Calculating the value of synergy: how increased takeover terms do not improve the value of a share offer to target shareholders and how bidder shareholders lose out

Expected synergy		
One-off net receipt – immediately £1.0m		
Increased profits per year £0.1m		
Present value of synergy (£1m + £1m) = £2m. That is 0.01/0.01 = 1.0, where the discount rate is assumed to be 10 per cent per year and the savings occur indefinitely.		
Shares	Bidder	Target
Number 5m 5m	5m	5m
Price (prior to bid) 260p 100p	260p	100p
Total market capitalization £13.0m £5.0m	£13.0m	£5.0m
Synergy	£2m	
Initial offer		
Offer terms (30% premium)		
Cash 130p		
Share price (after bid)	270p	130p
Shares: 1 new share in Bidder for 2 in Target (effectively 30% premium) Share price (after bid)	267p	133p
Improved offer		
Offer terms (43% premium)		
Cash 143p		
Share price (after bid)	257p	143p
Shares: 11 new shares in Bidder for 20 in Target (effectively 43% premium) Share Price (after bid)	258p	142p

133p, a premium of 33 per cent and Bidder's share price to 267p. This is £13m + £5m + £2m = £20m; 5m + 2.5m = 7.5m shares. £20m/7.5m = 267p. Table 5.1 also shows the effect of Bidder offering more than it can afford. Here there is an improved offer of 143p cash or an eleven for twenty share offer, effectively 43 per cent. The cash-only offer has the effect of causing Bidder's share price to fall from 260p to 257p. This is £13m + £5m + £2m = £20m. £20m – £7.15m = £12.85m. £12.85m/5m = 257p. In the case of the share offer, because it is so generous, Bidder's share price will fall to 258p which in turn reduces the value of Target's shares. This is £13m + £5m + £2m = £20m; 5m + 2.75m = 7.75m shares. £20m/7.75m = 258p.

The identification and forecasting of takeover targets

Clearly, if an investor were able to identify takeover targets sufficiently far in advance to enable them to buy shares in the target company before the announcement of the bid, they would be able to make huge profits. This is analogous to the ability of a gambler being able to accurately forecast the identity of cards being dealt or 'score draws' in order to complete the football pools.

Even though this has been likened to gambling, there is one important difference. In gambling, if the gambler is wrong, for example incorrectly forecasting the winner of a horse race, they lose the money they had bet. In the case of an investor who buys shares in a company they think may be taken over, they do not lose their stake (unless it inadvertently fails or they use a CFD or spread bet). The shares simply do not rise in price as was expected. It is also possible that if enough investors thought that the company would be the subject of a bid and bought shares in the target, it is quite likely that the share price would rise and a profit could be made even though the merger did not transpire[9] (see the graph of shares in Marks and Spencer in Figure 5.2). During December 1999 and January 2000 there was considerable press speculation that there would be a bid for Marks and Spencer. It did not transpire. This is a good example of a rumour not needing to be true to have the same effect.

Because the regulations prohibit it (see Chapter 6) and companies are required to announce a bid or the existence of bid discussions at a very early stage, an investor cannot rely on a company announcement to alert them to the possibility

9 It is quite common for a potential bidder to build a stake in a target, decide against a bid, and sell the shares at a profit due to the price rising in anticipation of the bid.

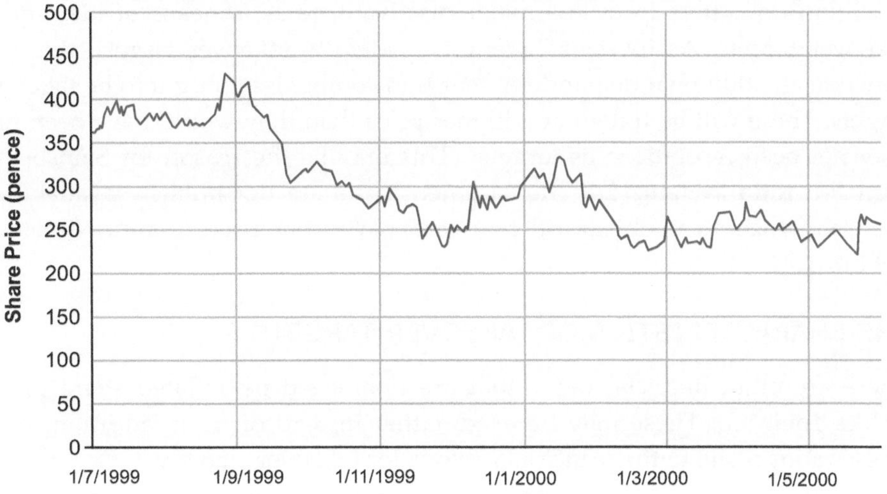

Figure 5.2 Marks and Spencer shares July 1999–May 2000

of a bid and be able to profit from the 30 per cent premium that is likely to be offered. In which case, is it possible using publicly available data, for example accounting and other financial information, for an investor to 'spot' a takeover target? There is some empirical evidence to suggest that this is possible.

MARKET TO BOOK RATIO: 'TOBIN'S Q'

The most obvious indicator of a company being unable to manage its resources profitably and becoming a likely takeover target is where its share price is low compared with the value of its assets. This may be measured by means of 'Tobin's q', the ratio of the total market value of the firm to the replacement cost of its assets. If a company's q is greater than one, then the value of the company exceeds the total value of its individual assets. This suggests that the company is regarded by the market as profitable. On the other hand, if a company's q is less than one, this suggests that the market places a very low value on the company, probably because it is unprofitable (or less profitable than its peers). This may suggest that the company is ripe for takeover. Another company should be able to acquire it and make it viable in some way. It is also possible that a bidder will acquire an undervalued company simply so as to sell off its assets at a profit. When asset-stripping was a popular reason for takeovers in the 1960s, a low Tobin's q was a particularly good sign of a possible takeover target (Marris 1964).

Tobin's q suffers from one major disadvantage as a means of identifying takeover targets. As investors attempt to identify takeover targets, this will generate an additional demand for shares in companies thought to be takeover targets. These will be traded at a higher price than they would have been had they not been recognized as targets. (This may be the reason for Sainsbury's high P/E ratio in Table 2.1). Replacement costs are not publicly available in the UK, which means historical costs will have to be used to approximate to Tobin's q.

THE CHARACTERISTICS OF TAKEOVER TARGETS

There are other financial ratios that are unaffected by inflated share prices unlike Tobin's q. These may be used, either instead of, or in addition to, it. These ratios relate to the principal reasons for takeover, namely:

Inefficient management/poor financial performance As the principal measure of efficiency is profitability, a firm with less than average profits may be more likely to be taken over than a company with higher than average profits. A company's P/E ratio reflects the market's opinion of its future profitability. A company with a low P/E ratio may be more likely to the subject of a bid than a company with a high one because it can be bought relatively cheaply.

Growth–resource mismatch This is an extension of the inefficient management hypothesis and relates to the notion of both low-growth/resource-rich and high-growth/resource-poor firms being likely acquisition targets (Levine and Aaronovitch 1981). As they have spare operating capacity, firms with low activity ratios may be attractive to ambitious management teams. Similarly, firms with low growth records are likely to be vulnerable to takeover. Although this may depend on each individual case, certain types of mismatch may be common and will be a factor in many mergers.

Inefficient financial structure Growth–resource mismatch may also extend to the way the firm is financed and to the adequacy of finance for the firm's activities. The prospects of a high-growth firm may be spoiled if it has inadequate financial support or base. It would be an attractive target to a firm with resources available to help. Similarly, a cash-rich company may be vulnerable as a target because it is attractive to a cash-starved acquirer. A bankrupt company may not only be vulnerable to but welcome a takeover. Again, it may be attractive to an acquirer because it is cheap and provides an opportunity to buy certain assets cheaply, if only to resell them at a profit.

Another aspect of the resources mismatch hypothesis relates to the extent to which the firm has taken advantage of the benefits of gearing or leverage. Low gearing may signal unused debt capacity, which may be attractive to a bidder that is highly geared.

Corporate size It is obvious that corporate size will have an effect in some way on the likelihood of a takeover or merger bid. A company is more vulnerable if it is small. The likelihood of acquisition decreases with increased size mainly because of the size-related transaction costs. There is another reason: the probability of acquisition decreases with increased size as the number of firms larger than the bidder decreases with size. On the other hand, a company may be more attractive simply because it is large and, in contrast to earlier periods, a feature of the 1980s merger boom was the very large size of some takeover targets (Hughes 1989).

Table 5.2 Variables affecting the likelihood of takeover

Hypothesis	Financial ratio
Inefficient management, poor financial performance	Profit before tax: Sales Profit before tax: Shareholders' equity Growth of profit before tax over last 3 years Price/Earnings ratio Average dividends over last 3 years: Shareholders' equity Growth of dividends over last 3 years
Growth-resource mismatch	Sales: Total assets Total remuneration: Sales Growth of sales over last 3 years Current assets: Current liabilities Current assets less current liabilities: total assets
Inefficient financial structure	Long term debt: Total assets Long term debt: Shareholders' equity Profit before tax + interest paid: Interest paid
Corporate size	Market capitalization prior to bid

Source: Barnes (1999).

Using financial characteristics to forecast takeover targets

Even though these ratios have been shown to be good financial indicators of the characteristics of takeover targets, they are less than perfect predictions because there are many different reasons for takeover. For instance, weak and unprofitable companies are vulnerable to takeover. On the other hand, a new young highly profitable company may be attractive to an ailing giant or a competitor that has an ailing growth record. If failure can be the reason for a takeover, so can success.

For many years, it was believed that statistical models could predict and identify takeover targets. The published studies had boasted high predictive accuracies ranging between 60 and 90 per cent. However, Palepu (1986) argued that these claims were largely unfounded because of statistical error. If the statistical studies had been performed correctly, their conclusions would have been similar to his own and shown that the successful identification of targets and the earning of abnormal returns were not possible. Palepu's model identified 625 firms as targets but only 24 were actually bid for. It is not surprising that his model did not earn abnormal returns. However, Bartley and Boardman (1990) and Walter (1994) have suggested that, whilst most of Palepu's methodological points are correct, his empirical conclusions may not be the final word on the subject. Walter (1994) used Palepu's methodological revisions and showed that US current cost data had a high predictive ability. Unfortunately, because of the losses sustained on a few of the incorrect forecasts, Walter's model earned quite modest excess returns overall. Four of the twenty-nine predicted firms were bid for compared with a total of ten bids out of his total sample of ninety-one. This represents a predictive ability far greater than chance, but because of the below-average performance of some of the firms that were incorrectly forecast and the relatively small population of companies in the hold out sample the overall abnormal return was small. Bartley and Boardman's (1990) results are also quite supportive of the view that published replacement cost accounting data have predictive ability, but only by inference. They had a high classifying accuracy (82.5 per cent) but did not test for the model's predictive ability. It is only the very largest firms in the USA that report current cost data and none do in the UK. See Figure 5.3 for an analysis of correct and incorrect classifications and what are known as Type I and Type II errors.

In order to judge whether a statistical model can be used in practice to identify takeover targets and earn an investor abnormal returns it is necessary to examine the methodology involved. Probably the most important consideration is a model's 'predictive ability' as opposed to its 'classifying accuracy'. Classifying accuracy refers the ability of a model to correctly classify cases drawn from its own estimating sample. Predictive ability, on the other hand, refers to the ability of the model at the time of its estimation to correctly predict targets drawn from a new group of sample companies for a subsequent period (the holdout sample), yielding an investor profits. To be used, the model must be available to the investor at the time of making an investment. It must have been estimated together with the cut-off.

The cut-off is the probability point above which a company may be classified as a likely takeover target. Its value defines the firm is to be classified as such. For example, say there is a 90 per cent probability of a bid, the firm should be classified as forecast to be subject to a bid; whereas a firm with a 10 per cent probability would be classified as not likely to be bid for. However, should a company with a 60 per cent probability be classified as a likely takeover target in which an investor would place money in the expectation of a bid? The choice of a cut-off value is, therefore, a difficult decision and should be influenced by the amount of risk and money the investor is prepared to invest. I may decide to have a higher cut-off in making my investment decisions than another person, perhaps they have more money to invest.

		Prediction	
		Bid	**No bid**
Outcome	**Bid**	Correct	Type I error
	No bid	Type II error	Correct

Figure 5.3 Type I and Type II errors

There are two stages involved and two distinct periods in the development and application of the statistical model. The first is the estimation period. At the end of it, the model and the cut-off are determined. These would then be applied during a subsequent period (the test period) to the holdout sample. As there is no reason for the model to remain stable, the test period should (and is assumed to) immediately follow the estimation period. It is quite possible for a model to have high classifying accuracy yet have poor actual predictive ability. Conditions in the market for corporate control may change quickly and factors affecting the likelihood of a merger at one point in time may be different to those at another point in time. (See Chapter 4 for more on stock market moods, crazes and fads.) Table 5.3 shows how classification accuracy and predictive ability vary.

Searching for takeover targets in practice has been likened to looking for a needle in a haystack. There are usually less than a hundred bids each year

Table 5.3 Published takeover prediction studies

Researcher	Country	Statistical method used	Classification accuracy (%)	Predictive ability (%)
Simkovitz and Monroe (1971)	USA	DA	77	63.2
Tzoannos and Samuels (1972)	UK	GLS	70	n/r
Stevens (1973)	USA	DA	70	67
Belkaoui (1978)	Canada	DA	72	70
Wansley and Lane (1983)	USA	DA	77.3	69.2
Dietrich and Sorensen (1984)	USA	Logit	92.5	n/r
Rege (1984)	Canada	DA	n/r	n/r
Bartley and Boardman (1986)	USA	DA	65	n/r
Palepu (1986)	USA	Logit	n/r	46
Bartley and Boardman (1990)	USA	DA	82.5	n/r
Ambrose (1990)	USA	Logit	65.1	75.6
Barnes (1990)	UK	DA	68.5	n/r
Ambrose and Megginson (1992)	USA	Logit	74.3	n/r
Walter (1994)	USA	Logit	65	66
Barnes (1998b)	UK	Logit	n/r	98.6
Barnes (1999)	UK	Logit	n/r	98.5
Barnes (2000)	UK	DA Logit	n/r n/r	97.8 98.5

DA, discriminant analysis, GLS, generalized least squares; n/r, not reported.

The statistical methods are briefly described in the Appendix.

on the LSE from the many thousands of listed companies. The probability of being a takeover target is low and the holdout sample needs to represent this. It needs to contain a representative number of companies in which the number of targets and non-targets reflects the population as a whole. The cut-off point also needs to reflect this. Most of the early takeover studies used a probability cut-off of 0.5. If the model stated that the probability of takeover was greater than 0.5, then this would be classified as a takeover prediction. Whilst this may be acceptable if the sample of targets and non-targets is equal, if the sample sizes are unequal – and they need to be if they are to be representative – a weighted cutoff needs to be used. In most of the earlier studies listed in Table 5.2, the holdout sample included an equal number of companies that were bid for as those that were not. The effect of this was to hugely overstate the model's predictive ability. Palepu (1986) demonstrates this by recalculating Steven's (1973) classifying accuracy of 70 per cent which was based on a sample of an equal number of targets and non-targets. It falls to 56 per cent if the proportion of targets to non-targets in the holdout sample were representative of the population as a whole.

There are a number of alternative ways of determining the cut off if the holdout sample is constructed to represent the population as a whole. Figure 5.4 shows the distribution of the probability distributions of those companies in the sample that were actually not bid for (Group A) and those that were (Group B). Palepu uses an empirically determined cut-off. This is known as 'the minimization of errors'. This is where the estimated probability distributions intersect, M in Figure 5.4. Although it does minimize total forecast errors, there is one important problem with determining the cut-off in this way. It does not necessarily maximize the investor's return! Consider the areas of the two distributions representing forecast error: a Type I error where the company was not forecast to be the subject of a bid but was bid for and a Type II error where the company was forecast to be bid for and was not in Figure 5.4. The minimization of errors criterion minimizes the aggregate errors. This is fine if they are equally costly but they are not. Type I errors are costly to an investor as they lose out on investing in a lucrative investment opportunity. In contrast, a Type II error is relatively cost free, especially if we assume that the investor has a relatively large sum to invest and is able to invest in all likely targets. Therefore, if an investor's returns are to be maximized, he should use the cut off, R, in Figure 5.4 where there are no Type II errors and the relatively large number of Type I errors is costless.[10]

10 A similar situation occurs in respect of bankruptcy prediction where the cost of an incorrect forecast of bankruptcy is costly to a lender who lends to a company which subsequently goes bankrupt. Avoiding lending to a company that the lender thought might become bankrupt but

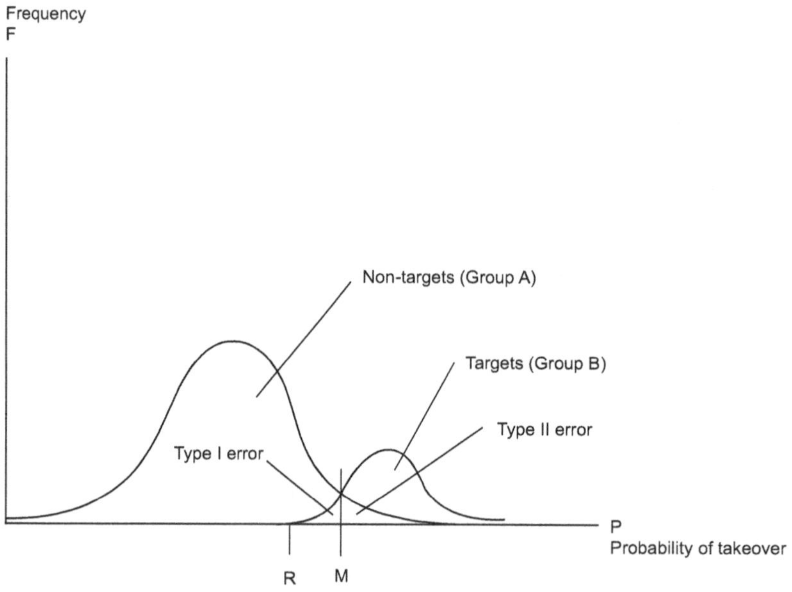

Figure 5.4 Diagram to show the distribution of actual targets and non-targets, the application of cut-off points and resultant Type I and II errors

Group A and B distributions represent actual target and non target firms. Here, Types I and II cut-offs are determined by the minimization of errors cut off, M in the diagram. If a different cut-off were employed, different Types I and II errors would result, for example if the cut-off were R there would be no Type II errors and more Type I.

Although the determination of the cut-off point by means of the minimization of errors or simply Type I errors may appear to be theoretically sound, both still suffer from one major problem. They need to be determined *ex ante* for the investor to purchase shares in the potential targets ahead of a bid. The cut-off can only be calculated precisely *ex post*, that is immediately after the test period. An *ex ante* cut-off will contain an estimation error, but this is the best that can be done.

There have only been a few studies that have used the minimization of Type I errors to determine the cut-off. Barnes (1998b, 1999) found that they did considerably better than chance and significantly improved the likelihood of

this turned out to incorrect may be annoying to a lender at the time but does not involve it in any lost money, nor any opportunity cost if it was able to lend the money elsewhere.

earning large abnormal returns. Nevertheless, the results were disappointing, even though he made various other attempts to improve the data, for example adjusting for industry differences by constructing industry-specific models. The most likely reason for these results was that there were too many conflicting factors affecting the likelihood of a bid and that these were changeable over time. That is, the models had high classifying accuracy, during the analysis periods at least, but they did not have sufficient predictive ability for an investor to make significantly large abnormal returns.

Using share price movements to identify takeover targets

In addition to accounting and other financial data that are publicly available, recent share price data are likely to have good predictive ability. This is especially so if movements in a company's share price occur prior to an announcement as a result of anticipating a bid. This may occur because of insider dealing, press speculation or an increase in the amount of dealing on the back of these. The total share price movement may be quick and once and for all at the time of the announcement according to the ECMH. Alternatively, the total share price change may be spread over a longer period beginning, perhaps, with the effects of insider information. If this were the case, it would be possible to use anticipatory price changes (or changes in the volume of trading or other measures of the volatility of trading in the share) as an indication of a forthcoming bid and earn abnormal returns. This is contrary to the implications of the ECMH, although it is not suggested that the market is efficient in the strong form and it is difficult (if not impossible) to distinguish between share price movements arising from the anticipation of a forthcoming takeover bid and those occurring for other reasons.

Palepu thought that share price changes occur too late for any forecasting model to use. He cited Jensen and Ruback's (1983) authoritative review of share price behaviour which suggested that prices adjust to the news of a merger during a relatively short period around the time of the announcement. For instance, Keown and Pinkerton (1981) found that in the US the abnormal share price performance was largely confined to one month immediately before the announcement of a bid. In which case there would hardly be time to trade on the information, or if there was, the gain would be severely reduced and even reduced to nought after transaction costs.

What is the UK evidence? Early studies suggested that targets' share prices experienced large gains over a long period prior to the announcement of a bid, implying that investors could advantageously trade on them. Franks *et al.* (1977) found abnormal gains in target companies of 26 per cent over the 5-month period up to the offer date. Limmack (1991) found that targets' abnormal returns were significant for the month before the month during which the announcement occurred – 3.64 per cent for completed bids and 5.4 per cent for unsuccessful or abandoned bids. (It matters little to an investor seeking abnormal return from a bid whether or not it is successful as the offer price stands during the offer period irrespective of whether the bid is ultimately successful.) In the preceding month they were again significant: 1.71 per cent for completed bids and 0.58 per cent for unsuccessful or abandoned bids. Barnes (1996) has shown that during the 1987–1992 period, share prices of target firms increased by 31 per cent over the period 2 months before the announcement to 1 month afterwards and 23 per cent (almost three-quarters of the total movement) occurred before the announcement. However, of that, a relatively small but nevertheless significant amount (2 per cent) occurred prior to 1 month before the bid. Thus, if these early movements had been identified at the time, there would have been sufficient time to act and a sufficiently large portion of the total price change still to occur to earn large abnormal returns. Figure 5.5 illustrates the trade-off between the amount of potential gains and how this is quickly eroded as the announcement date approaches.

Can share price movements be used in combination with an *ex ante* statistical prediction model to earn abnormal returns? Barnes (1998b) found that, somewhat surprisingly, neither the predictive model nor the addition of share price movements were capable of earning large abnormal returns. The predictive ability of the statistical model was only minutely improved by the addition of share price movement data if the investor used share price data up to one month prior to the announcement of a bid. This proposition was also tested by Holland and Hodgkinson (1994) who found that share prices of 'identified' targets (those for whom the press had reported the likelihood of a bid or that a large stake had been purchased in the target firm, or that the takeover classification model they had constructed had identified the firm as a target) experienced significant overperformance during the month before the announcement of a bid. Unfortunately, Holland and Hodgkinson's conclusions are impaired because they do not separate out of the 'identified' group, those firms included solely by reason of the classification model and whether those firms also overperformed. This is important because those firms would not have been known until after the event.

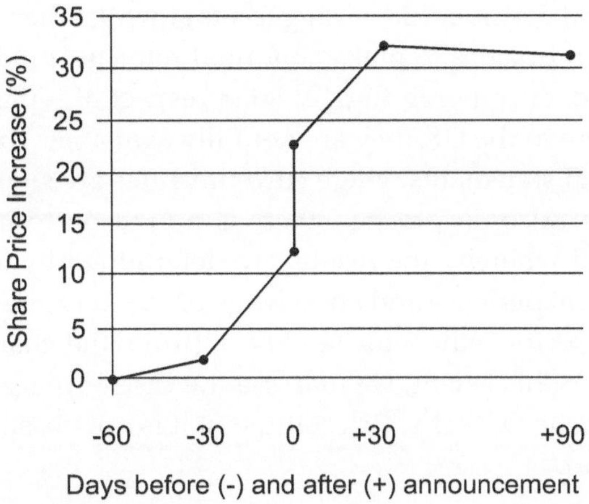

Figure 5.5 Increase in share price of target ahead of merger announcement (Barnes 1996)

Other events capable of prediction

Whilst most economic events cannot be predicted, some may at least be anticipated or inferred. Corporate bankruptcy is an example. Whilst an actual date may not be capable of prediction (thereby ruling out its use for profit-making, for example by short selling) it may be reasonably easy, and it is certainly feasible to anticipate failure, say if the firm has been consistently making losses, losing funds, losing its market share and so on. Nowadays there are many companies providing failure probability estimates based on similar types of statistical models I have described here which claim to predict up to four years ahead. Can these forecasts be used to outperform the market, or has it already digested the information and the share price has adjusted to the new probability of failure? Studies by Altman and Brenner (1981), Katz *et al.* (1985) and Zavgren *et al.* (1988) in the USA have shown that these models help investors avoid large losses by selling before bankruptcy occurs.

Conclusions

We have concentrated in this chapter on one of the largest events likely to affect a company, its finances, and its shareholders. In the first two sections we saw how such decisions are often not made in shareholders' interests and, whilst the shareholders of a target company stand to profit from a bid, the shareholders in the bidding company may not. We then proceeded to how an investor may forecast or identify takeover targets. Our review of the empirical studies and the methodological considerations suggests that whilst there are difficulties in using the model in practice to make abnormal returns, it may still be possible to do so. The US data certainly suggest so in respect of replacement cost data. Unfortunately, here in the UK they are not fully available. They should exist in published financial statements where current values are significantly different to historical costs. Also, in practice, there is no reason to make this exercise purely mechanical whereby the results are determined by a statistical model alone. Judgement, experience and knowledge of the stock market, firms in play, and the relevant sector may considerably improve the chances of success in spotting targets. To this extent, we may see the case of mergers and takeovers as an exception to the ECMH which states that it is not possible to make excess returns of this kind.

This chapter has demonstrated the problems the market for corporate control raises for the fair working of the stock markets. Invariably, there is a huge amount at stake for the companies involved, their directors and their shareholders. It is not surprising if directors and top management attempt to pursue their objectives at virtually any cost. They may also attempt to pursue their own objectives and agendas at shareholders' and other stakeholders' expense. They may try to exploit their positions. This requires regulation in some form. First, it is necessary that the market knows as soon as possible of a merger, otherwise insider dealing is likely to occur. Shareholders need to know whether a proposed bid is in their interests and if not how they may reject it. They need to be able to assess its success. A takeover bid often becomes a battle of wills between two boards of directors as they strive for shareholder acceptance. There need to be 'rules of the game' in which the 'battle' is conducted. These rules need to be sufficiently strong and robust to resist the efforts of companies to squeeze an unfair advantage. It is the purpose of the next three chapters to examine the issues here. First we will look at the law and regulation – not merely relating to the market for corporate control but generally. We will then examine the areas where the law and regulations are contravened.

References

Altman, E.I. and M. Brenner (1981) 'Information Effects and Stock Market Response to Firm Deterioration', *Journal of Financial and Quantitative Analysis*, 16: 35–51.

Ambrose, B.W. (1992) 'Corporate Real Estate's Impact on the Takeover Market', *Journal of Financial and Quantitative Analysis*, 27: 575–589.

Asquith, P. (1983) 'Merger Bids, Uncertainty and Stockholder Returns', *Journal of Financial Economics*, 11: 51–83.

Barnes, P.A. (1984) 'The Effect of a Merger on the Share Price of the Attacker Revisited', *Accounting and Business Research,* 15: 45–49.

Barnes, P.A. (1990) 'The Prediction of Takeover Targets in the UK by means of Multiple Discriminant Analysis', *Journal of Business Finance and Accounting,* 17(1): 73–84.

Barnes, P.A. (1996) 'The Regulation of Insider Dealing in the UK. Some Empirical Evidence concerning Share Prices, Merger Bids and Bidders' Advising Merchant Banks', *Applied Financial Economics,* 6: 383–391.

Barnes, P.A. (1998a) 'Why do Bidders do so Badly out of Mergers? Some UK Evidence', *Journal of Business Finance and Accounting,* 25(5 and 6): 571–594.

Barnes, P.A. (1998b) 'Can Takeover Targets be identified by Statistical Techniques? Some UK Evidence', *The Statistician,* 47(4): 1–19.

Barnes, P.A. (1999) 'Predicting UK Takeover Targets: Some Methodological Issues and an Empirical Study', *Review of Quantitative Finance and Accounting,* 12(3): 283–301.

Barnes, P.A. (2000) 'The Identification of UK Takeover Targets using Published Historical Cost Accounting Data: Some Empirical Evidence comparing Logit with Linear Discriminant Analysis and Raw Financial Ratios with Industry-Relative Ratios', *International Review of Financial Analysis,* 9(2): 147–162.

Bartley, J.W. and C.M. Boardman (1990) 'Replacement-cost Adjusted Valuation Ratio as a Discriminator among Takeover and Non-target Firms', *Journal of Business Finance and Accounting,* 17: 53–72.

Belkaoui, A. (1978) 'Financial Ratios as Predictors of Canadian Mergers', *Journal of Business Finance and Accounting,* 5: 93–107.

Berle, A.A. and G.C. Means (1932) *The Modern Corporation and Personal Property,* New York, Macmillan.

Capen, E., R. Clapp and W. Campbell (1971) 'Competitive Bidding in High-risk Situations', *Journal of Petroleum Technology,* 23, 641–53.

Franks, J.R. and C. Mayer (1996) 'Hostile Takeovers and the Correction of Managerial Failure', *Journal of Financial Economics,* 40(1): 163–181.

Franks, J.R. and R.S. Harris (1989) 'Shareholder Wealth Effects of Corporate Takeovers: the UK Experience 1955–85', *Journal of Financial Economics,* 18: 225–249.

Franks, J.R., J.E. Broyles and M.J. Hecht (1977) 'An Industry Study of the Profitability of Mergers in the United Kingdom', *Journal of Finance,* 32: 1513–1525.

Greenfield, L. (1992) 'Bidders Still have Deep Pockets Despite the Recession', *Acquisition Monthly,* May, 1.

Holland, K. and L. Hodgkinson (1994) 'The Pre-Announcement Share Price Behaviour of UK Takeover Targets', *Journal of Business Finance and Accounting,* 21: 467–490.

Hughes, A. (1989) 'The Impact of Merger: A Survey of Empirical Evidence for the UK', in J. Faurburn and J. Kay, eds, *Mergers and Merger Policy,* pp. 9–95, London, Oxford University Press.

Jensen, M.C. and R.S. Ruback (1983) 'The Market for Corporate Control: The Scientific Evidence', *Journal of Financial Economics,* 11: 5–50.

Katz, S.S., S. Lilien and B. Nelson (1985) 'Stock Market Behaviour around Bankruptcy Distress and Recovery Predictions', *Financial Analysts Journal,* Jan–Feb: 70–74.

Keown, A.J. and J.M. Pinkerton (1981) 'Merger Announcements and Insider Trading Activity', *Journal of Finance,* 36: 855–869.

Levine, P. and S. Aaronovitch (1981) 'The Financial Characteristics of Firms and Theories of Merger Activity', *Journal of industrial Economics,* 30: 149–172.

Limmack, R.J. (1991) 'Corporate Mergers and Shareholder Wealth Effects 1977–1986', *Accounting and Business Research,* 21: 239–251.

Marris, R. (1964) *The Economic Theory of Managerial Capitalism,* Glencoe, Free Press.

Palepu, K.G. (1986) 'Predicting Takeover Targets: A Methodological and Empirical Analysis', *Journal of Accounting and Economics,* 8: 3–35.

Rege, U.P. (1984) 'Accounting Ratios to Locate Takeover Targets', *Journal of Business Finance and Accounting,* 11: 301–311.

Roll, R. (1986) 'The Hubris Hypothesis of Corporate Mergers', *Journal of Business,* 59: 197–216.

Simkovitz, M.A. and R.J. Monroe (1971) 'A Discriminant Function for Conglomerate Targets', *Southern Journal of Business,* 38: 1–16.

Stevens, D.L. (1973) 'Financial Characteristics of Merged Firms: A Multivariate Analysis', *Journal of Financial and Quantitative Analysis,* 8: 149–158.

Tzoannos, J and J. Samuels (1972) 'Mergers and Takeovers: The Financial Characteristics of Companies Involved', *Journal of Business Finance and Accounting,* 1: 5–16.

Walter, R.M. (1994) 'The Usefulness of Current Cost Information for Identifying Takeover Targets and Earning Above-Average Stock Returns', *Journal of Accounting, Auditing and Finance,* 9: 349–377.

Wansley, J.R. and W.R. Lane (1983) 'A Financial Profile for Merged Firms', *Review of Business and Economic Research,* 65: 87–98.

Weston, J.F. (1966) 'Determinants of the Share Exchange Ratio in Mergers' in W.W. Alberts and J. Segall, eds, *The Corporate Merger,* pp. 119–138, Chicago, IL, University of Chicago Press.

Williamson, O.E. (1963) 'Managerial Discretion and Business Behaviour', *American Economic Review,* 53: 1032–1057.

Williamson, O.E. (1964) *The Economics of Discretionary Behaviour: Managerial Objectives in a Theroy of the Firm,* Englewood Cliffs, NJ, Prentice-Hall.

Zavgren, C.V., M.T. Dugan and J.M. Reeve (1998) 'The Association Between Probabilities of Bankruptcy and Market Responses – a Test of Market Anticipation', *Journal of Business Finance and Accounting,* 15: 27–45.

Appendix
Statistical Methodology

Economists usually use the market model or the CAPM to measure share price abnormal performance or synergy. A critical assumption of both statistical models is the stability of β which is interpreted as a measure of the riskiness of the share in that company. This assumption may not be justified. A merger or takeover significantly alters the make up of the firm. Two hitherto independent firms are being joined together; their new β will be a weighted average of their pre-merger β s (Asquith 1983).[11] Because β is likely to change and should do so, some researchers have abandoned the use of β and assume a value of unity; for example, Barnes (1984, 1996), Franks and Harris (1989) and Limmack (1991).

Table 5.3 shows that the statistical methods used to estimate the classification and predictive models are either Logit, discriminant analysis (DA), or generalized least squares (GLS). Logit and generalized least squares are estimated in a very similar way. Logit regression is estimated for the following equation:

$$\text{Ln}[p_i/(1 - p_i) = k_i = b_0 + b_1X_1 + b_2X_2 \ldots + b_nX_n$$

where p_i is the probability of a bid for firm i, b_0 is a constant and there are n independent variables. Each firm in the estimation sample is given a k value of one or zero according to whether it was bid for or not, respectively. The probability of a bid is therefore:

$p_i = 1/(1 + e^{-ki})$ where e is the base of the natural logarithm.

DA is estimated for the following equation:

$$z_i = d_1X_1 + d_2X_2 \ldots + d_nX_n.$$

The coefficients $d_1 \ldots d_n$ are estimated in an opposite way to Logit. Here they are estimated to best discriminate (or distinguish) between the bid-for and not bid-for sample companies. Again, each firm in the estimation sample is given

11 Weighted according to the size of the two companies by means of, say, their market capitalization.

a z value of one or zero according to whether it was bid for or not. For each firm in the holdout sample, its likelihood of being a takeover target may be measured by its estimated z-value which is estimated by multiplying its X_1, X_2 … X_n values by the estimated coefficients d_1, d_2, … d_n. This may be converted into a probability function, q, as the value of the exponent where $q_i = 1/(1 + e^{-z_i})$.

The Regulation of the Markets

CHAPTER 6

The market abuse regime covers markets well outside the scope of this book, such as the commodities and energy markets. This review attempts to cover those aspects related to the regulation of equities on the LSE.

Introduction

In order for the market to function properly, the information that it is provided with needs to be orderly and timely and companies and investors need to behave fairly and properly. In short, the market needs to be regulated. Before 1986 the Stock Exchange was virtually independent and self-governing. The Financial Services Act 1986 imposed a new regulatory regime that was self-regulatory in nature but placed within a statutory framework. There then followed a fairly tumultuous period involving various financial crises and many scandals posing operating and effectiveness problems for the new regulatory bodies. As a result, the new Labour government introduced statutory regulation by means of the Financial Services and Markets Act 2000 and the creation of a single statutory body, the Financial Services Authority (FSA) which replaced a host of self-regulatory bodies. In the case of the LSE, the FSA now has responsibility for the licensing and supervision of firms and individuals involved in securities trading, the vetting and approval of share and other securities' issues, the admission to listing of companies who shares are traded on the exchange, their compliance with the listing rules, and the integrity and efficiency of the securities markets generally.

This chapter reviews the legislation and regulations whose aim is to ensure that the LSE is efficient and free of market abuse. It therefore covers the legislation and regulations relating to the disclosure of information to the market. This is considered first. Next, we examine the law that has made insider dealing and market abuse criminal offences and, more recently, a civil offence. The latter should be seen in the context of the obligations of the FSA and the efforts of the EU legislators to ensure a uniformity of approach to market abuse across the European Union. As a result of the efforts of these two organizations, in addition to the law, currently there is a plethora of regulations, rules, guidelines and recommendations. I have attempted to avoid much of the minutiae of these and concentrate on the broad principles they are attempting to apply. This is not a legal textbook and should not be read as legal advice. The FSA guidelines and approach are still emerging as it strives for a more flexible and pragmatic approach to the way in which it expects those involved should behave. Nevertheless, I have attempted to present a feel for what the FSA and those involved currently consider acceptable and good practice relating to the controls within issuers and firms. The term 'issuer', which refers to the issuer of the securities, is used in the regulations rather than 'company'. The term 'firm' refers to financial intermediaries such as those acting as advisers, brokers and market makers.

Clearly, there is a movement away from detailed rules to more 'principles-based' regulation and broad-based standards (see Box 6.1). Firms need to be able to take the necessary precautions that are appropriate for their business. There will be greater reliance on informal FSA guidance in which firms will be encouraged to think for themselves. They will be given greater freedom and flexibility as to how the minimization of market abuse and leakage of information may be achieved. Firms' senior management will take responsibility for ensuring their firms identify risks and develop appropriate systems and controls to manage and mitigate these risks, notably conflicts of interest. The FSA is not prescriptive. Instead, it provides examples and illustration for firms to adapt for their businesses.

Box 6.1 The FSA's principles-based regulation

FSA Principles

↓

FSA Detailed Rules

↓

Firms' Systems and Controls

Of course, there are many laws and regulations, codes of practice etc. that relate to listed companies affecting the rights of shareholders and, therefore, the pricing of securities. The most important are company law itself which is contained in the Companies Acts and related legislation, and the additional requirements imposed on a company as a condition for Stock Exchange listing. These are not covered here, although the listing requirements that directly relate to market abuse are reviewed. Finally, this chapter briefly reviews the rules and codes of practice relating to the situation where a listed company is involved in a takeover or merger bid. This is a particularly important area given the purpose of this book, as it is often the point at which insider dealing and market abuse occur.

Disclosure of information to the market by listed companies

Before a company's shares are first allowed to be traded on the LSE and when new shares are listed, it has to publish a detailed document containing information about itself, its business and its finances. This document, called the *Listing particulars,* is designed to provide all information considered relevant to an investor's decision whether to buy shares in the company. This principle of full information is fundamental to the fair working of the market. Although a company is not required to issue new listing particulars regularly, it is required to provide to the market all price-sensitive information in a proper and orderly way and ensure that people dealing in its shares are fully and properly provided with all the necessary information to determine its current value. Under the listing rules, a listed company must notify a Regulatory Information Service (RIS) of any major or significant developments that are not already public knowledge and affect its financial position, its financial condition, the performance of its business or its expectations of its future performance that would lead to a movement in its share price. A RIS is an organization or firm through which listed companies can release their regulatory announcements. Since 2002 listed companies have had a choice of RIS, bringing to an end the LSE's monopoly on the release of information through its own Regulatory News Service.

To be listed or quoted on the Official List of the Stock Exchange (a full listing), a public company has to comply with the UK Listing Authority (UKLA) Listing Rules. (The FSA, acting as the competent authority for listing, is referred to as the UK Listing Authority.) These contain the:

- requirements and procedures for obtaining a listing;
- obligations of the company and its officers, once admitted;
- circumstances giving rise to the suspension and termination of listing.

The Listing Rules were traditionally set by the Stock Exchange itself but are now administered by the FSA and effectively have the force of law. The Listing Rules dictate such matters as the contents of the prospectus in an initial public offering (IPO), ongoing obligations such as the disclosure of price-sensitive information, and communications on new share offers, rights issues, and potential or actual takeover bids for the company. The new Listing, Prospectus and Disclosure Rules came into effect in 2005, replacing the UKLA Sourcebook. They reflected changes made following the FSA's review of the listing regime and implemented the EU Prospectus Directive and certain aspects of the EU Market Abuse Directive. Of relevance here is Listing Rule 9 which requires listed companies to comply with the disclosure and transparency rules. It also requires listed companies to comply with the Model Code. This Code imposes restrictions on dealing in the securities of a listed company beyond those imposed by law. Its purpose is to ensure that persons discharging managerial responsibilities do not abuse, and do not place themselves under suspicion of abusing, inside information they may have – especially in periods leading up to an announcement of the company's results. Such people are restricted from dealing during a 'close period'. That is, essentially, the period of 60 days immediately preceding a preliminary announcement of the company's annual results or, if shorter, the period from the end of the relevant financial year up to and including the time of announcement. Some background on the FSA and the UKLA is presented in the Appendix to this chapter.

ANNUAL REPORT AND ACCOUNTS AND INTERIM REPORT

Following the Transparency Obligations Directive (Disclosure and Transparency Rules) Instrument 2006 (FSA 2006/70), a listed company is now required to issue an annual report and accounts as well as a report covering the first 6 months of each financial year. The annual accounts must be published no later than 4 months after the end of the financial year and the half-yearly report must be published within 2 months of the end of the relevant financial period.

Previously, a listed company was required to notify the RIS as soon as possible following board approval of the preliminary statement of its annual results, the announcement of the half-yearly results and any decision relating to the payment of a dividend. The preliminary announcement is now optional, although in the absence of such an announcement, a listed company is required to publish inside information as soon as possible to comply with its market abuse obligations.

If the half-yearly report is audited, the announcement to a RIS and related press releases must include the auditors' report in full. However, if the auditors have merely reviewed the half-yearly report, a copy of the report must be provided when the announcement is made to the RIS.

OTHER INFORMATION

The rules concerning the disclosure of other information and how it is to be submitted to a RIS and the FSA are contained in the FSA's Disclosure and Transparency Rules. Rule 2 is of particular importance and relates to the disclosure and control of 'inside information'. This replaces what was referred to in the old Listing Rules as 'price-sensitive information'. In practice, there is little difference between the two terms although the new concept of inside information is couched in more general terms. Inside information is defined as information of a precise nature which is not generally available; relates, directly or indirectly, to an issuer or to one or more of its securities; and would, if generally available, be likely to have a significant effect on the price of the issuer's securities or related securities. Information is precise if it indicates circumstances that exist or are expected to occur; and is specific enough to determine the possible effect on the price of the security. Information is regarded as likely to have a significant effect on price if it is information that a reasonable investor is likely to use it as part of the basis of their investment decisions.

Rule 2.2 requires an issuer to notify a RIS as soon as possible of any inside information which directly concerns the issuer. The guidance note to Rule 2.2 makes it clear that there is no figure (for example percentage change) that can be set to determine a 'significant effect'. Instead, it introduces a new test: the 'reasonable investor test'. This states that when deciding whether a piece of information is likely to have a significant effect on price, the issuer should assess whether it is likely to be used by a reasonable investor as part of the basis of their investment, and is, therefore, likely to have a significant effect on the share price. The guidance note also sets out what the issuer should take into account in determining this, for example the issuer's size, recent developments and market sentiment about the issuer. It also outlines information which is likely to be considered relevant to a reasonable investor's decision, including information relating to the issuer's assets and liabilities and any major new developments in its business.

The guidance note permits a short delay for the issuer in making an announcement in order to clarify the situation when it is faced with an unexpected and significant event. It recommends that a holding announcement should be used where an issuer believes that there is a danger of inside information leaking before the facts and their impact can be confirmed. The guidance also stipulates what the holding announcement should contain, such as including as much detail of the subject matter as possible, and the reasons why a further announcement cannot be made. Rule 2.5.1 permits an issuer to delay the public disclosure of inside information so as not to prejudice its legitimate interests. This is subject to certain provisos; for example that such omission would not be likely to mislead the public and that the issuer is able to ensure the confidentiality of that information. Rule 2.5.3 sets out certain circumstances where early disclosure could prejudice an issuer's legitimate interests, such as negotiations in progress and decisions taken by the board of directors that need the approval of shareholders.

Where a delay is permitted under Rule 2.5.1, an issuer may selectively disclose that information to certain persons confidentially, provided that this is in the normal course of their employment, profession or duty; for example to the issuer's advisers, persons with whom the issuer is negotiating, employee representatives, statutory and regulatory bodies, major shareholders, the issuer's lenders and credit-rating agencies. Rule 2.3 requires that inside information announced through a RIS should be available on the issuer's Internet site by the close of the next business day. If a RIS is not open for business and an issuer needs to notify information under Rule 1.3.6 the issuer must distribute the information as soon as possible to: (i) not less than two national newspapers in the UK; (ii) two newswire services operating in the UK; and (iii) the RIS for release as soon as it opens. The fact that a RIS is not open for business is not sufficient ground for delaying the disclosure or distribution of inside information. If an issuer fails to make a RIS announcement as required by the Disclosure and Transparency Rules within the period the FSA considers would affect the interests of investors or the smooth operation of the market; or if there is (or is likely to be) a leak of inside information and the issuer is unwilling or unable to issue an appropriate RIS announcement within a reasonable period, the FSA may suspend trading in the securities affected (Rule 1.4).

Rule 1.3.4 requires that an issuer must take all reasonable care to ensure that any information it notifies to a RIS is not misleading, false or deceptive and does not omit anything likely to affect the significance of the information. Rule 2.4 requires an issuer to take reasonable care to ensure that disclosure of inside information is synchronized as far as possible in other relevant jurisdictions. However, whilst the reasonable care rule implies verification, verification does not justify delay. Rule 1.3.5 requires that an issuer must not combine, in a manner likely to be misleading, a RIS announcement with the marketing of its activities.

Rule 2.7.1 relates to press speculation on market rumour and whether the issuer becomes obliged to make a disclosure. The issuer needs to decide whether the speculation or rumour has caused a situation to arise where the issuer has inside information. The guidance suggests that where speculation or rumour is largely correct and the information underlying it is inside information, then the issuer should no longer delay disclosure and the information should be disclosed as soon as possible. If the speculation or rumour is false and is not likely to amount to inside information, the issuer would be able to delay disclosure. In other words, companies are not expected to respond to every piece of inaccurate speculation or false rumour. However, in certain circumstances an announcement which goes beyond merely a 'no comment' may be required. For example, where the speculation or rumour is largely accurate which implies that there may have been a leak of confidential inside information.

The control of inside information

The FSA's Disclosure and Transparency Rule 2.6.1 requires an issuer to establish effective arrangements to deny access to inside information other than those who require it for the exercise of their functions within the issuer. Rule 2.6.2 requires an issuer to have in place measures which enable public disclosure to be made through an RIS as soon as possible in case the issuer is not able to ensure the confidentiality of the relevant inside information. It is, therefore, essential that issuers have effective systems and controls to control inside information, to determine whether or not an announcement is required, to control the content of such announcement and the mechanics for releasing it in other jurisdictions (if necessary) and on the issuer's website. Guidance to Rule 2.2.8 requires directors of the issuer to monitor carefully and continuously whether changes in the issuer's circumstances have triggered the need for an announcement. Guidance to Rule 2.2.9 recommends that the FSA should be consulted at the earliest opportunity if an issuer is in any doubt as to the timing of any announcement.

Rule 2.8.1 requires an issuer to ensure that it (and those acting on its behalf) prepares a list of people working for them who have access to inside information on either a regular or occasional basis. Rule 2.8.5 states that an insider list must be kept for at least five years from the date on which it is first drawn up or updated, whichever is the later. Rule 2.8.3 sets out the content requirement for each insider list. It stipulates that every insider list must refer to the identity of each person having access to inside information, the reason why the person is on the insider list and the date on which the insider list was created and updated. The issuer needs to include the principal contacts at any other firm acting on its behalf that have access to inside information. However, so long as the issuer has made effective arrangements with that firm, it does not need to record all the individuals who have access to inside information there.

Rules 2.8.9 and 2.8.10 require an issuer to ensure that each person whose name is on the insider list acknowledges the legal and regulatory duties involved and is aware of the sanctions attaching to the misuse or improper circulation of such information. This may involve providing employees with a summary of these requirements, and then requiring them to formally acknowledge it by way of signature. Alternatively, the issuer could amend employees' employment contracts to include such an acknowledgement. Another approach is to update the staff handbook and inform employees of this and require them to confirm that they have received notice of the update. In the case of the issuer's advisers, the adviser's engagement letter should contain a recognition of the adviser's obligation to take the necessary measures to obtain such an acknowledgement from any of its relevant employees or consultants.

In order for an issuer's procedures to comply with the disclosure rules, they must:

- be capable of identifying potential inside information arising from such matters as:
  - i) the publication of regular trading reports,
  - ii) projects that may involve inside information and being able to decide when inside information exists during the life of the project,
  - iii) ad hoc events and be able to identify those individuals most likely to be aware of them who are able to deal with the uncertainty involved.
- be capable of providing for timely escalation of relevant information.
- allocate responsibility for decisions relating to inside information such as determining whether information is actually inside information and whether a delay in an announcement is justified, approving announcements and making other decisions, for example suspension. The issuer may consider creating an Inside Information Committee or Disclosure Committee. It also needs to decide the extent to which board members are involved in these decisions.

- be capable of managing the inside information once it is identified. Insider lists need to be compiled, the announcement needs to be prepared, and a prohibition on dealing brought into effect.

The issuer should have a policy on communications to ensure that everyone involved in communications is operating within an agreed framework. The overall approach should be set out defining responsibilities, sign-off procedures, the involvement of advisers, the maintenance of a log of forward-looking information, verification, and an agreed approach to handling rumours.

In addition to this, issuers need to comply with the FSA's Listing Principles which should be adhered to both in the spirit and to the letter to ensure a fair and orderly market. These state that a listed company must:

- Take reasonable steps to enable its directors to understand their responsibilities and obligations as directors.
- Take reasonable steps to establish and maintain adequate procedures, systems and controls to enable it to comply with its obligations.
- Act with integrity towards holders and potential holders of its listed equity securities.
- Communicate information to holders and potential holders of its listed equity securities in such a way as to avoid the creation or continuation of a false market in such listed equity securities.
- Ensure that it treats all holders of the same class of its listed equity securities equally in respect of the rights attaching to such listed equity securities.
- Deal with the FSA in an open and co-operative manner.

Inside information for a firm may occur in many ways; for example the discussion of financial plans with an advising bank or the stake-building by a bidder or a potential bidder. Leakage of information within a firm may arise from the passing of information (either by word of mouth or a document) by one member of staff to another member of staff or to an outside person. It may also occur through an insecure IT system.

Managing the risk of insider dealing and market manipulation by either a firm or an individual within it should involve policies and procedures relating to such matters as:

- Telephone tapping.
- Transaction recording.
- Review of unusual trades.
- Whistleblowing procedures.
- Staff vetting checks.
- Exit interviews.
- The use of temporary workers.
- Media contact, including the use of dedicated staff for this purpose.
- Internal audit review of policies, systems and controls.

The firm should have a clear policy relating to personal account dealing. This should include whether and, if so to what extent, an employee may deal in shares. The policy should be defined and contained in a set of formal written procedures. This would usually be part of the contract of employment and suitably acknowledged. The firm should consider whether there should be a blanket ban on dealing, a ban for certain sectors depending on their responsibilities within the firm, or allow dealing subject to permission and attestation. The firm should also consider whether the ban or restriction extends to an employee's immediate family accounts and to accounts over which they have powers of attorney. The firm may also consider requiring staff to use a specified firm of brokers.

For inside information to be properly managed and leaks prevented:

- Insider lists need to be properly maintained. They should be prepared on a clear 'need to know' policy. Lists should be regularly updated.
- Information barriers need to reasonable, workable and effective. For Chinese Walls to be effective they should at least be geographically separated. The term Chinese Wall is used to describe procedures enforced within a firm to separate its departments and restrict access to non-public, material information, in order to avoid the illegal use of inside information. Areas for discussions should be restricted and, if possible, the research department should be offsite. There should be a clearly defined wall-crossing policy and set of procedures. Code names should be used where necessary

but not in such a simple way as to allow the principal to be easily identified.

- Information technology needs to be secure. There should be secure data rooms. There should be restricted IT access with immediate removal on departure or change. Passwords should be fully protected and encryption should be done where necessary, particularly for laptop security. The systems should provide for an audit trail of persons accessing sensitive files.
- Document access needs to be secure and procedures need to be in place. There should be a clean desk policy which is applied in practice. The disposal of documents needs to be performed securely. There need to be formal procedures for removing information from offices, laptops and memory sticks. The distribution of emails and documents (hard and electronic copies) needs to be controlled.
- There needs to be proper training and updating of professional and support staff in respect of the issues, hazards and the cost–benefit problems involved.
- There should be formal procedures in place for passing information to third parties. The greatest risk of leakage may be at the preliminary stage; for example, when carrying out conflict checks and conducting 'beauty parades'. When dealing with third parties involved, for example printers, confidentiality letters are necessary but should not be regarded as sufficient on their own. It is necessary to perform due diligence on the controls within a third party's organization. It may be necessary to explain their responsibilities for managing confidential information to them and for them to acknowledge their legal and regulatory responsibilities in writing, including the maintenance of their own insider lists, and to deliver these to the firm.

The FSA Principles of Business also relate to firms' market conduct and market abuse. These state that a firm must:

- conduct its business with integrity;
- conduct its business with due skill, care and diligence;
- take reasonable care to organize and control its affairs responsibly and effectively, with adequate risk-management systems;
- maintain adequate financial resources;

- observe proper standards of market conduct;
- pay due regard to the interests of its customers and treat them fairly;
- communicate information to its clients in a way that is not misleading;
- manage conflicts of interest fairly, both between itself and its customers and between a customer and another client.

The FSA's Principles for Approved Persons also relate to market conduct and market abuse by firms. These state that:

1. An approved person must act with integrity in carrying out his/her controlled function.
2. An approved person must act with due skill, care and diligence in carrying out his/her controlled function.
3. An approved person must observe proper standards of market conduct in carrying out his/her function.
4. An approved person must deal with the FSA and with other regulators in an open and co-operative way and must disclose appropriately any information of which the FSA would reasonably expect notice.
5. An approved person performing a significant influence function must take reasonable steps to ensure that the regulated business of the firm for which he/she is responsible in his/her controlled function is organized so that it can be controlled effectively.
6. An approved person performing a significant influence function must exercise due skill, care and diligence in managing the business of that firm for which he/she is responsible in his/her controlled function.
7. An approved person performing a significant influence function must take reasonable steps to ensure that the business of that firm for which he/she is responsible in his/her controlled function complies with the regulatory requirements imposed on that business.

Insider dealing as a criminal offence

Insider dealing was not made unlawful in the UK until 1980 when under Part V of the Companies Act 1980 it became a criminal offence in certain specified circumstances. These provisions were later consolidated as the Company Securities (Insider Dealing) Act 1985 (CSA) which was subsequently amended by the Financial Services Act 1986. The CSA provisions were superseded by the Criminal Justice Act 1993, Part V (CJA) which implemented the EC Directive on Insider Dealing. The UK legislation has also been revised to incorporate the provisions of the 2003 European Directive on market abuse but it has not changed in principle, or in any significant way, other than to extend the responsibility of the UK authorities to investigate individuals in the UK linked to market abuse conducted elsewhere in the EU.

Under Section 52 of the CJA, an individual who has information as an insider is guilty of insider dealing if they:

- deal in securities with information which, if it were made public, would be likely to have a significant effect on the price of the securities and if the insider deals as, or uses, an intermediary,[1]
- encourage another person to deal in the securities,[2] or
- disclose the information to another person other than in the proper performance of their employment.

'Inside information' is defined by the CJA as information which:

- Relates to a particular security or a particular issuer of securities;[3]
- Is specific or precise;[4]
- Has not been made public; and
- If it were made public, would have a significant impact on the share price, that is is price-sensitive.

1 It follows that the Act does not apply to private off-market transactions without the use of a professional intermediary. It also follows that stockbrokers and market makers (and anyone employed by them) are included.

2 'Encouragement' does not have to involve the disclosure of inside information. The offence is also committed whether or not the person encouraged actually decides to deal.

3 It does not include information that relates generally to the market, for example general economic information. However, if the information is likely to have a disproportionate effect on the company or sector, it may constitute inside information.

4 For example, an individual may be regarded as having inside information about an event even if he does not know all the surrounding or background details.

'Made public' means:

- Published in accordance with the rules of the regulated market;
- Contained in records which are open to inspection by the public;
- Readily acquired by those likely to deal in securities; and
- Derived from information that has been made public.

Information may be treated as made public if it:

- Can be acquired by persons exercising diligence or expertise;
- Is communicated to a section of the public and not to the public at large;
- Can be acquired only by observation;
- Is communicated only on the payment of a fee; or
- Is published only outside the UK.

Further, an insider must know that they have inside information if they have it because of:

- Being a director, employee or shareholder of the issuer of securities, or
- Having access to the information because of their employment, office or profession, or
- Having it directly or indirectly from one of the above.

The CJA 1993 attempted to block the loopholes in the 1985 Act by extending the classes of individuals who could be regarded as party to the offence. As this would have the effect of making almost all share dealing by directors and others associated with the company unlawful, the CJA 1993 prescribed certain defences in order to protect individuals who were legitimately trading in the shares. Section 53 provides three 'defences' to the circumstances in which an individual may be guilty of insider dealing by virtue of dealing in securities. These are where the individual who is dealing is able to show that at the time of dealing:

- They did not expect it to result in a profit attributable to the information that they possessed (section 53(1)(a)),

- They had reasonable grounds to believe that the information had already been disclosed (section 53(1)(b)),
- They would have done what they did even if they had not possessed the information (section 53(1)(c)).

There are three similar defences under section 53(2) for a person who encourages another person to deal in securities.

There are two defences where an individual discloses inside information to another person other than in the proper performance of his employment. These are, where the individual is able to show that they did not expect at the time of the disclosure:

- anybody to deal in the securities, and
- any such dealing to result in a profit attributable to the information.

There are also three situations which merit 'special defences' under Schedule 1 of the Act:

- If they are able to show that they acted in good faith in the course of their business as a market maker.
- If the information which they had was market information[5] and it was reasonable for an individual in their position to have acted as they did despite having that information as an insider at that time. (This provision is to enable persons involved in a takeover to be able to deal.)
- If they acted as a 'stabilizing manager' supporting the price of newly issued securities in conformity with the price stabilization rules. Price stabilization is a process whereby the market price of a security is manipulated in order to achieve a successful IPO. The manipulation of the market price is done purely to slow down a decline in the price of the security. It is done by the lead manager buying or selling the newly issued securities in the open market, by over-allotment and creating short positions. Stabilization creates the impression that there is demand for the securities at a particular

5 'Market information' relates to information relating to the fact that certain securities have (or have not) or are about to be bought or sold; the range of prices involved and the identity of the persons involved.

price or at various prices. Price stabilization is allowed because it promotes the orderly operation of the market, it helps reduce investor nervousness, meet demand and counteract short selling.

Market abuse as a criminal offence under the Financial Services and Markets Act 2000 (FSMA)

Market abuse is made a criminal offence under Section 397 of FSMA which replaces section 47(2) of the Financial Services Act 1986. Section 397 refers to a person (or induces another person) who:

a) makes a statement, promise or forecast which they know to be misleading, false or deceptive, or

b) dishonestly conceals any material facts whether in connection with a statement, promise or,

c) recklessly makes (dishonestly or otherwise) a statement, promise or forecast which is misleading, false or deceptive.

The section also states that it is a defence if they can show that they:

a) reasonably believed that their act or conduct would not create an impression that was false or misleading as to the matters mentioned in that subsection;

b) acted or engaged in the conduct:

   i) for the purpose of stabilizing the price of investments; and

   ii) in conformity with price stabilizing rules; or

c) acted, or engaged in the conduct, in conformity with control of information rules.

Market abuse as a criminal offence under the Fraud Act 2006

The Fraud Act 2006 became law in January 2007. It replaced a number of complicated and overlapping deception offences. These offences had proved inadequate to tackle the wide range of possible fraudulent activity today or failed to keep pace with rapidly developing technology. In their place the Act established a new general offence of fraud, which can be committed in three ways:

1. Fraud by false representation (section 2).
2. Fraud by failing to disclose information (section 3).
3. Fraud by abuse of position (section 4).

Section 4 has particular relevance to market abuse and insider dealing. It states that a person is in breach of this section if they:

a) occupy a position in which they are expected to safeguard, or not to act against, the financial interests of another person,
b) dishonestly abuse that position, and
c) intend, by means of the abuse of that position to:
    i) make a gain for themself or another, or
    ii) cause loss to another or to expose another to a risk of loss.

A person may be regarded as having abused their position even though their conduct consisted of an omission rather than an act.

Although it is most likely that a person committing market abuse or insider dealing would be charged under more specific legislation, these offences may fall under the general offence of fraud.

Market abuse as a civil offence under the Financial Services and Markets Act 2000 (FSMA)

The CJA largely failed as a deterrent because of its reliance on the criminal law (Stamp and Jaggers 2005). This was recognized by parliament when it introduced civil penalties for insider dealing as part of its market abuse regime under the FSMA.

The FSMA extends the powers of regulators to combat market abuse and insider dealing as a form of market abuse. FSMA 118 introduces two new civil offences of market manipulation: false or misleading impression and the distortion of the market. As civil offences, they run in parallel to the statutory criminal offences contained in the CJA 1993. The civil offence need only be proved on 'the balance of probabilities'. It is unnecessary to show dishonest intention to commit market abuse: negligent action or inaction may be sufficient. It is irrelevant where the behaviour occurred. It is merely necessary to be 'in relation to qualifying investments traded on a prescribed market'.

FSMA 118(1) defines market abuse as behaviour (whether by one person alone or by two or more persons jointly or in concert) that:

- occurs in relation to qualifying investments on a prescribed market (FSMA 118(1)(a)), and
- Falls within any one or more of the seven types of behaviour set out in FSMA 118(2) to 118(8).

Broadly, inside information under the FSMA is information of a precise nature which:

- Is not generally available.
- Relates directly or indirectly to one or more issuers of the qualifying investments or to one or more of the qualifying investments themselves.
- Would, if generally available, be likely to have a significant effect on the price of the qualifying investments (that is, qualifying instruments actually issued by the issuer) or on the price of related investments (FSMA 118C(2)).

Information is precise if it:

- Indicates circumstances that exist (or are likely to exist) or an event has occurred (or is likely to occur), and
- Is specific enough to enable a conclusion to be drawn as to the possible effect of those circumstances or that event on the price of the qualifying investments or related investments (FSMA 118C(5)).

Information is regarded as being generally available if it can be obtained by research or analysis conducted by or on behalf of users of the market (FSMA 118C(8)).

An insider is any person who has inside information:

- As a result of their membership of an administrative, management or supervisory body of an issuer of qualifying investments.
- As a result of their holding in the capital of an issuer of qualifying investments.
- As a result of having access to the information through the exercise of their employment, profession or duties.
- As a result of their criminal activities.
- Which they have obtained by other means and which they know or could reasonably be expected to know is inside information (FSMA 118B).

Under FSMA 119, the FSA is required to produce a code, The Code of Market Conduct, (the Code) which specifies behaviour amounting to market abuse.

The Code adopts the convention of numbering its paragraphs and preceding the number with the letters 'MAR'. The Code is not exhaustive in its descriptions of behaviour amounting to market abuse. Where the Code describes behaviour that, in the FSA's opinion, does not amount to market abuse, that behaviour is regarded conclusively as not amounting to market abuse (FSMA 122(1)). Otherwise, the Code may only be relied on in so far as it indicates whether or not behaviour should be taken as amounting to market abuse. Each provision in the Code is designated with a suffix of the letter E, G or C. Paragraphs marked with the letter E specify descriptions of behaviour that, in the opinion of the FSA, amount to market abuse and factors that, in the opinion of the FSA, are to be taken into account in determining whether or not behaviour amounts to market abuse. Paragraphs marked with the letter E indicates whether or not particular behaviour should be taken to amount to market abuse. Paragraphs marked with the letter G indicate guidance given under FSMA 157. If a person acts in accordance with general guidance in the circumstances contemplated in that guidance, the FSA will regard that the person has having complied with the rule or other requirement to which the guidance relates. Paragraphs marked with a letter C describes behaviour that, in the opinion of the FSA, does not amount to market abuse. These descriptions are conclusive because such behaviour is to be taken, for the purposes of FSMA, as not amounting to market abuse. Not all of the Code is reproduced here, merely those parts that indicate the principles involved. In addition to the Code, from time to time, the FSA releases information on the operation of the market abuse regime through its newsletter *Market Watch*. The Committee of European Securities Regulators (CESR) has also issued helpful guidelines (see the Appendix to this chapter).

In addition to the primary offence of market abuse, FSMA creates a secondary offence of taking, or refraining from taking, action which requires or encourages another person to engage in market abuse (FSMA 123). The secondary offence may be committed through early or selective disclosure of inside information, such as information required to be disclosed under the Disclosure or Listing Rules. The market abuse provisions apply to anyone, including a corporation or individual, whether authorized by the FSA or not.

Table 6.1 The seven types of market abuse

1. Insider dealing	Where an insider deals or attempts to deal on the basis of inside information
2. Improper disclosure	Where an insider improperly discloses inside information to another person
3. Misuse of information	Behaviour based on information that is not generally available that would affect an investor's decision about the terms on which to deal
4. Manipulating transactions	Trading, or placing orders, to give a false or misleading impression of the supply or demand for an investments, raising its price to an abnormal level
5. Manipulating devices	Trading, or placing orders, which employ fictitious devices or any other form of deception or contrivance
6. Dissemination	Knowingly providing information that gives a misleading impression about an investment
7. Distortion and misleading behaviour	Behaviour that gives a false or misleading impression of the supply or demand for an investment or distorts the market in an investment

The seven types of behaviour are summarized in Table 6.1. Each will now be examined in more detail.

INSIDER DEALING

This is where an insider deals or attempts to deal in a qualifying or related investment on the basis of inside information relating to the investment in question (FSMA 118(2)) (MAR 1.3.1).

The dealing must be based on the inside information to the extent that the insider has consciously taken advantage of it. Dealing means acquiring or disposing of the investment whether as principal or agent or directly or indirectly, and includes agreeing to acquire or dispose of the investment, and entering into and bringing to an end a contract creating it (Section 130A, FSMA).

Indications that a person's behaviour is not 'on the basis of' inside information are:

- If the decision to deal or attempt to deal was made before the person possessed the relevant inside information.
- If the person concerned is dealing to satisfy a legal or regulatory obligation which came into being before they possessed the relevant inside information.
- Where a person is an organization, if none of the individuals in possession of the inside information had any involvement in the decision to deal, or behaved in such a way as to influence the decision (MAR 1.3.3E).

Where the inside information is the reason for, or a material influence on, the decision to deal or attempt to deal, the FSA will view this as an indication that the person's behaviour is 'on the basis of' inside information (MAR 1.3.4E). The use of an effective Chinese Wall or similar effective arrangement to hold the inside information away from individuals who are involved in, or who influence the decision to deal, is viewed as an indication that the decision to deal by an organization is not 'on the basis of' inside information (MAR 1.3.5E).

The Code sets out a number of descriptions of behaviour that do not amount to market abuse insider dealing in the context of the legitimate business of market makers, execution of client orders and takeover and merger activity (MAR 1.3.6C to MAR 1.3.19E). In relation to the latter, the Code states that behaviour based on inside information relating to another company in the context of a public takeover bid or merger for the purposes of gaining control of that company or proposing a merger with that company does not of itself amount to market abuse (including seeking irrevocable undertakings from shareholders, making arrangements for the underwriting or placing of securities that are to be offered as consideration and making arrangements for a cash alternative) (MAR 1.3.17C).

IMPROPER DISCLOSURE

This is where an insider improperly discloses inside information to another person ('tipping off') otherwise than in the proper performance of his employment, profession or duties. (FSMA 118(3)) (MAR 1.4.1). The following are in the opinion of the FSA examples of improper disclosure:

- disclosure of inside information by the director of an issuer to another in a social context; and
- selective briefing of analysts by directors of issuers or others who are persons discharging managerial responsibilities (MAR 1.4.2).

MISUSE OF INFORMATION

This is behaviour based on information that is not generally available but would affect an investor's decision about the terms on which to deal (FSMA 118(4)) (MAR 1.5.1).

This relates to behaviour that does not constitute insider dealing or improper disclosure above. It is behaviour:

- based on information which is not generally available to those using the market but which, if available to a regular user of the market, would be regarded by them as relevant when deciding the terms on which to deal, and
- likely to be regarded by a regular user of the market as a failure on the part of the person concerned to observe the standard of behaviour reasonably expected of a person in their position (FSMA 118(4)).

The information must be that which a regular user would consider to be relevant in determining the terms of a deal. The following factors would be taken into account in determining whether a regular user would regard information as relevant information:

- The extent to which the information is reliable, including how near the person providing the information is, or appears to be, to the original source of that information and the reliability of that source.
- If the information differs from information which is generally available and can therefore be said to be new or fresh information.
- In the case of information relating to possible future developments which are not currently required to be disclosed but which, if they occur, would lead to a disclosure or announcement being made.
- If there is no other material information which is already generally available to inform users of the market (MAR 1.5.6E).

MANIPULATING TRANSACTIONS

This is trading, or placing orders to trade, that gives a false or misleading impression of the supply of, or demand for, one or more investments, raising the price of the investment to an abnormal or artificial level (FSMA 118(5)) (MAR 1.6.1).

This type of behaviour will not occur where the behaviour is for legitimate reasons and in accordance with accepted market practices. The following are indications that the behaviour is legitimate:

- Where the transaction relates to a prior legal or regulatory obligation.
- Where the transaction is executed in a way that takes into account the need for the market as a whole to operate fairly and efficiently.
- The extent to which the transaction generally opens a new position, so creating an exposure to market risk, rather than closes out a position and so removes market risk.
- Where the transaction complies with the rules of the relevant prescribed markets about how transactions are to be properly executed (MAR 1.6.6E).

The following are indications that the behaviour is not legitimate:

- If the purpose of the transaction to induce others to trade in, or to position or move the price of, a qualifying investment.
- If there is another, illegitimate, reason behind the transactions or order to trade.
- If the transaction is designed to create a false or misleading impression (MAR 1.6.5E).

This creates two separate types of behaviour:

1. *False or misleading transactions*. These mainly refer to buying and selling activity by an individual or group of individuals so as to give a false impression of the volume of trade in the security. The US term is 'flipping'. Types of transactions include:

- Buying or selling qualifying investments at the close of the market with the effect of misleading investors who act on the basis of closing prices.
- Wash trades. That is, a sale or purchase of a qualifying investment where there is no change in beneficial interest or market risk, or where the transfer of beneficial interest or market risk is only between parties acting in concert.
- 'Painting the tape'. That is, dealers buying and selling a specific security amongst themselves in order to create an illusion of high volume trading, thereby attracting investor interest.
- Entering orders into an electronic trading system, at prices which are higher than the previous bid or lower than the previous offer, and withdrawing them before they are executed, in order to give a misleading impression (MAR 1.6.2E).

2. *Price positioning*. These include:
   - Transactions or orders to trade that secure a dominant position over the supply of or demand for a qualifying investment which have the effect of fixing, directly or indirectly, purchase or sale prices or creating other unfair trading conditions.
   - Transactions where both buy and sell orders are entered at, or nearly at, the same time, with the same price and quantity with the same party, or colluding parties, unless the transactions are legitimate trades carried out in accordance with the rules of the relevant trading platform (such as crossing trades).
   - Entering small orders into an electronic trading system at prices which are higher than the previous bid or lower than the previous offer, in order to move the price of the qualifying investment.
   - An abusive squeeze. That is, a situation in which a person:
     i) has a significant influence over the supply of, or demand for, or the delivery mechanisms for a qualifying investment or related investment;

ii) has a position (directly or indirectly) in an investment under which quantities of the qualifying investment or related investment, are deliverable; and

iii) engages in behaviour with the purpose of positioning at a distorted level affecting the price at which others have to deliver, or take delivery to satisfy their obligations in relation to a qualifying investment;

- Parties who have been allocated qualifying investments in a primary offering, colluding to purchase further tranches of those qualifying investments when trading begins, in order to force the price of the qualifying investments to an artificial level and generate interest from other investors, and then sell the qualifying investments;
- Transactions or orders to trade employed so as to create obstacles to the price falling below a certain level, in order to avoid negative consequences for the issuer, for example a downgrading of its credit rating, and
- Trading on one market or trading platform with a view to improperly influencing the price of the investment or a related traded on another prescribed market (MAR 1.6.4).

MANIPULATING DEVICES

This is trading, or placing orders to trade, which employs fictitious devices or any other form of deception or contrivance (FSMA 118(6)) (MAR 1.4.5). These include:

- Taking advantage of access to traditional or electronic media by voicing an opinion about a qualifying investment or issuer while having previously taken positions on that investment without having disclosed the conflict of interest in a proper way.
- 'Flipping' as mentioned above.
- A transaction or series of transactions that are designed to conceal the ownership of a qualifying investment, so as to circumvent the disclosure requirements.
- A 'pump and dump' scheme. This was described in Chapter 1.
- A 'trash and cash' scheme. This was described in Chapter 1 (MAR 1.7.2E).

DISSEMINATION

This is issuing information that conveys a false or misleading impression about an investment or the issuer of an investment knowing the information to be false or misleading (FSMA 118(7)) (MAR 1.4.6).

Examples of dissemination include:

- A person posting information on an internet bulletin board or chat room about the takeover of a company knowing it to be false or misleading.
- A person responsible for the content of information recklessly submitting to a RIS false or misleading information relating to qualifying investments (MAR 1.8.6).

DISTORTION AND MISLEADING BEHAVIOUR

This is behaviour that gives a false or misleading impression of either the supply of, or demand for, an investment; or behaviour that distorts the market in an investment (FSMA 118(8)) (MAR 1.4.5).

SAFE HARBOURS AND EXCEPTIONS

Behaviour which falls within a safe harbour cannot amount to market abuse. To comply with MAD, the safe harbours in the previous UK market abuse regime have been either been deleted or downgraded to factors that the FSA will take into account in determining whether behaviour amounts to market abuse. MAD, itself, provides for only two safe harbours. These are:

1. the buying back of outstanding shares (repurchase) by a company in order to reduce the number of shares on the market, and
2. 'price stabilization' activities.

SANCTIONS FOR MARKET ABUSE

If the FSA believes that market abuse has occurred, it may:

- Investigate.
- Have the matter heard in its Regulatory Decision Committee.
- Impose an unlimited civil fine. The level of fine will depend on a number of factors including the wealth of the individual, the

seriousness of the abuse, the frequency of the breach and the extent to which that behaviour was deliberate or reckless. The imposition of a penalty does not make any transaction void or unenforceable. The FSA has the discretion to publish the name of the person and details of the offence.

- Make a public statement that that person has engaged in market abuse.
- Apply to the court for an injunction to restrain threatened or continued market abuse.
- Apply to the court to make an order for the restitution in respect of any losses suffered or profits made as a result of market abuse.

To further aid its investigation of alleged market abuse, in August 2003 the FSA signed a memorandum of understanding with the City of London Police Fraud Squad formalizing the powers of the police to arrest people, on the FSA's behalf, in cases of suspected market abuse, insider dealing, money laundering or illegal deposit taking. Under FSMA, the FSA has power to detain suspects for questioning in relation to market abuse.

If the FSA decides to take action against a person, under FSMA 127 that individual has a right to refer the matter on appeal to the independent Financial Services and Markets Tribunal.

SUSPICIOUS TRANSACTION REPORTING

MAD has introduced a new requirement for financial intermediaries to report to the FSA any suspicious transactions in which market abuse may have taken place. A firm that arranges or executes a transaction with or for a client in a qualifying investment traded on a prescribed market must notify the FSA without delay if it has reasonable grounds to suspect that the transaction might constitute market abuse. When deciding which transactions to report, the firm has to decide whether there are reasonable grounds for suspicion. Defensive reports without reasonable suspicion are unacceptable. This requirement overlaps with the obligation under the Proceeds of Crime Act 2002 to report suspicions of money laundering to the Serious Organised Crime Agency.

The City Code on Takeovers and Mergers

The City Code on Takeovers and Mergers governs how takeover bids in the UK are carried out. It is drawn up by, and is primarily enforced by, the Panel on Takeovers and Mergers. The Panel is responsible for the general administration of the City Code. This includes the monitoring of relevant dealings and, where necessary, conducting investigations. It is also available for consultation and to give rulings on points of interpretation before or during a takeover or merger. The City Code is also now required to comply with the EU Directive on takeovers. It directly incorporates part of the Directive.

The purpose of the City Code is to ensure good business practice in the conduct of takeovers and mergers, especially during the offer period. Traditionally, the City Code has not had the force of law. However, the Panel may institute disciplinary proceedings when it considers that there has been a breach of the City Code. As the FSA has endorsed the City Code, it may, at the request of the Panel, take enforcement action against a person authorized under the FSMA who contravenes the City Code or a Panel ruling. Such action may include public censure, fines, the removal of authorization, the imposition of injunctions and orders for restitution. Also under the Companies Act 2006 sections 942–992 which implements the EU Directive, the Panel is to have certain prescribed regulatory functions in relation to takeovers and is empowered to do anything that it considers necessary or expedient in relation to its prescribed functions. These include the power to make rules in relation to takeover regulation and to make provision in its rules for it to give a direction preventing a person from breaching the rules.

The City Code has ten general principles. These are:

1. All shareholders of the same class of an offeree company must be treated similarly by an offeror.
2. During the course of an offer, or when an offer is being contemplated, neither an offeror, the offeree, nor any of their advisers may issue information to some shareholders that is not issued to all others. (This principle does not apply to the provision of information in confidence by the offeree to a bona fide potential offeror or vice versa.)
3. An offeror should only announce an offer after careful and responsible consideration and it should only be made when the offeror has

reason to believe that it can implement the offer. (Responsibility for this also rests with the offeror's financial adviser.)

4. Shareholders must be given sufficient information and advice to enable them to reach a properly informed decision and must have sufficient time to do so. No relevant information should be withheld from them.

5. Any document or advertisement addressed to shareholders containing information or advice from an offeror or the offeree company or their respective advisers must be prepared with the highest standards of care and accuracy.

6. All parties to an offer must ensure that a false market in the securities of an offeror or offeree company is not created. All the parties involved must ensure that any statements they make do not mislead shareholders or the market.

7. At no time after an offer has been communicated to the offeree company, or after its board has reason to believe it is imminent, may any action be taken by the board of the offeree company, without the approval of the shareholders in general meeting, to frustrate an offer or prevent shareholders being given the opportunity to decide on the merits of the offer.

8. All actions must be conducted in good faith and the oppression of a minority interest is unacceptable.

9. The directors of the offeror and offeree companies must always, in advising their shareholders, act only in their capacity as directors without regard to their own or other interests. They should consider the shareholders' interests taken as a whole, together with those of employees and creditors when giving advice. The directors of the offeree company should give careful consideration before they enter into any commitment with an offeror (or anyone else) which would restrict their freedom to advise their shareholders in the future.

10. Where control of a company is acquired, a general offer to all other shareholders is normally required. Before an offeror makes such an offer, they should ensure that they are able to implement such an offer.

The main requirements of the City Code relating to a bid are that:

- All shareholders must be offered equally good terms, as defined by the code.
- All shareholders must be given equal access to information.
- A timetable is adhered to that sets time limits for each phase of the bid.
- Bidders and members of a concert party must disclose their dealings.
- The bidder must set an acceptance level (of over 50 per cent) at which the bid becomes unconditional.
- A mandatory offer must be made if a shareholder's or concert party's holdings exceed 30 per cent.
- The board of the target company may not use 'poison pills' and other actions to frustrate a bona fide bid, unless they have shareholder approval. A poison pill is a device used by a company to avoid a takeover, for example the issue of preferred stock that gives shareholders the right to redeem them at a premium after the takeover.

In addition to these, under the Disclosure and Transparency Rules, a person must notify the issuer of the percentage of voting rights they hold if they acquire or dispose of shares in the issuer to which voting rights are attached (or another events occurs changing the breakdown of voting rights) if the percentage of voting rights reaches or falls below 3 per cent.

Conclusions

It was the purpose of this chapter to review the relevant legislation and rules relating to market efficiency and market abuse. Clearly, there have been changes in recent times, essentially relating to the imposition of a statutory backed regime which attempts to be flexible in order to respond to changes and developments within the markets and the unification of the regulations across Europe. The extent to which the latter will be successful is a matter for the future. However, the criminal provisions have now been operating (although in the process of development) for some time, as have the FSA's obligations as the principal regulator and prosecutor of market abuse as a civil offence. The effectiveness of these is the subject of the next chapter.

References

Stamp, M. and T. Jaggers (2005) 'United Kingdom', *International Insider Dealing*, pp. 107–162, Old Woking, City and Financial Publishing.

Appendix
The FSA and the UKLA

As a result of the passing of the Financial Services and Markets Act 2000 (FSMA), the FSA has become the UK's 'competent authority' for the listing of securities in place of the LSE. In this capacity the FSA is known as the UK Listing Authority (UKLA). The FSA made several changes to the Listing Rules and introduced the UKLA Guidance Manual. The Listing Rules and UKLA Guidance Manual together form the UKLA Sourcebook. This is now known as 'the Purple Book' (instead of 'the Yellow Book' to which the old Listing Rules were referred).

As the competent authority, the UKLA is required under the FSMA to

- maintain an official list of securities;
- regulate the admission of securities to the official list; and
- monitor the subsequent adherence to the Listing Rules by issuers.

As part of this general duty, the UKLA has responsibility for:

- the admission of securities to listing;
- the cancellation and suspension of listings; and
- the approval of listing particulars, prospectuses and sponsors.

The UKLA also has the power to impose penalties on issuers of listed securities, applicants for listing, and directors for breach of the Listing Rules and it may publicly censure a sponsor, issuer or director in certain circumstances.

To obtain a listing for securities (other than those being offered for the first time which require a prospectus under the Public Offers of Securities Regulations 1995), listing particulars need to be submitted to and published by the UKLA (Sections 79 and 80 FSMA). These particulars must contain all the information that investors and their professional advisers would reasonably require to make an informed assessment about the issuer and the rights attaching to the securities.

FSMA gives the UKLA draconian new powers to impose penalties for breaches of the Listing Rules. Prior to FSMA the sanctions under the Listing Rules for breach were to require the company to publish information, to censure the company or any director privately or publicly and the suspension or cancellation of listing. These are still part of the Listing Rules, but now the UKLA may impose a penalty under FSMA of 'such amount as it considers appropriate' (Section 91) on:

- an issuer of listed securities,
- an applicant for listing,
- a director of the issuer or applicant who was knowingly involved in the breach.

The Purple Book specifies certain UKLA disclosure requirements in annual reports in addition to those required by the Companies Act 1985. The important ones are:

- A commentary on forecasts, where the results differ from the published forecast or estimate by more than 10 per cent.
- Details of directors' interests in shares and share options.
- A report by the company's remuneration committee giving specified details on directors' remuneration.
- Major interests in shares in excess of 3 per cent.
- A corporate governance statement as to how the company has applied the principles in Section 1 of the Combined Code.

European guidance on the market abuse directive

The Committee of European Securities Regulators (CESR) is an independent body set up by the EU. Its role is to:

- Improve co-ordination among securities regulators to enhance day to day consistent supervision and enforcement of the Single Market for financial services.
- Act as an advisory group to assist the EU Commission : in particular in its preparation of draft implementing measures of EU framework directives in the field of securities.

- Work to ensure more consistent and timely day-to-day implementation of community legislation in the member states.

It has issued two sets of guidance on the common operation of the Directive throughout the EU. In 2005, it issued a set of guidance relating to market manipulation: examples of practices that CESR members consider on suspicious transaction reporting (for example painting the tape, pump and dump and trash and cash. In 2007, CESR issued a second set of guidance relating to insider dealing – what constitutes inside information under the market abuse directive, when are there reasons to delay the publication of inside information, and when does information relating to a client's pending orders constitute inside information and insider lists.

Market Abuse

CHAPTER 7

It is the purpose of this chapter to review the reported instances of insider dealing and market abuse. First the criminal cases will be reviewed, then the civil cases brought by the FSA.

Market abuse takes various forms and may be performed in many ways, not least because of the different motives that may be involved. The directors of a plc may wish to inflate its share price for many reasons, for example at the time of a takeover bid, to boost the value of their own investments. They may also wish to deflate another company's share price, say at the time of a merger when they are attempting to buy its shares. They may achieve these and many other objectives in the seven ways outlined in Chapter 6. They may also manipulate the company's report and accounts and other financial information. How this is done is left to Chapter 8. Private individuals and dealers may also want to create a false impression of the size of the market and the volume of trading in a company's shares, to influence their price.

Earlier formative cases

Insider dealing was not made illegal in the UK until 1980 and market abuse was not made illegal and a criminal offence until 1986. Until then, market abuse may or may not, depending on its form, have contravened company law and/or the City Code. The latter, at that time, was only a voluntary code and widely regarded as ineffective in curbing such behaviour.

The famous cases of the 1980s and early 1990s actually involved market abuse and in particular share support operations. Well before the Guinness-Distillers case it was generally believed, even by academics, that a bidder's share price would rise during the period prior to the announcement of a bid as a result of pre-arranged buying support (Firth 1976, Barnes 1978, which is reviewed in Chapter 3).

The Guinness-Distillers share support scheme

The Guinness-Distillers case was one of the most famous financial scandals of the twentieth century. It is less well known that the issues centred on market abuse and the Department of Trade and Industry's (DTI) Inspectors' reports provide a valuable insight into how it was conducted. The scheme is briefly described here.

In the early 1980s, Distillers plc, the Scotch whisky manufacturers, was generally regarded as a fairly obvious takeover target for any company large enough to absorb the group. It was an obvious target for Guinness, the drinks company, as it attempted to revitalize its business. As early as 1981, Ernest Saunders, Guinness' chairman and chief executive, spoke of acquiring Distillers. Argyll plc, the Scottish food group, was also interested in Distillers and on 2 December 1985 it announced a bid. The offer, mainly comprising of shares in Argyll, valued Distillers at 513p per share with a cash alternative of 485p. It was not until 20 January 1986 that Guinness announced a rival offer. The terms of the offer were better than those of Argyll. They were: 8 new Guinness shares and £7 cash for every 5 shares in Distillers with a cash alternative of 584.8p. On 6 February 1986 Argyll responded by raising its offer to 11 new Argyll shares plus 10 new Argyll convertible preference shares and £15 cash for every 10 Distillers shares, and on 7 February 1986 Argyll stated that it and its concert parties had accumulated a 4 per cent holding.

On 14 February 1986 the government announced that the Guinness bid for Distillers would be referred to the Monopolies and Mergers Commission (MMC). Guinness attempted to assuage the MMC's concerns by offering to dispose of certain Distillers' brands in the UK if the bid were successful, thereby keeping the new group's share of the UK whisky market below 25 per cent, the matter of concern to the MMC. After a legal dispute about this, Guinness on 20 February 1986 was able to make a new, higher offer of 5 Guinness shares and £5.16 cash for every 3 shares in Distillers with a cash alternative of 630.3p per share. Guinness offered a further alternative of part, or all, of the cash element in convertible preference shares. On 21 March 1986 the Government announced that the second Guinness bid would not be referred to the MMC. Argyll responded by also offering an improved, but final, bid: 125 new ordinary shares, 100 convertible preference shares and £162.75 cash for every 100 shares in Distillers with a 660p cash alternative.

The Argyll bid was significantly better than that of Guinness and a debate within Guinness ensued. Saunders wanted to increase Guinness' offer but it was pointed out that apparently improved terms would not necessarily raise the value of the bid because it would have the effect of diluting the earnings per share and, probably therefore, the share price.[1] The Inspectors pointed out that Mr Saunders:

> *Appeared unable to understand the dilution argument, despite lengthy explanations by Morgan Grenfell, Cazenove and Mr Roux (Guinness' finance director). He refused to accept Morgan Grenfell's advice that an increased cash alternative would not find underwriters. Mr Saunders' histrionic reaction at one stage was to ask loudly for the telephone number of S.G. Warburg, hinting that a less pusillanimous merchant bank would do his bidding.*
>
> DTI (1997, paragraph 4.17)

Eventually, Mr Saunders yielded to the argument and it was agreed that Guinness would not raise its offer. An announcement to this effect was made on 3 April 1986. Both offers were now final and Argyll's cash alternative was better than that of Guinness.

It transpired that Guinness had not left the outcome to fate. Underpinning its moves was a massive, but illegal, share support operation. It had two objectives:

1. to provide an inducement to Distillers shareholders to accept the offer by raising the apparent value of Guinness shares and, therefore, the value of the offer, and
2. to maintain the share price both during and immediately after the placing of the sub-underwriting of the cash alternative.

The offer was underwritten (at 278p per Guinness share) by Morgan Grenfell who needed to lay off some of this by sub-underwriting. A fall in the share price might have resulted in it falling below the underwritten price making the sub-underwriting difficult, if not impossible.

The aim of the share support operation was, therefore, to boost the Guinness share price. The Inspectors state that it was argued to them that the market can, and does, discount the effect of that activity 'which everyone knows and

1 An increase in the number of shares (denominator, n) has the obvious effect of reducing the earnings per share (the ratio e/n) as the historically profits (e) remain the same. See Chapters 2 and 6.

expects to occur'. The DTI Inspectors make the point that all parties to the bid and their advisers believe otherwise. If a bid is supported in this way, those involved must believe that it would have an effect.

It is ironic that at one stage Guinness actually accused Argyll of attempting to manipulate its share price. On 11 April 1986, Guinness issued a press release stating that over the previous week 2.5 million shares in Argyll had been bought by Samual Montagu and Charterhouse Japhet, Argyll's merchant bankers which had been disclosed in accordance with Rule 8.21 of the City Code. The press release said: 'Guinness would like to know ... What the share price of Argyll, and hence the value of Argyll's offer for Distillers, would be if these purchases had not been made.' The Inspectors comment that in the light of the huge support operation for the Guinness share price, the press release is remarkable.

After the sub-underwriting had been placed and the market had 'stabilized', there was little need for substantial support for the Guinness share price. However, on 6 February 1986 when Argyll raised its offer to approximately 640p with a 600p cash alternative, the Guinness alternative was significantly lower. Mr Saunders was most concerned, placed great pressure on his 'supporters' and during the following week more than 4.8 million shares in Guinness were bought to push up the price. When the Guinness offer did became final, obviously its success depended on the share price and support was crucial from the beginning of April. Purchases by supporters increased. According to the Inspectors, in the ten-and-a-half weeks of the bid to 3 April 1986, Guinness supporters had bought just under half a million shares. In the last two-and-a-half-weeks they bought 521 million more. In total this represented 25 per cent of Guinness' entire issued share capital!

At that time, an undisclosed share price support operation was in breach of the City Code, a voluntary code, and the Stock Exchange Rules. However, Section 151 of the Companies Act 1985 made it illegal for a company to give financial assistance for the purchase of its own shares. Section 152 of the Act defines 'financial assistance' as 'gifts, guarantees, security or indemnities, and any other financial assistance given by a company'. The share support operation also fell foul of the Prevention of Fraud (Investments) Act, 1958, which made it an offence for any person to induce or attempt to induce another person to acquire shares by any statement, promise or forecast which he knows to be misleading, false or deceptive, or by the dishonest concealment of material facts.

The conduct of companies, directors, advisers and others involved in a bid was laid down at the time by the City Code on Takeovers and Mergers (usually

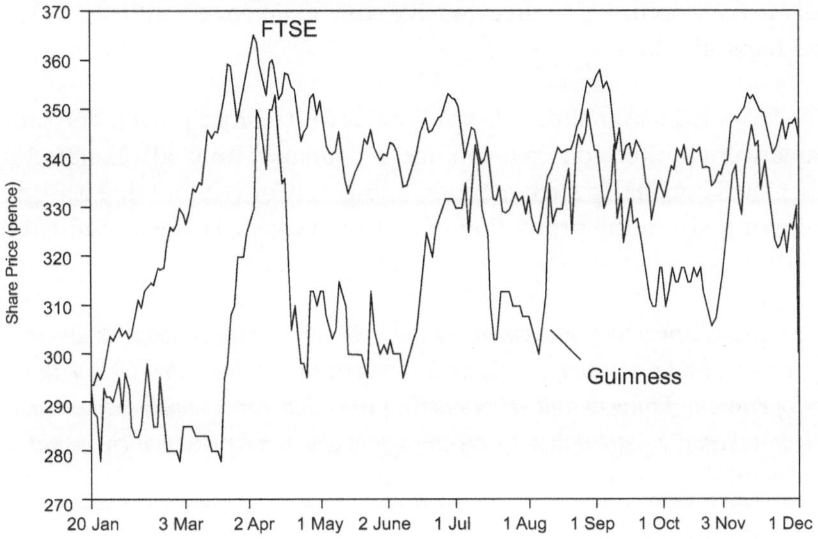

Figure 7.1 Guinness Share Price and rebased FTSE index during 1986 (DTI 1997)

referred to simply as The City Code) which was administered by The Panel on Takeovers and Mergers (usually referred to simply as The Panel). Although it was fully recognized and accepted as providing the key regulatory framework, it was often claimed that it was ignored and had no bite.

Undoubtedly, the actions by Guinness contravened the City Code and in particular Principle 6, which stated that 'all parties to a take-over transaction must use every endeavour to prevent the creation of a false market in the securities of an offeror or offeree company'. Rule 8 of the City Code required the immediate disclosure to the Stock Exchange, the Panel, and the press, of dealings in the shares of the companies involved by both the parties directly involved and any 'associates' which included:

> *all persons (whether or not acting in concert) who directly or indirectly own or deal in the shares of the offeror or offeree company in a take-over and who have (in addition to their normal interests as shareholders) an interest or potential interest, whether commercial, financial or personal, in the outcome of the offer.*

The City Code did not address the solicitation of other parties to purchase shares in order to support the share price. The Inspectors remark 'Such activity appears to have occurred on an extensive scale in takeover battles of the period, and perhaps still does.'

The Stock Exchange Rules also did not have statutory power. The sanctions available were limited to expulsion and reprimand. Rule 301(2) stated that 'a member shall not deal in such manner, knowingly or without due care, as shall promote or assist in the promotion of a false market'. This was defined under Rule 301(3) as

> *A market in which movement of the price of a share is brought about or sought to be brought about by contrived factors, whether by the operation of buyers and sellers acting in collaboration with each other or otherwise, calculated to create a movement of price which is not justified by assets, earnings or prospects.*

The regulators learned of the action of Guinness and its supporters from the US arbitrageur stockbroker, Ivan Boesky, after his arrest for insider dealing by the US authorities. In a plea bargain, Boesky told of the Guinness share support arrangements and his involvement in them and an investigation was started.

Ernest Saunders, the financiers and part of the share support group, Gerald Ronson and Sir Jack Lyons, and stockbroker Anthony Parnes were ultimately charged with participating in the operation. In its case against them, the DTI alleged Saunders had agreed to pay Parnes £3.35m for his role. The DTI also alleged that Lyons, a financier, had received £3m for his part in the scheme and companies in Ronson's Heron group which bought £25m worth of Guinness shares during the bid were to be paid a £5m 'success fee' for their support.

The verdicts on the 112th day of the case ended what was at the time the most expensive court action in British legal history, costing around £7.5m. Saunders, Ronson and Lyons were convicted of conspiracy, theft and false accounting. Parnes was found guilty of theft and false accounting. Sir Jack Lyons was stripped of his knighthood. Saunders served only 5 months of a 10-year sentence (it was later halved on appeal) after he was diagnosed as suffering from pre-senile dementia. (He later went on to advise a number of companies.) Gerald Ronson, who later rebuilt his Heron property empire, was fined £5m and served 6 months of a 1-year sentence. Anthony Parnes, a stockbroker, had his two-and-a-half year sentence cut to 21 months at a 1991 appeal.

Blue Arrow

Blue Arrow was also a major scandal of the 1980s. It was a direct result of the 1987 stock market crash and involving market abuse. In August 1987 County NatWest (CNW), National Westminster Bank's (NW) merchant banking subsidiary, underwrote a £837m rights issue by Blue Arrow, a rapidly expanding employment agency. The money was needed to fund the purchase of Manpower, a much larger American company. At that time, this was the largest ever rights issue. The offer closed on 28 September 1987 at which time only 38.04 per cent of the issue had been taken up. CNW announced the following day that 48.9 per cent of the issue had been subscribed for and that the balance had been sold on the market. CNW did not reveal that it had been left holding 13.4 per cent of Blue Arrow's share capital.

As a result of the stock market crash of 19 October 1987, the price of Blue Arrow shares dropped considerably and Natwest Investment Bank Ltd, the holding company for NW's investment banking operations, incurred substantial losses, £47.4m in 1987 and £17.7m in 1988. Between February 1988 and August 1988 internal inquiries into the circumstances of the Blue Arrow rights issue were carried out by NW and reports were submitted to the Bank of England and the DTI. The resulting scandal led the DTI to appoint inspectors to investigate the affair and the prosecution of three companies and many individuals by the Serious Fraud Office (SFO). The inspectors concluded that the market had been misled and the obligations of those involved to disclose were not complied with.

The DTI Inspectors' report was published in July 1989 (DTI 1989). It led to the resignation of three executive directors of NW. The bank's chairman, Lord Boardman, who was not criticised in the report, also resigned, because he believed that he should take ultimate responsibility. The report led to criminal charges being brought although some of these were later withdrawn. In February 1992, after a long and complex trial, four men (three of them from CNW) were convicted of misleading the market by disguising the failure of the rights issue. Later, all four appealed, and their convictions were overturned. In August 1992, formal verdicts of not guilty were entered.

Subsequent share support schemes

It is an interesting question as to whether at the time of the Guinness-Distillers case and afterwards, share support operations were as common as were claimed. The empirical evidence tentatively suggests not. Barnes (1996) found that whilst there was some positive abnormal performance in bidder share prices prior to an announcement, this was not the case where shares only were offered as consideration. However, post-announcement abnormal performance data are significantly different for bids where only shares are offered. Between one and three months afterwards, when the offer has expired, the share price fell for shares only bids by 1.9 per cent whereas it rose by 1.3 per cent for bids as a whole.

Criminal prosecutions for insider dealing

Contrary to general belief there were successful prosecutions under the original legislation, the Companies Act 1980, although these were relatively small and there were many other unsuccessful cases. There were also successful prosecutions under the Company Securities (Insider Dealing) Act 1985, the most notable being the Geoffrey Collier case, described later. However, the larger cases have been prosecuted under the Criminal Justice Act 1993 in conjunction with the Criminal Law Act 1977 section 1 which makes it an offence to conspire to commit an act which would be a substantive offence in criminal law. All together, there have been twenty-one successful cases. The most significant cases are described here.

Butt and others

This case centred on a city professional, Asif Butt, former vice-president of compliance at Credit Suisse First Boston. Butt was found guilty of using confidential information about clients over a period of about three-and-a-half years. Mr Butt worked in the secure zone of the bank known as the Compliance Control Room. This existed to ensure the secrecy of dealings. However, it gave Butt access to highly confidential inside information that was price-sensitive relating to the status and performance of companies that the bank were advising. Mr Butt fed the information to friends outside the bank, Ian Beale, Alexander Coleman, Richard Judson and Daniel Masters, who either bought shares or placed spread bets of up to £600 000 before important financial announcements. Nineteen transactions were presented at the trial. Seven involved advance knowledge of profits warnings and twelve concerned confidential information that a company was about to become the subject of a hostile bid or recommended takeover. Companies included Chubb, EMI, Johnson Matthey, Charter, Grantchester, Sedgwick and Royal Bank of Scotland's bid for NatWest. The friends used a schoolboy code in correspondence in which Butt was 'The Walrus' and Masters 'The Jackal'. The total profits made were estimated at £388 488 and losses at £100 681, the net gain being £287 807, in which Butt's share was excess of £237 000. According to the prosecution, the actual figure could run into millions of pounds.

Smith, Spearman, Spearman and Payne

In January 2004, three of the defendants were found guilty of conspiracy to commit insider dealing. Payne worked as a proof-reader at a firm of commercial printers where he saw drafts of prospectuses and offer documents prior to the announcement of a bid on the LSE. He passed this information on to the other defendants, who were not city professionals but business people working outside London, who bought shares. Twenty-seven takeover/merger transactions were presented at the trial. Profits earned by the defendants amounted to a total of £336 000. The Court of Appeal upheld sentences of 18 months' imprisonment for Smith and Catherine Spearman, and 21 months for Payne. Richard Spearman, who had pleaded not guilty, was found guilty on 4 June 2004 after a retrial and sentenced to 30 months' imprisonment. Substantial confiscation orders and cost orders were also made.

Gray, Liggins, Rowlands and Riding

David Gray was a stockbroker, William Liggins a fund manager, Catherine Rowlands an investment analyst and Mark Riding a fund manager. They were part of a 'network of friends' ready and willing to pass insider information between themselves. They were charged in respect of two separate incidents in 1988. The first was the planned takeover of two cellular phone companies by the Hawthorn Leslie Group plc. The second was the Australian group Goodman, Fielder, Wattie's bid for Rank Hovis McDougall. The case resulted from a DTI investigation into dealings in shares of Pleasurama, a leisure group, at a time when Mecca Leisure was making a takeover bid. The DTI said there had been many other highly suspicious dealings in Pleasurama shares, and not all the individuals involved had been charged.

Ronald Jenkins

On 17 July 1987 Ronald Jenkins, a former private secretary of Lord Cayzer, chairman of the British & Commonwealth Shipping group (B&C) pleaded guilty to insider dealing in October and November 1986. In the first instance, Jenkins used confidential price-sensitive information he had obtained from Lord Cayzer indicating that there was to be a senior management shake-up at B&C, at which time he bought 7500 shares. A week later after news of the reorganization had been made public Jenkins sold the shares at a profit of £4000. In the second instance, Jenkins bought shares in the name of the friend with whom he lived in a company B&C intended to buy. Jenkins was fined £10 000 and ordered to pay £2000 costs.

Geoffrey Collier

On 1 July 1987 Geoffrey Collier, joint managing director of Morgan Grenfell Securities, part of the Morgan Grenfell merchant banking group, was charged and found guilty under the Company Securities (Insider Dealing) Act 1985. He was given a 12-month suspended sentence and fined £25 000 with £7 000 costs. Mr Collier admitted two charges involving shares in the AE engineering group and Cadbury Schweppes. Four similar charges were left on file.

On Sunday 2 November, Mr Collier and Mr Richard Holmes, his joint managing director at Morgan Grenfell, attended a meeting at *The Daily Mirror*, Holborn, London, to discuss the takeover of engineering firm AE by Robert Maxwell. That night Mr Collier stayed at Mr Holmes' house in Wimbledon. At 6 a.m. the following day Mr Holmes was telephoned and told a bid was to be announced. At about 6.15 a.m., without Mr Holmes' knowledge, Mr Collier rang Mr Cassell, a colleague at the Los Angeles branch of his former employer, Vickers de Costa, and instructed them to buy 60 000 AE shares through a nominee company as soon as possible. Mr Cassell placed an order on behalf of Vickers Da Costa with London brokers Scrimgeour Vickers for 60 000 AE shares at a price up to 239p. The transaction was booked in Vickers Da Costa's records in the name of Pureve Investments, a Cayman Islands company. 'Pureve' was 'Everup' spelled backwards and had been formed by Mr Cassell and Mr Collier when they jointly bought an apartment. It was subsequently controlled by Mr Collier alone. At 8.15 a.m. trading began in London with AE shares valued at 239p. When the Maxwell bid was announced 15 minutes later, the shares had increased to 265p. Mr Cassell sold for £159 000, making a gross profit of £15 000. Not surprisingly the purchase, minutes before the announcement, and the sale minutes afterwards, attracted attention and colleagues at Morgan Grenfell in London traced the deal to Pureve.

Collier offered to make restitution if Morgan Grenfell was not informed. When told that this was not possible, he went to Mr Christopher Reeves, joint chairman of the Morgan Grenfell group, and confessed. He did not say anything about any earlier transactions. One of these involved Cadbury Schweppes. In August 1986, Morgan Grenfell was asked by a US company, General Cinema

Corporation, which was interested in taking over Cadbury Schweppes, to build up a 4.9 per cent holding in Cadbury, paying up to 230p per share. After Morgan Grenfell started buying there was press speculation about a possible bid and buying was temporarily stopped. During the lull, Mr Collier telephoned Mr Cassell and asked him to buy £30 000 of Cadbury Schweppes shares for him. Mr Cassell ordered call option contracts for shares in the name of Pureve Investments. The shares, in which Cassell and Collier had invested between them for £45 775, were sold at a loss of £15 000 when the price fell. Four similar charges were left on file.

This was the first major conviction for insider dealing since it became illegal in 1980. It was also the first since the implementation of the Financial Services Act 1986 which gave DTI inspectors powers to compel witnesses to provide evidence and supply documents. It was reported at the time that the sections of the Act granting these powers were brought into force two months ahead of schedule primarily to facilitate the investigation.[2] As it turned out, the case against Mr Collier was straightforward and did not require the new powers.

Porter and Daw

Stephen Porter and Julian Daw were employees of the LSE in its companies announcement office, handling price-sensitive information about listed companies before releasing them via the Regulatory News Service (RNS). Both were charged with insider dealing. Another LSE employee, Anthony Hadnutt, whose job involved monitoring suspicious share movements, was charged with disclosing information.

In July 1997 Mr Porter received information concerning merger talks between Capital Transport Rental Group (CTR) and General Electric Capital Corporation. He passed that information on to Mr Daw before putting out an announcement on the RNS. Mr Daw, who no longer worked for the Exchange at the time, then passed the information on to a third party who arranged for shares in CTR to be acquired. The shares were sold the next day for a profit of £6000, although there was no evidence that Mr Porter or Mr Daw profited from the sale. In November 1997, the process was repeated in relation to a potential takeover of Faber Prest. On this occasion, however, no shares could be acquired before the announcement went out on RNS.

2 *The Financial Times*, July 2, 1987, p. 10.

Mr Daw was fined £1000 for each of the two offences, plus costs of £3000. Mr Porter was sentenced to six months in prison and Mr Hadnutt was cleared.

Other smaller or older cases

John Dickinson, a director of a company in the Harris and Sheldon group, was found guilty of dealing in its shares. He was given a suspended six-month sentence and ordered to pay £100 costs.

John Bryce, at the time a partner in an Edinburgh firm of investment managers, was charged with using inside information to deal in Winterbottom Trust shares. He was found guilty but given an absolute discharge.

John Titheridge and his wife, Joyce, were found guilty of two offences relating to the purchase of 12 500 ordinary shares in Joseph Stocks and Sons prior to an agreed takeover bid from Fitch Lovell. Joyce Titheridge was at the time a secretary to a corporate finance director at the advising merchant bank.

Maurice Naeger was a director of W. H. Smith when the group launched a bid for Martin the Newsagent plc. The bid was unsuccessful as Martin later agreed to a takeover by Guinness. Mr Naerger, who pleaded guilty, was charged with buying 1500 of Martin's shares at 125p each in 1984 and selling them to the Guinness brewing group for 350p.

William Reardon-Smith was found guilty of insider dealing in the shares of Reardon Smith Line, a Cardiff-based shipping company. The DTI, which had brought the charge, claimed that in May 28 1985 Mr Reardon-Smith sold 85 000 shares in the company with the advantage of inside information.

Keith Robinson was found guilty of insider dealings in the shares of Mercantile House Holdings, the financial services group for acting on unpublished, price-sensitive information obtained from Mr Barkshire, then Mercantile's chairman and his brother-in-law. Mr Robinson had bought shares on 5 January 1987. The following day, CrownX, the Canadian financial services and health care group, announced that it had acquired 14.9 per cent of Mercantile. Mrs Robinson, his wife, was also charged, pleaded not guilty, and was acquitted.

John Hales, a management consultant, was found guilty of using unpublished price-sensitive information when he bought shares in Minet Holdings. St Paul, a US insurance company, had reached an agreement in principle on 24 November 1987 to take over Minet. The following day, a St Paul executive asked Mr Hales to devise an incentive scheme to ensure that senior Minet executives stayed on after the takeover. Within hours, Mr Hales bought 2500 Minet shares at 300p a share. He sold them three weeks later at 450p with a £3415 net profit.

Malcolm Gooding, a former dealer for a financial services group, admitted eight charges of insider dealing in shares in Hawtal Whiting Holdings, a design and engineering services company, over a three-day period during September 1987 for a profit of £456. Gooding bought shares in Hawtal after a conversation advising a director in the company that a proposed takeover of Hawtal by First Security Group would not be a good idea.

John Lukins, the holder of 3000 shares, and his brother, Peter, the holder of 5000 shares, sold their shares in the leather firm Pittard Garnar after a friend who was a director of the company told one of them of an impending profits fall in the company. They sold at 108p, the day before the shares fell to 77p.

Peter Sewell, a solicitor, bought 23 000 shares of plastics and components group Camotech on May 29 1987, using information he knew to be unpublished. He had been informed by Frederick Stebbing, his accountant and a director of Camotech, that it was about to bid for Fort Hill Aircraft Holdings, an airplane-seat manufacturer. Although he did not trade personally, Stebbing also bought Camotech shares for his god-daughter's baby girl.

Ian Morrisey and Lorelie Staines bought shares and persuaded others to buy shares in building products supplier Aaronson Brothers after learning of a planned takeover bid to be launched by Glunz AG, a German wood company. The pair gained the information about the bid from a friend, Mr Martin Priddle, an accountant with KPMG Peat Marwick, at a garden party. Aaronson shares rose from 50p to 80p after the bid announcement in August 1990.

Geoffrey Atkinson and John Hawksby, at that time share registrars, were convicted on three counts relating to dealing in shares in Queen's Moat Houses plc having knowingly obtained unpublished price-sensitive information relating to the timing of the dispatch of dividend payments.

Tim Blackstone bought 150 000 shares in Murray Financial Corporation shortly after being appointed as its PR adviser in August 1999. He was one of only a small group of people who knew that Murray Financial, run by Ken Murray, a godfather to one of Mr Blackstone's children, was planning a £30m bid for Leek Building Society.

Table 7.1 Analysis of the successful criminal cases according to the way the information was acquired*

	%
Ring of 'City professionals'	10.5
Acting on information from an adviser or another insider	42.1
Director and/or his associates	15.8
Acting on information from a director	26.3
Acting on information from a regulator	5.3
	100.0

* There were 21 cases. Two of these have been omitted because of the absence of sufficient information.

The cases overall

In 2001 the FSA took over the role of policing insider dealing from the DTI. It was generally believed that the DTI had brought few prosecutions either because it has failed to find proof that the suspect had genuine inside information when they dealt or that the Stock Exchange was unable to discover the true beneficial owners behind the companies that carried out the suspicious deals.

Table 7.1 provides an analysis of the successful criminal cases according to the way the information was acquired. It has always been believed that 'City professionals' such as merchant bankers, accountants and lawyers, who are privy to price-sensitive information, have continued to use offshore companies and nominees in this manner since the 1950s. By means of nominee holdings and intricate networks, the tracing of organized dealing rings, the swapping of information, is simply not possible. The only successful prosecutions of insider dealing of City professional 'rings' are the Asif Butt and others and the Gray, Rowlands, Liggins and Riding cases. Perhaps the largest case is that of Spearman, Smith and Payne although they are business people from outside London and not City folk. Most of the remaining cases are, in the words of the FSA, 'small fry'.[3] To these should be added a relatively large number of unsuccessful prosecutions, although, again most of these are small, mainly representing difficulties with the early legislation. These are shown in Table 7.2. To this extent the overall record can only be regarded as unsuccessful and suggests a significant fall in the number of prosecutions during recent years.

3 'Tough talking', *The Lawyer*, 29 September 2003.

Table 7.2 Unsuccessful criminal prosecutions for insider dealing since 1980 when it was made illegal: persons acquitted

Year	Number of cases	Number of individuals
1984	3	4
1988	1	1
1989	5	6
1990	2	3
1991	2	3
1993	1	1
1996	1	1
Total	15	19

Criminal prosecutions for market abuse (effectively) under Section 397 of the Financial Services and Markets Act 2000

There have been even fewer of these cases, although those that have come to court are arguably larger and more significant.

Table 7.3 Successful criminal prosecutions for market abuse since 1986 when it was made illegal

Date	Name	Offence	Penalty
18 August 2005	C. Rigby, G. Bailey	Recklessly making a statement to the market which was misleading, false or deceptive in a material particular, contrary to Section 397(1) of the Financial Services and Markets Act 2000	42 months' imprisonment reduced to 18 months on appeal 2 years' imprisonment
7 December 2005	J. Hipwell, T. Shepherd, A. Bhoyrul	Conspiracy to contravene Sect 47(2) of the Financial Services Act 1986 contrary to Sect 1(1) of the Criminal Law Act 1977. (Sect 47(2) of the Financial Services Act 1986 has now been replaced by Sect 397 of the Financial Services and Markets Act 2000)	6 months' imprisonment (upheld on appeal) 3 months' imprisonment 180 hours' community service

RIGBY AND BAILEY

Carl Rigby was Chairman and Chief Executive Officer and Gareth Bailey was the Chief Financial Officer of AIT, a software design company listed on the LSE. On 2 May 2002, AIT issued a trading statement which stated that its next reported turnover and profit figures were going to be in line with the market's expectation of £47m and £6.7m, respectively. The statement was false and misleading because it had taken into account revenue and profit from three contracts that had not yet been entered into so as to legally bind the parties. These were: Centraal Beheer valued at £1.1m; Datapoint, £2.5m; and St James's Place, £1.2m. Under normal accounting practice, the revenue and profit under those contracts would not have been included. On 31 May 2002, an update was issued stating that the 2 May statement was no longer accurate because the contract with Centraal Beheer had not been confirmed, leading to a £1.1m shortfall in revenue and profit. It also noted that short-term cash requirements were unlikely to be covered by AIT's available borrowing facilities and other cash resources. The statement caused the share price to fall from 492.5p to 96.5p. On 13 June 2002 a further statement was issued announcing that AIT would not publish preliminary results that day, as was previously expected, because of issues that had arisen in the company's audit. It said that there would be a further shortfall in revenue and profit, partly because the company had failed to satisfy itself that the value of a license agreement with Datapoint worth £2.5m could be recognized in the year-end results. As a consequence, the share price fell again, from 105p to 38.5p. Following the announcements, the company was forced by its bankers to restructure and to seek financing. A new board formally took over in September 2002 and new CEO and CFO were appointed. In August 2005, Rigby and Bailey were convicted of recklessly making a statement, promise or forecast which was misleading, false or deceptive contrary to Section 397 of the Financial Services and Markets Act 2000.

HIPWELL AND BHOYRUL: THE 'CITY SLICKERS' SHARE PRICE SCAM

This case involves two journalists and a friend who bought shares, tipped them through their newspaper column and then sold them. James Hipwell and Anil Bhoyrul were financial journalists employed by *The Daily Mirror*, to write a regular column called 'City Slickers'. They were also the authors of a book on investment (Hipwell and Bhoyrul 2000). The column was devoted to reporting rumours and making recommendations to readers to buy and sell shares based on these. At some point, Hipwell and Bhoyrul were joined by Shepherd, a friend (a former day-trader in shares), who gave them tips and ideas and helped to broadcast these on the Internet.

The Daily Mirror is a 'redtop' tabloid (Chan and Goldthorpe 2007). It is typically read by people with relatively little interest and expertise in investment and the workings of financial markets and relatively little money to invest. Nevertheless, the City Slickers column became well known. Its tips were regarded as exceptionally good to such an extent that they were ranked in a survey as second only to *The Financial Times* at that time. Anyone who followed them regularly would probably have made a substantial profit.

The most famous case is that of Viglen Technology plc, a computer company, run by Sir Alan Sugar, a high-profile businessman. Sugar was well-known to readers of *The Daily Mirror* not only because of having been a hands-on chairman of Tottenham Hotspur Football Club but also because Viglen was probably the best-known UK hardware company and recognized as highly successful. In January 2000, when excitement in Internet developments was at its peak, City Slickers informed its readers under the headline 'Sugar to Head Next Gold Rush' that Viglen was about to set up a company to market its products over the Internet. The price of Viglen shares virtually doubled almost immediately. It also emerged that the editor of *The Daily Mirror*, Piers Morgan, had bought £67 000 worth of shares in Viglen the day before the City Slickers tip. City Slickers boasted 'Sir Alan Sugar made the fastest £100m in City history yesterday because of us'. As a result of this, there were rumours that various people at *The Daily Mirror* had taken advantage of the situation and articles and complaints about their behaviour appearing in the press.

The LSE had noticed the 'very significant rise' in the Viglen share price. It alerted the DTI's Companies Investigation Branch who duly appointed inspectors to ascertain whether there had been a contravention of the insider dealing legislation. As a result of their findings, a criminal investigation was undertaken by the DTI. The investigators discovered that Hipwell, Bhoyrul and Shepherd regularly bought shares the day before they tipped them in the City Slickers column and then sold them soon afterwards at a profit as the price rose. In the opinion of the investigators, the tip was a deliberate act of manipulating the market by inflating or 'ramping' the share price from which they were able to profit (DTI 2001).

The Daily Mirror sacked Hipwell and Bhoyrul in early 2000 for gross misconduct. They and Piers Morgan were also criticised by the Press Complaints Commission for breaking its Code of Conduct. The DTI decided not to pursue Mr Morgan but Hipwell, Bhoyrul and Shepherd were charged with conspiracy under section 1(1) of the Criminal Law Act 1977 to contravene section 47(2) of the Financial Services Act 1986.

The seven-week trial began in October 2005 and received widespread press interest, not least because it was perpetrated by journalists on a national newspaper involving its editor, who had a high media profile. It was claimed that Hipwell, Bhoyrul and Shepherd had conspired between August 1999 and February 2000 to buy shares in 44 companies that they later tipped in their column or on Internet sites. Hipwell made £41 000, Anil Bhoyrul £15 000 and Terry Shepherd around £17 000. They also accused Hipwell and Bhoyrul of writing stories, on more than one occasion, simply to ramp the value of shares in a particular company 'quite irrespective of the accuracy ... of the story'. All three were found guilty. Bhoyrul, who had admitted conspiracy before going to trial, was sentenced to 180 hours' community service. Hipwell was jailed for six months and Shepherd for three months. Lawyers for Hipwell later argued the disparity of the two men's sentences was hard to justify. The Appeal Court judge upheld the sentence.

Table 7.4 Successful civil actions by FSA for market abuse since 2000

Date	Name	Offence	Fine
23 April 2003	ABN Amro Equities (UK) Mr M. Ackers	Market manipulation contrary to former FSA Principle 3 requiring firms to maintain high standards of market conduct	£900 000 £70 000
10 February 2004	Mr R. Middlemiss	Using inside information to sell shares contrary to Section 118 of FSMA	£15 000
7 July 2004	Mr P. Bracken	Using inside information to buy shares contrary to Section 118 of FSMA	£15 000
2 August 2004	Mr M. T. Davies	Using inside information to buy shares contrary to Section 118 of FSMA	£1000
24 August 2004	Shell Transport & Trading; Royal Dutch/Shell Group of Companies	Providing false or misleading information to the market contrary to Section 118 of FSMA and the Listing rules	£17 000 000
12 November 2004	Evolution Beeson Gregory Ltd Mr C. Potts	Distorting the market in a company's shares contrary to Section 118 of FSMA	£500 000 £75 000

Table 7.4 *Concluded*

16 December 2004	Mr R. Hutchings Mr J. Smith	Abusive dissemination of information contrary to Section 118 of FSMA	£18 000 £15 000
21 December 2004	Mr R. Bonnier Indigo Capital LLC	Providing misleading statements which created a false impression to the market contrary to Section 118 of FSMA	£290 000 £65 000
1 March 2005	Mr D. Isaacs	Dishonestly obtaining inside information contrary to Section 118 of FSMA and the Code of Market Conduct	£15 000
18 May 2005	Mr A. Mohammed	Using inside information to buy shares contrary to Section 118 of FSMA	£10 000
21 December 2005	Mr J. Malins	Using inside information to buy shares contrary to Section 118 of FSMA	£25 000
11 April 2006	Deutsche Bank AG Mr D. Maslen	Failing to observe proper standards of market conduct contrary to the FSA Principles for Business 2 and 5	£6 363 643 £350 000
1 August 2006	GLG Partners LP Mr P. Jabre	Using inside information to buy shares contrary to Section 118 of FSMA and FSA Principles 2 and 3 for approved persons	£750 000 £750 000
19 August 2006	Mr J. Parker	Using inside information to deal in shares and engage in spread betting contrary to Section 118(1) and (2) of FSMA	£300 000 reduced to £250 000
23 November 2006	Mr S. Pignatelli	Presenting information to clients as if it were inside information contrary to FSA General Principles 2 and 3 for approved persons	£20 000
20 March 2007	Mr R. Casoni	Failing to observe proper standards of market conduct contrary to FSA General Principle 3 for approved persons	£52 500

Civil actions by FSA for market abuse since 2000

Most cases of market abuse have been prosecuted at the civil level. Those that have been successful are listed in Table 7.4.

ABN AMRO EQUITIES (UK); MR M. ACKERS

The London office of ABN Amro, the Netherlands-based investment banking and securities trading group, ABN Amro Equities (UK), and known as AAE and the then joint head of the UK equity trading desk, Michael Ackers, accepted improper instructions from a US sales trader at ABN Amro Inc. The apparent purpose was to push the closing market price of certain shares to a higher level than would otherwise have been the case. This happened on three separate occasions between April and October 1998 in respect of four stocks, Carlton Communications plc, British Biotech plc, Volkswagen and Metro, and involved several different traders.

MIDDLEMISS

Mr Middlemiss was an employee of, and also owned shares in, Profile Media Group plc (PMG). During the week beginning 22 April 2002 he became aware of potential problems relating to the financial performance and finances of PMG's largest subsidiary, Profile Pursuit Inc. On 2 May 2002 PMG issued a press statement warning that its financial results for the year to 30 June 2002 'are likely to be materially below expectations'. As a result of the announcement, PMG's shares fell from 14.5p to 4.75p. Prior to the announcement, Mr Middlemiss sold 70 000 of his 274 800 shares in PMG, avoiding a potential loss of £6825.

Mr Middlemiss was fully aware of PMG's policy requiring employees to seek prior permission before trading in PMG shares. Previously, he had sought permission from its Chief Executive Officer or Finance Director before dealing. On this occasion, he did not seek approval as he knew that permission would not have been granted.

BRACKEN

Mr Bracken, in his role as Group Head of Communications at the Whitehead Mann Group (WMG), learned on 26 September 2002 that it was likely to issue a negative trading statement in the near future. Within an hour of receiving this information Mr Bracken had approached his broker placing an order to short sell 5000 shares in WMG at 190p to settle by 10 October. WMG made an announcement at 8.15am on 27 September 2002 that its expected profit would be similar to that for 2001 because of difficult trading conditions. At 9.47 a.m.

on the same day, Mr Bracken instructed his broker to buy 5000 WMG shares at 138p to close out his short position. He made a profit of £2430.

In early November 2002 Mr Bracken received the detailed figures for WMG's interim results and learned that its CEO was to step down and a new CEO be appointed. On 11 November Mr Bracken again approached his broker and instructed them to short sell 3000 WMG shares at 123p to settle by 25 November. At 7.02 a.m. on 12 November, WMG announced its interim results for the half-year ending 30 September 2002 and the appointment of a new CEO. The shares then fell from 130p to 117.5p by the close of trading and to a low of 105p by 21 November. At 1.51 p.m. on 21 November, Mr Bracken instructed his broker to close out the position with the purchase of 3000 WMG shares at 107p. He made a profit of £393.

By carrying out both these transactions Mr Bracken, a regular investor, was in breach of WMG's internal rules requiring employees to seek permission before dealing in its shares.

DAVIES

Mr Davies was Group Financial Controller of Berkeley Morgan Group plc (BMG). During November and December 2003, Mr Davies assisted in the preparation of BMG's interim results. By 5 January 2004 when he bought shares in BMG, Mr Davies knew that the exceptional items contained in BMG's accounts in the previous year which had an adverse effect on its results would not be recurring and that BMG's interim results were favourable. The following day the results were announced and BMG's share price rose 29 per cent over the day from 52.5p to 67.5p. On 7 January Mr Davies sold his 4000 shares in BMG at 63p, making a net profit of £420.

SHELL

This fine was imposed on Shell as a result of what was described as 'unprecedented misconduct' in relation to misstatements of its proved reserves. When Shell first publicly revealed on 9 January 2004 that it had misstated its reserves, its share price fell 7.5 per cent, from 401p to 371p, reducing its market capitalization by approximately £2.9bn.

A number of factors made Shell's abuse of the market particularly serious. It had made false or misleading announcements in relation to its hydrocarbon reserves and reserves replacement ratios between 1998 and 2003. These announcements were made despite indications and warnings from 2000 to

2003 that they were false or misleading. Shell did not correct the information it had disclosed until the publication of its results for the period 9 January to 24 May 2004 when it announced the recategorization of 4470 million barrels of oil equivalent, approximately 25 per cent of its proved reserves.

EVOLUTION BEESON GREGORY (EBG), C. POTTS

From 25 September to 21 October 2003, EBG, through Mr Potts, implemented a strategy to short sell shares in Room Service plc (RS), resulting in EBG short selling 252 per cent of RS's issued share capital. The strategy was undertaken without a reasonable settlement plan to ensure delivery of the shares sold, but in anticipation of RS issuing new shares following its AGM on 20 October 2003, thereby allowing demand to be met. The issue of shares did not occur and RS shares were suspended from AIM on 22 October 2003.

EBG's short selling of Room Service shares went beyond a level where it was capable of delivering those shares, resulting in the supply side of the market being distorted and leading to EBG's failure to deliver shares to 250 investors. EBG co-operated with the FSA throughout the investigation, and paid out approximately £150 000 to disadvantaged investors. This was the first occasion that the FSA had acted against a firm or individual for distorting the market. The FSA had previously taken action in respect of misuse of confidential information and for making false and misleading statements.

HUTCHINGS AND SMITH

During the period March to May 2003 I Feel Good (Holdings) plc (IFG) was involved in takeover talks with Dennis Publishing Limited (Dennis). These resulted in Dennis taking over IFG in May 2003. Mr Smith was involved in these negotiations as company secretary and finance director of IFG, and Mr Hutchings was an FSA-approved person working as an equity analyst at Evolution Beeson Gregory at the time.

Mr Hutchings and Mr Smith knew each other as friends and former colleagues and were in frequent contact throughout April 2003 by phone, text and emails. On 11 April Mr Hutchings bought 114 942 shares in IFG. Smith and Hutchings exchanged 11 text messages on 14 April during which Mr Smith is likely to have told Mr Hutchings to look out for an announcement the next morning concerning a potential offer. IFG made an announcement at 10.37 on 15 April that it had received an approach which may lead to an offer for the company. IFG's share price rose by 29 per cent from 4.25p to 5.5p.

Mr Hutchings contacted Mr Smith on 28 April by email looking for information on the progress of the takeover talks; Mr Smith confirmed that a bid from Dennis had been accepted by the board of IFG at an offer price of 8p per share. On receipt of this information Mr Hutchings bought 80 000 shares on 28 April for 6.25p, 80 000 on 29 April at 6.25p, and 166 666 shares at 6p on 30 April. He did not consult his compliance department about any of these purchases, although he was aware that he was in possession of price-sensitive information, and had deliberately staggered his share purchases to avoid detection. Mr Hutchings made a profit of just under £5000 on 6 May when he sold the shares.

BONNIER, INDIGO

Mr Bonnier was a managing partner of Indigo with sole responsibility for its proprietary investments and compliance with statutory reporting requirements. On Indigo's behalf, Mr Bonnier traded in Regus' shares and CFDs referenced to Regus' shares. The majority of the CFD purchases during the period were from Cantor Fitzgerald Europe Limited (Cantors) whose terms of business meant that Cantors retained ownership of all shares bought to hedge its CFD position.

During this period Mr Bonnier made 12 inaccurate notifications to Regus informing them that Indigo had bought Regus' shares. The notifications indicated that Indigo's shareholding in Regus had increased from 3.51 per cent on 18 November 2002 to 15.12 per cent on 6 January 2003 and 12.8 per cent on 8 January 2003. The notifications related to the size of Indigo's CFD holdings and not actual shares. Regus in turn disclosed the notifications to the market as required under Listing Rule 9.11. In fact, Indigo's shareholding in Regus decreased and never amounted to more than 2.3 per cent and on 8 January 2003 there were none.

ISAACS

Mr Isaacs, an experienced investor, regularly used Internet bulletin boards to exchange information with other investors. One of his acquaintances was a Trafficmaster employee who received the minutes of its internal management meetings. Over the summer of 2003, Mr Isaacs became aware of confidential information contained in two different sets of minutes.

On the first occasion, Mr Isaacs saw minutes dated 4 August whilst in this person's kitchen. The minutes contained information concerning Smartnav, Trafficmaster's flagship navigation product, and several leading car brands that were set to offer its installation. Mr Isaacs memorized this information and posted it on the Internet bulletin board ADVFN on 3 September.

Mr Isaacs obtained access to a second set of minutes, published on 8 September 2003, which noted that the 'slightly better than expected' interim results were to be published on 11 September. It also gave details of further Smartnav transactions. Mr Isaacs admitted to obtaining this information and posting it on ADVFN on 10, 12 and 18 September.

MOHAMMED

Mr Mohammed was an employee of PricewaterhouseCoopers and a member of its Delta plc audit team. In November 2002 he obtained confidential information that Delta intended to sell its electrical division and on 29 November 2002 he bought shares in Delta. The sale of the electrical division was announced on 10 December 2002 whereupon Mr Mohammed sold his shares, making a profit of £3750.

MALINS

Mr Malins, the only executive director of Cambrian plc based in the UK, committed market abuse by buying shares in Cambrian based on his inside knowledge of the company's financial condition and business performance on 23 March 2005 and 31 March 2005, both of which were during a close period.

On the morning of 23 March 2005, Mr Malins chaired a meeting to discuss a new share placing by the company, at a premium to the share price. Following the meeting, he bought 50 000 shares in Cambrian. The order was filled in two tranches by 15.14 p.m. The announcement was made at 16.10 p.m. Mr Malins did not seek permission from Cambrian to buy the shares, as is required during a close period, and he knew that the placing had not been announced when he made his purchase. Mr Malins, who continued to hold the shares, would have made £6000 had he sold his shares following the announcement.

On 30 March Mr Malins chaired a board meeting to finalize the accounts and interim results, which showed profits to be greater than market expectations. He sought permission to buy 20 000 shares in Cambrian and was granted this on the basis that the purchase would take place following the announcement of the interim results. He bought the shares at 9.22 a.m. on 31 March 2005 before they had been published. If he had sold his shares in Cambrian after the announcement, Mr Malins would have made a profit of £400.

DEUTSCHE BANK AG; MASLEN

The FSA found Deutsche Bank AG (Deutsche) guilty of breaching FSA Principle 5 for failing to observe proper standards of market conduct, and Principle 2, for failing to conduct its business with due skill, care and diligence. These breaches arose from two separate transactions conducted by Deutsche during March 2004. The FSA also found Mr David Maslen, Deutsche's Head of European Cash Trading at the time, guilty of failing to observe proper standards of market conduct in the first transaction.

The first transaction was in relation to a book build in Scania AB (Scania) B shares. Book building is the process by which an underwriter attempts to determine at what price to offer an IPO based on demand from institutional investors. This is done by accepting orders from fund managers indicating the number of shares they desire and the price they are willing to pay. An accelerated book build is where this is done over a few hours.

Deutsche breached FSA Principle 5 due to Mr Maslen, who had an active role in the Scania book build, giving instructions for proprietary trading which occurred at a sensitive time during the book build. This trading was not transparent to the market and was of a size and manner that contributed to material changes in the Scania B share price during the book build. It prevented potential investors from gaining a full understanding of the nature of supply and demand for Scania B shares that was independent of Deutsche. Deutsche was also found to have breached FSA Principle 2 as, despite Mr Maslen's role in the book build, he gave the instructions to commence the trading without either notifying or seeking clearance from Deutsche compliance or senior management or checking Deutsche's own restricted list.

Deutsche was also found to have breached FSA Principle 2 for making announcements during the course of the book build about the Scania transaction that were incomplete or inaccurate. Deutsche also released an announcement to its own sales force, which was subsequently communicated to clients, about its holding of Scania shares before notifying the Stockholm stock exchange.

Scania B shares are listed on Sweden's Stockholmbörsen, which is not a prescribed market. On 4 March 2004, Deutsche agreed to purchase 63.7 million Scania B shares for £1.1bn from Volvo AB and to dispose of them through an accelerated book build. Potential investors were guided to the likely allocation price of the book build by setting a marketing range for the book build shares. While Deutsche was conducting the book build, Scania B shares were being traded on the open market. During the course of the morning the share price dropped to below the marketing range and Mr Maslen instructed a Deutsche trader to commence buying shares in Scania on the open market. This was undertaken using two external Swedish brokers. The trading by Deutsche at times represented 90 per cent of trading in Scania B shares and contributed to the Scania price moving to within the book build marketing range. The way in which Deutsche traded was not transparent to the market and potential investors were unable to obtain a full understanding as to the supply and demand and price of the shares independent of Deutsche. The trading in Scania B shares was also in breach of Deutsche's own internal restrictions.

During the book build, information was provided to potential investors by Deutsche's Equity Sales team. This sales force was updated using Deutsche's internal messaging system. This information was incomplete or inaccurate in relation to the level of demand in the book. Furthermore, on 5 March 2004 certain customers were notified of Deutsche's holding in Scania B shares by Deutsche's sales force before it made an announcement to the Stockholmbörsen.

The second transaction involved the stabilization of Cytos Biotechnology AG (Cytos) shares which were offered by Deutsche on 25 March 2004 and were stabilized on the Swiss SWX exchange through a Deutsche trader in Zurich. Deutsche failed to ensure that the trader conducted the trades in accordance with its internal procedures, and its staff involved in the trades failed to escalate the matter in a timely fashion. Deutsche failed to ensure that the trader conducting the stabilization trades understood and followed its internal procedures. The supervising London staff, although aware of the trading, failed to escalate the matter to the proper level.

In reaching its decision, the FSA took into account Deutsche's conduct which included reporting the matter to the FSA; taking disciplinary action against individuals; undertaking an internal review of its systems; and introducing new senior management in the area.

GLG PARTNERS LP, JABRE

On 11 February 2003 Mr Jabre was 'wall crossed' by Goldman Sachs International as part of the pre-marketing of a new issue of convertible preference shares in Sumitomo Mitsui Financial Group Inc (SMFG). Mr Jabre was given confidential information and agreed to be restricted from dealing in SMFG securities until the issue was announced. Mr Jabre breached this restriction by short selling around £16m of SMFG ordinary shares between 12 and 14 February 2003. When the new issue was announced on 17 February 2003, Mr Jabre made a substantial profit for the GLG Market Neutral Fund he managed.

PARKER

James Parker, a senior accountant and a long-serving employee at the set-top box maker Pace Micro Technology was fined £250 000 for insider dealing, after losing his appeal to the Financial Services and Markets Tribunal.

Mr Parker sold his shares in the company after discovering that a major competitor had withdrawn from takeover talks with Pace. Pace subsequently revealed news of the collapsed bid talks to the market, at the same time as issuing a profit warning, sending the shares plummeting. Shortly before the announcement Parker also took out spread bets.

The FSA calculated that Mr Parker made a profit of £153 942 from the trades, and fined him £300 000. Although the Tribunal upheld the FSA's ruling that Parker had acted in breach of market regulations, it reduced the fine from £300 000 to £250 000 after recalculating Mr Parker's gains as £121 742. Pace Micro was also fined £450 000 by the FSA in January 2005 for not keeping investors informed of material information. (See penalties imposed by the FSA for breaches of their Listing Rules later in this chapter.)

PIGNATELLI

The FSA's disciplinary action related to Mr Pignatelli's conduct after receiving an email on 24 May 2005 from an analyst concerning a US company. The FSA found that Mr Pignatelli breached Principle 2 of the Statements of Principle for Approved Persons (duty to act with skill, care and diligence in carrying out a controlled function) by failing to consider whether the email contained inside information, despite what the FSA considered to be 'warning signals'. Mr Pignatelli immediately relayed the information to eight people, including clients, four of whom sold or short sold shares in the company that evening. In the FSA's view, Mr Pignatelli relayed the information in a way that gave the impression that it was inside information. This breached Principle 3 of the FSA's Statement of Principles for Approved Persons (duty to observe proper standards of market conduct in carrying out a controlled function. See Chapter 6).

In view of the circumstances that Mr Pignatelli's misconduct occurred only on one day and the fact that he had never previously been the subject of disciplinary action from a regulator, the FSA decided to fine him £20 000.

CASONI

The FSA found Roberto Casoni, a former equities analyst, guilty of failing to observe proper standards of market conduct whilst acting as an Approved

Person. This was in breach of Principle 3 of the FSA's Statement of Principles for Approved Persons (duty to observe proper standards of market conduct in carrying out a controlled function. See Chapter 6).

Mr Casoni was a research analyst for Citigroup's Global Equity Research (Citigroup) in London, where he was head of the Italian small-mid cap team covering the Italian leasing sector. On 9 January 2006 Mr Casoni began the approval process for Citigroup's coverage of the Italian factoring bank, Banca Italease (BI). Prior to its publication, Mr Casoni disclosed details of his valuation methodology, final recommendation and the target price. In one case he also told a client the expected date of publication. Citigroup published its research, containing a buy recommendation with a target price of €39 per share. BI's price at the time was €25.70.

In reaching its decision, the FSA took into account the fact that Mr Casoni neither intended to manipulate BI's share price nor did he obtain any financial gain from his misconduct. As Mr Casoni co-operated fully with the FSA and agreed to settle this matter at an early stage of the investigation, his fine was reduced from £75 000 to £52 500.

Summary

Table 7.5 provides an analysis of these cases. It shows that by far the majority relate to insider dealing offences as opposed to market abuse. Presumably, this is because of the less stringent requirements for proof of insider dealing in a civil action compared with a criminal action. The four cases that relate to action contrary to FSA principles, as opposed to being contrary to FSMA, are presumably lesser offences. Certainly those relating to improper disclosure appear to be less severe than the insider dealing offence.

Table 7.5 Analysis of successful civil actions by the FSA for market abuse since 2000 according to the seven types of market abuse

	Contrary to Section 118 of FSMA	Contrary to FSA Principles
Insider dealing	8	
Improper disclosure	1	2
Misuse of information	0	
Manipulating transactions	0	2
Manipulating devices	0	
Dissemination	2	
Distortion and misleading behaviour	1	
Total	12	4

Breaches of listing tules

The FSA has imposed penalties on individuals and companies for breaching the listing rules relating to market abuse. These are listed in Table 7.6.

Table 7.6 Penalties imposed by the FSA for breaches of Listing Rules

Date	Name	Offence	Penalty
11 April 2003	Marconi plc	Failure to release price-sensitive information regarding a change in its expectation as to its performance to the market, without delay, as required by Rule 9.2(c) of the Listing Rules.	Censured
12 December 2003	SFI Group plc	Contravention of Rule 9.3A of the Listing Rules by failing to take reasonable care to ensure that the Preliminary Results Announcement was not false or misleading.	Censured
29 March, 2004	Sportsworld Media Group plc Mr G. Brown	Contravention of Rule 9.2 of the Listing Rules by failing to notify the market of changes in its business performance and expectations.	Censured £45 000
19 May, 2004	Universal Salvage plc Mr C. Hynes	Contravention of Rule 9.1A of the Listing Rules by failing to notify the market of the loss of a major contract which was likely to lead to a substantial movement in the price of its listed securities.	£90 000 £10 000
27 January, 2005	Pace Micro Technology plc	Contravention of Rules 9.2c and 9.3A of the Listing Rules by failing to ensure that the announcement of its Interim Results included all relevant information.	£450 000

MARCONI

In this case a large listed company failed to provide important information to investors on a timely basis. The FSA decided that Marconi had breached paragraph 9.2(c) of the Listing Rules when it failed to notify the Company Announcements Office without delay of a change in its expected performance for the half year ending September 2001 and full year ending March 2002.

Marconi changed its expectations as to its performance in the afternoon of 2 July 2001 but did not make an announcement until after the market had closed on 4 July 2001 and, after its stock had been suspended for a full day. On

5 July 2001, there was a twenty five-fold increase in the volume of trading in its securities and a 54 per cent fall in the share price. The FSA's view was that from the afternoon of 2 July 2001 Marconi should have taken steps to ensure that announcement had been made by, at the latest, the evening of 3 July 2001.

SFI GROUP PLC

SFI breached the Listing Rules by failing to take reasonable care to ensure that its Preliminary Results Announcement issued on the 30 July 2002 was not false or misleading. This presented an overstated and overoptimistic view of its financial results and its future prospects, not only as at 30 July 2002, but also in relation to the results for the two previous financial years. This was because:

- SFI's accounting systems and controls had for some time failed to reliably determine its current and historical financial position as a whole.
- For some time, SFI's accounting systems and controls had not been robust enough to support internal forecasts and projections that proved misleading and false.
- These failures in SFI's accounting systems and controls had existed for at least two years prior to the Preliminary Results Announcement and it was only in November 2002 that SFI eventually identified the discrepancies which caused the announcement to be misleading and false.

While there was no evidence to suggest these breaches were deliberate, there was a serious failure to take the reasonable care required by a listed company. Having considered the circumstances, including SFI's financial position, the FSA decided not to impose a financial penalty but, instead, to issue a public statement of censure. The FSA also acknowledged that SFI and their advisors had co-operated with the investigation.

SPORTSWORLD AND BROWN

Sportsworld breached the Listing Rules by failing to notify the market of changes in its business performance and expectations as to its pre-tax profit until 28 January 2002, despite having been aware of the situation since 24 December 2001.

Mr Brown, its CEO, was responsible for ensuring Sportsworld observed the Listing Rules. Mr Brown's and Sportsworld's failure to inform investors and other market participants of changes in its performance and expectations as to performance without delay could have caused investors to make decisions based on inaccurate information. Sportsworld's forecasts, agreed by the Board, for the year ending June 2002 indicated expected pre-tax profits of £16.1m, £5.5m in the first half and £10.6m in the second half. The company was positive about these in a statement on 3 October 2001 when its preliminary results were announced and again on 29 November 2001 at the time of its AGM. These announcements influenced the market's expectation of Sportsworld's likely profits.

Sportsworld's senior management had received its November management accounts on 24 December 2001. These were disappointing and indicated that Sportsworld was experiencing significant losses rather than the expected profit and only a greatly improved performance in the second half of the year would enable it to meet expectations. Despite the situation becoming even more apparent in the weeks following 24 December 2001, the Board did not meet until 25 January 2002 to discuss the company's changed circumstances and a trading statement. Sportsworld announced a reduced full-year profit forecast of between £9m and £10m on 28 January 2002.

The FSA decided that Mr Brown, as the CEO, failed in his duty under the Listing Rules to ensure that the Board were kept fully informed of developments and whether these changes were price-sensitive and should have been released to the market without delay. It was not enough for Mr Brown or the company to remain optimistic that lost ground would be made up in the rest of the financial year as a sufficient reason for not informing the market of the company's adverse performance. The market should have been allowed to judge for itself whether the belief was justified. Mr Brown was fined £45 000. The FSA would also have imposed a substantial financial penalty on Sportsworld for the breach were it not for its lack of financial resources.

UNIVERSAL AND HYNES

Universal breached the Listing Rules by failing to notify the market of the loss of a major contract which was likely to lead to a substantial fall the price of its listed securities. Mr Hynes was the director responsible for ensuring that the company notified the market without delay once the obligation was triggered on 16 April 2002. Universal did not make the announcement until 23 April 2002. When it was made, the announcement also reported worse than expected trading figures and Universal's share price fell 55 per cent on the day of the announcement.

Universal is involved in the vehicle salvage business. In 1998 it won a contract with Direct Line which by March 2002 accounted for approximately 40 per cent of the vehicles Universal handled. Direct Line first told Universal that it intended to terminate this contract at a meeting on 18 March 2002 attended by Mr Hynes. Universal tried in correspondence to persuade Direct Line not to terminate the contract, but Direct Line confirmed the termination in a letter received by Universal on 16 April 2002.

In the meantime Universal had conducted an analysis as to the likely financial impact of the contract being terminated and explored options for costs savings with a view to presenting the findings to a Board Meeting on 18 April 2002. However, on receiving confirmation of the termination of the contract, Universal took no steps to obtain advice from West LB, its corporate advisers, bring forward the Board Meeting or to take any other preparatory measures. At the board meeting, it was agreed to seek advice from West LB as to whether to make an announcement to the market regarding the loss of the Direct Line contract and its poor trading figures for the final quarter of the financial year. Mr Hynes was given responsibility for consulting with West LB. He contacted West LB later that day and met with them on the afternoon of Monday 22 April. At that meeting West LB advised Universal to make an announcement to the market. The announcement was released through the RIS at 3.24 p.m. on Tuesday 23 April.

PACE

Pace breached the Listing Rules because it failed to ensure its Interim Results announcement on 8 January 2002 included all relevant information when it did not reveal that its trade credit insurance in respect of one of its largest customers had been withdrawn. It also failed to update the market without delay of a change in its expected profits which had occurred on 4 February 2002.

Pace is involved in the manufacture, development and distribution of digital television set-top boxes. Its primary customer base at that time was composed of a small number of large European and US companies. NTL was one of its largest customers and accounted for nearly half of Pace's turnover and profit in late 2001. In October 2001, NTL placed orders for 450 000 set top boxes, to be delivered in the first three months of 2002, on which Pace's forecasted revenues for the financial year ending 1 June 2002 were dependent. In early December 2001, NTL, which was suffering well-publicized financial difficulties, reduced the size of the order to 300 000 boxes. On 19 December 2001, Pace's trade credit insurer, NCM, informed Pace that it was withdrawing insurance cover in respect of all of Pace's future shipments to NTL including the October 2001 order. This withdrawal meant that future payments owed by NTL were no longer guaranteed. The matter was not drawn to the attention of the company's corporate brokers and the withdrawal of insurance cover was not mentioned in the Interim Results statement published on 8 January 2002, which stated that the expected turnover for the year ending 1 June 2002 would be broadly similar to the previous year's turnover of £524m. The forecast figure depended on revenue from NTL's purchase of the 300 000 boxes. On 4 February 2002, Pace did revise its revenue forecast for its financial year ending 1 June 2002, to £455m, which was 12.5 per cent less than that the market expection of £520m. When Pace informed the market on 5 March 2002 of this, its share price fell 67 per cent on the day.

Summary

The use of its powers to issue fines for breaching the listing rules is another means by which the FSA may regulate market abuse. Of the five cases on which it has acted, three relate to failure to notify the market. The remaining two cases relate to failure to ensure that the announcement is not misleading. It is difficult to tell whether there have been no breaches in other areas or it has not been possible for the FSA to take action.

Conclusions

It is unclear from the data whether insider dealing and market abuse are increasing or decreasing in recent years. The data do suggest that whilst there have been a few criminal cases, the main effort by the FSA is the civil route, emphasizing prevention through controls within firms as opposed to investigation and prosecution.

The FSA appears to have been as vigorous as it can in the use of its powers of prosecution. Of the five cases that were decided in 2006 the FSA lost two, which is an indication of the difficulty of obtaining evidence for a successful prosecution, one of which resulted in a decision by the Financial Services and Markets Tribunal that the FSA had acted unreasonably.

On the other hand, there were only five decisions during 2006 which related to individuals and only one involving a firm suggests that the FSA is finding it difficult to prosecute the latter. The most recent cases against Pignatelli and Casoni suggest that even if the offence does not amount to market abuse contrary to section 118 FSMA it may still breach the FSA's Principles for Approved Persons.

There is one aspect of market abuse that is only partly covered by the regulations. Although the Rigby and Bailey case was brought under the new FSMA regulations, the provision of misleading financial statements and their manipulation is often more subtle but nevertheless pervasive. It was mentioned in earlier chapters, particularly those relating to the ECMH, that a change in accounting policy or method is likely to have an effect on share prices. We will look at these issues in the next chapter.

References

Barners, P.A. (1978) 'The Effect of a Merger on the Share Price of the Attacker', *Accounting and Business Research,* 7: 162–168.

Chan, T.W. and J.H. Goldthorpe (2007) 'Social Status and Newspaper Readership', *American Journal of Sociology,* 112: 1095–1134.

(DTI) Department of Trade and Industry (2001) *Mirror Group Newspapers plc: Investigations under Sections 432(2) and 442 of the Companies Act 1985,* London, HMSO.

(DTI) Department of Trade and Industry (1989) *County NatWest Limited County NatWest Securities Limited, Investigations under Sections 432(2) of the Companies Act 1985,* London, HMSO.

(DTI) Department of Trade and Industry (1997) *Guinness PLC: Investigation under Sections 432(2) and 442 of the Companies Act 1985,* Report made and submitted to the Secretary of State on 21 July 1997 by David Davidson QC and Ian Watt FCA, London, HMSO.

Firth, M. (1976) *Share Prices and Mergers,* Farnborough, Saxon House.

Hipwell, James and Anil, Bhoyrul (2000) *The City Slickers: Make a Million in Twelve Months,* London, Blake Publishing.

The Role, Use and Abuse of Financial and Accounting Data: Information Asymmetry

CHAPTER

8

Three people were invited to be interviewed for a job with a large plc.

The first, a mathematician, was asked 'What are two and two? He replied 'Easy – four'.

The second interviewee, a statistician, was asked the same question: 'What are two and two?', they asked. He replied 'Why – four'.

The third, an accountant, was then interviewed. Again he was asked the same question, 'What are two and two?' 'What number would you like?' he replied.

The accountant got the job.

The relationship between published financial or accounting information and share price movements is a complex one. It is affected by analyst's forecasts and expectations putting pressure on companies to adjust reported earnings numbers. It was also argued in Chapter 3 that share prices are affected by the way corporate profits and balance sheet data are actually measured and the way in which they are reported. Companies are naturally given a certain amount of discretion as to how they report and measure their performance. However, this is limited by auditors[1] who are required to check whether a listed company's financial statements provide a 'true and fair view' and comply with the rules and conventions that determine generally accepted accounting practice. This chapter examines the areas for legitimate discretion and false or deceptive information, the techniques involved and the role of auditors. It begins with an

1 I have used the word 'auditor' to refer to the audit firm and the corresponding pronoun 'it'.

examination of the pressures on management and others to provide misleading financial information.

Pressures on management at certain points in the trade cycle

At particular stages in the trade cycle, exceptional pressures on the company to perform occur and their directors to meet expectations. At the time of high growth in corporate profits, it may be relatively easy to meet market expectations. Initially, these may be relatively low and, in any case, the company is doing well. It will, therefore, have little difficulty in meeting expectations. Later, because of its growth in profitability and that of other companies, expectations will mount. At first, the company may be able to meet these. However, as expectations rise further, either the company's performance continues to rise with them or, if not, there is pressure on a company's directors to continue to report increased earnings (see Figure 8.1). During Period A, the company is able to meet expectations. It is also more than able to meet expectations in Period B because expectations are so low. However, it becomes difficult in Period C, not because the company is doing badly but because the market continues to have rising expectations whereas the company's results are levelling off. Later, when there is a recession, there is pressure on the company to report good results not only because the market is expecting growth (as it has become used to them) but, because of the recession, the company is unable to make as much profit as it would have been able to previously. This is Period D in Figure 8.1. In Period E, the market has come to accept the downward trend and adjust to the new situation.

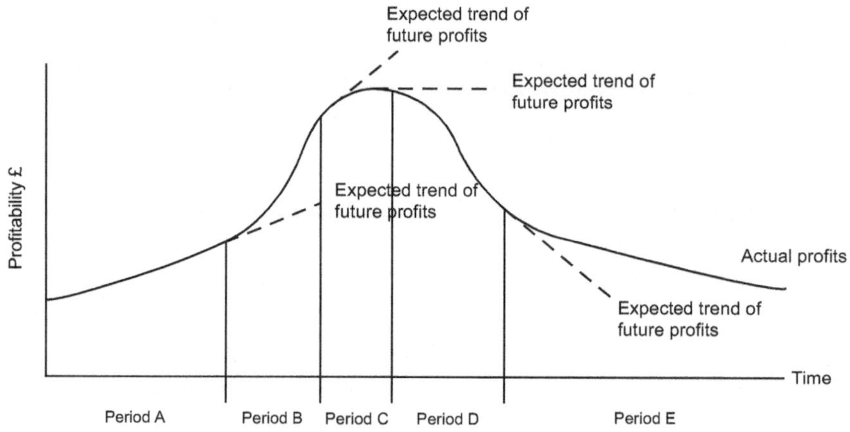

Figure 8.1 Diagram showing the trend of a company's real profits over time and expectations about profits during future periods (A to E)

There are a number of ways in which management may handle the pressures in Periods C and D.

1. State at the outset that the company is unable to meet expectations because they are unrealistic, or
2. Attempt to meet expectations either by
   a) 'smoothing' reported results, or
   b) simply manipulating the reported results.

It is possible that 2(a) may be done sufficiently to assuage expectations and be performed within the law, whereas 2(b) is probably not legally possible. Often, the former is referred to as 'creative accounting' which we may define as the exercise of discretion (to the extent that this is possible) to account as favourably as possible but *within* the law, accounting regulations, and standard accounting practice. Creative accounting is to be distinguished from 'financial statement fraud' which is one step further and relates to accounting favourably in some way for transactions that the law or mandatory regulations do not permit. A useful analogy may be that of tax avoidance (legal) and evasion (illegal).

Income smoothing

This section assumes that the reader understands basic accounting. Further explanation of the accounting principles involved for the reader less familiar with these is provided in the footnotes.

The process of income smoothing within limits, and if done correctly, is usually lawful. It is generally believed that it is practiced widely, even though it is contrary to the spirit of the law and the auditor's criterion of true and fair. Income smoothing refers to the actions of management to 'smooth' their reported profits by adopting techniques and making certain judgements and estimates that have the effect of understating profits when these are high and overstating profits when they are low (see Figure 8.2). This has the effect of damping down expectations as to future growth in periods of boom and, as a result, creates secret reserves that are available to be used when the company is facing having to report bad results and being able to report better results than it would otherwise have done. It should also be noted from Figure 8.2 that, overall, the total profits are the same but those reported are less volatile. As was shown in Chapter 2, all things being equal, this raises the value of the company in the eyes of an investor as its future returns appear to be more certain and, as a result, they would require a smaller compensation for risk.

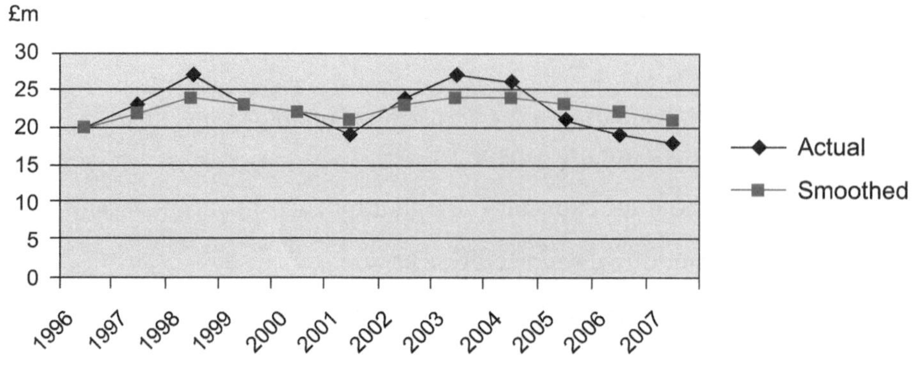

Figure 8.2 Income smoothing

For a long time this was not only regarded as perfectly acceptable and good practice but the mark of a financially sound company. Secret reserves have been defined as the 'undisclosed understatement of net worth resulting from for example the excessive writing-down of assets, the overstatement of provisions and liabilities and the writing-off of additions to fixed assets as expenses' (Parker 1984, p. 156). They were an extreme form of prudence or conservatism, whose existence continued to be merely hinted at by the use of phrases such as 'sundry creditors and credit balances', and were common practice until the Second World War. For instance, the finance director of Boots was quoted for saying that his business was 'stuffed full' of secret reserves unknown to shareholders (Chapman 1974) and highly reputable companies such as P&O, Imperial Tobacco, J. Lyons and John Summers amongst many others carried them during the 1920s (Napier 1991, Edwards 1989). The authoritative accounting text during the immediate post-Second World War period was *Spicer and Pegler's Practical Book-keeping and Commercial Knowledge* (Bigg *et al.* 1952). It contained over a page on secret reserves, listing ways of setting them up and explaining the reasons for not creating them. For example, in discussing the revenue surpluses of subsidiary companies, it said 'these are ignored in good years and brought to credit in the lean years. Such surpluses lend themselves to manipulation in unscrupulous hands' (1952, pp. 203–4). This was followed by a statement that:

> *On the other hand, the practice ... is undoubtedly advantageous in many instances, especially for banks ... since it enables the dividends to be maintained without violent fluctuations ... and prevents the disclosure of exceptional losses, which though alarming to the uninitiated do not in fact shake the stability of the concern.*
>
> Bigg et al. (1952, p. 203)

The effect and purpose of secret reserves was to distort reported profits and balance sheet values. It was not surprising, therefore, when the Companies Act 1948 effectively outlawed them (except for banking, insurance and shipping companies) by requiring fixed assets to be shown at cost or valuation, provisions for depreciation and the charge for depreciation for the year be separately disclosed, reserves were to be distinguished under separate headings and transfers to and from reserves and provisions must be disclosed.

Even though nowadays listed companies would deny using secret reserves, they would acknowledge the subjective nature of the judgements and estimates necessarily contained in their financial statements. Table 8.1 shows the effect on reported earnings and reported net assets (the balance sheet 'bottom line') of changes in the basis of computing such items as annual depreciation, provisions for expenses and other costs, in particular bad and doubtful debts, and the capitalization (or non-capitalization) of costs. Whilst accounting standards state how these items should be computed and outlaw certain methods, they do recognize that their estimation in practice is based on judgement. Table 8.1 shows how a pound less current depreciation increases both reported profits and net assets by the same amount. In order to compute depreciation, the company has to decide over how many years the asset is likely to last and its eventual disposal value, net of any disposal costs. Obviously, it is difficult to accurately estimate these and it may be necessary for management to revise their estimates at some stage. It is also necessary for management to decide whether depreciation occurs evenly over the lifetime of the asset or it occurs more in the early years, when the asset is new, compared with later years when it is older, as in the case of a motor car.

Table 8.1 Impact of changes of charges to reported profit and net assets

	Charges against current profits	Effect on reported income	Effect on reported net assets on balance sheet
Depreciation	More	Less	Less
	Less	More	More
Provision for bad debts	More	Less	Less
	Less	More	More
Capitalization of costs	More	Less	Less
	Less	More	More
Closing stock value	More	More	More
	Less	Less	Less

A company is required to make provisions for all possible and foreseeable costs and losses that it has incurred and relate to the accounting period.[2] Again, a reduction of the provision by one pound not only reduces the current charge for that expense against profits by one pound but it also increases the company's net assets value by the same amount. Consider two sectors in which it is not only difficult to do this accurately but where the sums involved are likely to significantly affect the reported profits and net worth of the business. The first is banking and the problem of estimating the proportion of loans a bank has made that are unlikely to be repaid. At the time of writing, banks are increasing their provisions for bad debts as a result of the sub-prime crisis. They are also publicly acknowledging that they do not fully know the extent of these bad debts. The second case is fashion retailing. It is difficult to forecast how quickly, or whether at all, certain items will sell. If not, the company will stand to lose. It is necessary, therefore, for the company to identify, or estimate in some way, those goods it holds that are effectively obsolete or worthless.[3] A reduction of one pound in the valuation of stock will reduce profit and net assets by one pound. Similarly, an increase in the value of stock by one pound will result in an additional pound on profit and net assets.

Although these problems relate to specific sectors, most companies will be faced with the problem of estimating expenses and losses that relate to the current accounting period for which they have not yet received invoices or claims or even knows they exist. For example, costs in respect of faulty service, or damages incurred.[4]

Finally, consider the decision that management have to make when deciding whether an expense is a revenue item that is to be charged against current profits, or whether it should be capitalized, that is, not charged against current profits but carried forward as an asset to be charged against profits in the period when it is effectively used.[5] Consider the cost of repainting a building. Is it normal maintenance, in which case it is to be charged against revenue, or

2 This is to conform with the principles of prudence and conservatism in financial reporting.

3 Accounting principles require a company to value its stock in hand at the lower of cost and net realizable value. If an item of clothing cannot be sold, its net realizable value is likely to be virtually zero.

4 In accordance with the 'matching' principle, profit is computed as the income from sales that have actually been made during the accounting period less the costs *incurred in earning these.* In respect of direct costs such as raw materials, these will be the cost of those items actually used in making the goods. In respect of other costs that are not directly related to output in this way, such as those relating to the overall running of the company, for example rent, salaries, heating and lighting, these are the costs that relate to their use during the accounting period, even though they were actually paid for in another accounting period.

5 This is an application of the matching principle, although it could conflict with the conservatism or prudence principle. Therefore, in practice, capitalization should be done only if management

does it constitute an improvement to such an extent that the building's value has been significantly increased and the costs should be added to the value of the building stated on the company's balance sheet? Again, a pound less charged against revenue and instead capitalized increases reported profits and net assets by the same amount.

Whilst management are faced with having to estimate these, it is even more difficult for the auditor to check whether such estimates and judgements are fair, especially if it is in management's interests that they should be biased in a particular direction, for example have the effect of overstating current profits. In the banking and fashion industry examples, it is obvious that the auditor will have less experience and skill than management in assessing bad debts and obsolete stock and would find it difficult to justify its judgement if it disagrees with those of management. It would also be difficult for the auditor to discover other costs for which the company has not yet been invoiced or charged, or even the reason why a building has been repainted.

There is considerable empirical evidence in the academic literature for the existence of income smoothing. Although researchers do not have direct access to the actual decision-making, they may estimate the amount of income smoothing and infer its existence in terms of the variations in the amounts of provisions and 'discretionary' items in the financial statements. Most of this evidence comes from the US but a UK study (Beattie *et al.* 1994) found that 'the incentives to smooth are positively related to the magnitude of the effect of classificatory choices, that is the effect must reach a certain level before smoothing behaviour is triggered' (p. 791).

The auditor and the financial statements

The traditional way by which owners are protected from theft or diversion of their money by senior managers is through their annual financial accounts. Managers are required by law to 'account' to owners as to how they have managed their funds; that is their stewardship of the organization's funds. Because managers may attempt to mislead the owners, auditors are appointed to independently check whether the accounts are true and fair. In fact, the historical origins of accountability, stewardship and auditing lie in the working of the English medieval manor, a classic situation of the separation of ownership and control. The auditor was appointed by the Lord of the Manor or his steward

---

believes that the benefits to be received from that expenditure in a future period are certain, or virtually certain.

to prevent him from being defrauded by the bailiffs. (The bailiffs managed the day-to-day workings of the manorial estate. The steward oversaw the general workings of the estates.) The Lord would usually be absent from the manor for most of the time, either because he was Lord of many manors and lived on another one, or he was absent abroad as was the custom. The auditor protected his Lord's estate by listening to the bailiffs' detailed accounts as they were questioned and examined by the steward on the results of the year's harvest, the amounts received in rents and fines and spent on maintenance of the estate (Bennett 1937, p. 158). Hence, the origins of the word 'auditor': from the Latin *audire*, to hear.

Today auditing is very different but its purpose is precisely the same – to see whether management have properly managed the resources they have been entrusted with and to protect owners and other stakeholders from being robbed, defrauded or misled. The implication is that audited financial statements are more credible than unaudited financial statements. The directors may want to convey certain messages about how they have managed the business but, just like the medieval bailiff, they may have reason to tell a biased story or simply want, or need, to mislead the owners. It is the auditor's job to prevent this. The problem here is that auditors are appointed by the directors and there is often a very close relationship between the financial director and the auditors. Often a financial director is an ex-partner or ex-employee of the company's auditors. The audit market has for some time now been contracting and is competitive on price; the accompanying consultancy work that they could expect to receive is, therefore, very important. All this is very different to the days of the Lord of the Manor. The bailiff would not be allowed to appoint the auditor. He would certainly not be allowed to grease the hands of the auditor by giving it other paid work. The whole process was based on transparency. The auditor had to decide one simple thing: whether to accept the bailiff's account about what he had done with his Lordship's money. It could be truly independent.

In addition to the problem of being at a disadvantage when checking management's estimates when they are under pressure to bias their financial statements, there are other difficulties facing the auditor and affecting its ability to act independently. The auditor has to balance two things:

1. If it does not comply with management's wishes it may lose the audit. The directors could deselect it, switch auditors and appoint another firm.
2. If it does comply with management's wishes and is party to a cover-up or misinformation in some way, it could be sued for negligence

by shareholders or other groups for the damage they have suffered. Additionally, individual members of the audit firm could be censured, struck off as an auditor etc., which may severely harm the firm's reputation and future business. In short, the reputational costs could be enormous.

The auditor is placed in a dilemma. On the one hand it does not want to lose the audit. On the other hand, it does not wish to be sued for negligence. Little wonder auditors err on the side of caution and qualify small, less important, clients but take a risk with their larger clients. There is some UK evidence that provides an insight into the extent the auditor behaves independently in difficult circumstances. As part of its approval of the accounts, the auditor has to decide whether the company is able to continue to trade in the foreseeable future (that is the next 12 months from the balance sheet date). If the auditor thinks the company is unable to survive that long it has to say so by means of making what is known as, a going concern qualification in its audit report. This has to be stated in the audit report in some way. Peel (1989), Citron and Taffler (1992), Barnes and Huan (1993), and Lennox (1999) show that in the UK many companies that receive going concern qualifications continue despite the fact that their auditors have effectively stated that they are 'no-hopers', that is, they were forecast to fail but did not. These are known as 'Type I errors' (see Figure 8.3). Companies that receive adverse reports are typically small. Perhaps less remarkably, many companies that have failed or collapsed and did not receive a going concern qualification are typically very large, that is they were forecast not to fail but did. These are known as 'Type II errors'. The situation is similar in the US where seven of the ten largest recent US corporate failures at the turn of the last century (including Enron) did not receive qualified audit reports.

So why is this? The literature offers two basic reasons:

1. The possibility of incompetence, due to a lack of practical appreciation and understanding of the industry in which the client company operates – 'the incompetence hypothesis', or

2. The ability of the auditor and the client firm to get their own way – the bargaining power hypothesis. The company does not want a qualified audit report, especially if it is dependent on bank and other types of loan to survive. It will push the auditor as far as possible not to issue one. It will threaten to switch to another auditor and may even provide other incentives, for example lucrative consultancies.

Increasing relative auditor bargaining power ⟶

Increasing probability of failure ↓

		Prediction (audit report)	
		Non-failure	Failure (qualification)
Outcome	Non-failure	Correct	Type I error
	Failure	Type II error	Correct

Figure 8.3 The effect of increasing relative auditor bargaining power on the auditor's going-concern prediction (qualified or clean report) relative to the outcome and the probability of failure

Research strongly rejects the incompetence hypothesis (for example, Mutchler 1984, 1985; Campisi and Trotman 1985; Barnes and Huan 1993) in favour of the bargaining power hypothesis. Goldman and Barlev (1974) were probably the first to recognize that these conflicts would be resolved by the two sides according to their bargaining power. They note: 'the ability of auditors to withstand such pressures is a function of the parties to the conflict' (Goldman and Barlev 1974, p. 707). Bargaining power relates to the strength of a negotiator to obtain advantageous terms: it is the ability of a negotiator to secure an opponent's agreement to his own terms. Here it relates to the ability of the auditor to withstand the pressures placed on it by its client, notably the threat of audit switch, and issue a qualified report nevertheless. At one extreme, the auditor is able to withstand all pressures, perhaps because they have such a high reputation and are not prepared to risk this being threatened, and/or the client company is relatively small or unimportant. At the other extreme, it relates to the auditor submitting to the pressures imposed on them by the client, who is relatively large and important to the auditor. As a result, the direction of the error depends upon the auditor's relative bargaining power: a Type I error, where the auditor's bargaining power is relatively high, and a Type II error, where the auditor's bargaining power is relatively low (see Figure 8.2). Although Goldman and Barlev produced no statistical evidence, they thought at that time there was 'an asymmetry in favour of the firm ... inherent in these relationships' (1974, p. 707). More recently, Barnes and Lee (2007) have obtained statistical evidence for the UK that supports the theory. Table 8.2 shows that almost nine out of ten companies whose financial results included a qualified auditors' report did not fail. These companies were significantly smaller than the average. Of those companies that received unqualified audit reports, 3 per cent failed. These were companies significantly larger than the average.

There has been a considerable increase in concentration of the accountancy profession amongst the very large firms over recent years, both in the USA (Wolk *et al.* 2001) and the UK (Pong 1999). It has also become necessary for large or listed companies to be audited by one of these firms. So the choice for the company which may be considering switching (or threatening to switch) its auditors may not be that great, providing increased bargaining power to the audit firm in discussions about accounting treatment and creative accounting opportunities. There has also been increasing emphasis by the accountancy

Table 8.2 Companies that received an auditor's report for 2000 distinguishing between (i) those that received qualified or favourable audit report relating to their continuity, and (ii) those that were/were not dissolved or placed in receivership during 2001–2003

Qualified reports with correct prediction	193
Qualified reports with incorrect prediction (Type I errors)	1456
Total qualified reports	1649
Type I errors as a % of total qualified reports	88.30%
Unqualified reports with correct prediction	38 757
Unqualified reports with incorrect prediction (Type II errors)	1278
Total unqualified reports	40 035
Type II errors as a % of total unqualified reports	3.19%
All auditor reports	41 684
Errors as a % of all auditor reports	6.56%

profession on the development and documentation of accounting standards and Generally Agreed Accounting Practice as a way of reducing the scope for creative accounting. The effect of these developments may be to protect the auditor's independence and bolster its bargaining power. Unfortunately, whilst at first glance this may be seen as desirable, it may have the effect of forcing companies into financial statement fraud.

Conclusions

It was the purpose of this chapter to examine the scope for manipulation of financial statements as a means of affecting investors' perceptions and share prices. I distinguished between what may be regarded as within the law – this was defined as creative accounting – and outside the law – financial statement fraud.

The empirical evidence suggests that income smoothing is common. Presumably the majority of it is creative accounting, although there is no evidence to suggest this. In fact, the anecdotal evidence of the late 1980s and early 1990s in Chapter 4 suggests that in many cases it may be unlawful.

This chapter also showed how significant areas of a company's financial statements are based on judgements and estimates and how these may be varied in accordance with management's objectives to under- or overstate reported profits. It was also shown that auditors whose job is to check and certify company accounts may not be as independent as might be assumed. The reader may look no further for evidence for this possibility than the collapse of Arthur Andersen, the largest accounting and auditing firm in the world, as a result of its damaged reputation in the scandals at Enron and elsewhere.

References

Barnes, P.A. (2004) 'The Auditor's Going Concern Decision and Types I and II Errors: the Coase Theorem, Transaction Costs, Bargaining Power and Attempts to Mislead', *Journal of Accounting and Public Policy,* 23(6): 415–440.

Barnes, P.A. and H.D. Huan (1993) 'The Auditor's Going Concern Decision: Some UK Evidence Concerning Independence and Competence', *Journal of Business Finance and Accounting,* 20(2): 213–228.

Barnes, P.A. and H. Lee (2007) Auditor Independence and the Going Concern Decision: Some UK Evidence concerning Types I and II Audit Errors and Bargaining Power, Working Paper, Nottingham Business School.

Beattie, V., S. Brown, D. Ewers, B. John, S. Manson, D. Thomas and M. Turner (1994) 'Extraordinary Items and Income Smoothing: a Positive Accounting Approach', *Journal of Business Finance and Accounting,* 21(6): 791–810.

Bennett, H.S. (1937) *Life on the English Manor: a Study of Peasant Conditions 1150–1400,* London, Cambridge University Press.

Bigg, W.W, H. Wilson and A.E. Langton (1952) *Spicer and Pegler's Practical Book-Keeping and Commercial Knowledge,* 11th edn, London, H.F.L. Publishers.

Campisi, S. and K.T. Trotman (1985) 'Auditor Consensus in Going Concern Judgements', *Accounting and Business Research,* 15(3): 303–310.

Chapman, S. (1974) *Jesse Boot of Boots the Chemist,* London, Hodder and Stoughton.

Citron, D.B. and R.J. Taffler (1992) 'The Audit Report Under Going Concern Uncertainties: An Empirical Analysis', *Accounting and Business Research,* 22(3): 337–345.

Edwards J.R. (1989) *A History of Financial Accounting,* London, Routledge.

Goldman, A. and B. Barlev (1974) 'The Auditor–firm Conflict of Interest: Its Implications for Independence', *The Accounting Review,* 49(3): 707–718.

Lennox, C.S. (1999) 'The Accuracy and Incremental Information Content of Audit Reports in Predicting Bankruptcy', *Journal of Business Finance and Accounting,* 26(5 and 6): 757–778.

Mutchler, J.F. (1984) 'Auditors Perceptions of the Going Concern Decision', *Auditing: A Journal of Practice and Theory,* 3(1): 17–30.

Mutchler, J.F. (1985) 'A Multivariate Analysis of the Auditor's Going Concern Opinion Decision', *Journal of Accounting Research,* 23(2): 668–682.

Napier, C.J. (1991) 'Secret Accounting: the P&O Group in the Inter-war Years', *Accounting Business and Financial History,* 1(3): 303–333.

Parker, R.H. (1984) *Macmillan Dictionary of Accounting,* 2nd edn, London, Macmillan.

Peel, M. (1989) 'The Adverse Report Debate: Some UK Evidence', *British Accounting Review,* 21(4): 329–350.

Pong, C.K.M. (1999) 'Auditor Concentation: A Replication and Extension for the UK Audit Market', *Journal of Business Finance and Accounting,* 26(3 and 4): 450–75.

Wolk, C.M., S.E. Michelson and C.W. Wootton (2001) 'Auditor Concentration and Market Shares in the US: 1988–1999', *British Accounting Review,* 33(2): 157–174.

The Way Forward

CHAPTER 9

Is market efficiency unaffected by market abuse? The early chapters of this book examined market efficiency and other models in an attempt to understand behaviour in practice. It was clear from these that whilst in one sense a sophisticated exchange such as the LSE could hardly be anything other than efficient, in another sense it was not. The market could not be perfectly informationally efficient, never mind perfectly allocatively efficient. Furthermore, the more recent studies relating to the ECMH suggest that it is not as efficient as was previously thought. It was also suggested in the last chapter that the manipulation of financial data may be common – especially during those periods of the trade cycle when management and companies are under particular pressure to perform. These, together with the actions of the FSA and the number of cases brought to court, suggest that market abuse may be on a significantly large scale. It is the purpose of this chapter to consider the proposition that the market is inefficient in both the strong and semi-strong forms. If so, can we quantify the amount of insider dealing and market abuse? How best should they be regulated and are the regulations in place sufficient?

The magnitude of market abuse and insider dealing

There are regular claims in the press of insider dealing, usually in respect of takeover bids. Here are some examples sufficiently old for us to see the outcome. On 6 February 2005 *The Financial Mail* mentioned four recent cases:

1. On 12 January 2005, it was announced that Aggregate Industries, the British sand and gravel group, had been approached about a possible bid. In the week before the announcement, the shares had jumped 8 per cent and rose another 4 per cent on the day before the news.

2. On 13 December 2004, LA Fitness, the health group, announced that it had received several approaches. The previous week its shares had risen 5 per cent and on the day before the news, 2.5 per cent.

3. On 13 December 2004, The LSE announced an approach from Deutsche Borse. In the week before this was announced, its shares rose 5 per cent.

4. On 31 December 2004, Apax, the venture capital group, announced it was considering a bid for Woolworths. Over Christmas week, Woolworths' shares had jumped 5 per cent.

Despite claims by *The Financial Mail* that 'a small army of Square Mile professionals' buy shares ahead of official announcements and 'the pattern can be seen in almost every major bid' nothing appears to have happened or, at least, there was no public statement to that effect.

Claims of market abuse are also common. The following story which appeared in *The Independent* is typical. A shareholder relations executive rang various financial analysts to steer their forecasts down. A day later the executive told a journalist to ring the analysts for a story, saying he had heard on the grapevine that they had cut their forecasts. Although it broke the spirit of the rules, it made sure that the share price was managed and the market was not wrong-footed.

Dubow and Monteiro (2006) at the FSA have attempted to quantify the amount of insider dealing and market abuse by means of a 'market cleanliness' indicator. Using similar methodology to that previously described (the market model, see Chapter 3) Dubow and Monteiro computed cumulative abnormal returns (CAR) around the date of the announcement - the pre-announcement window (two trading days prior to the day of announcement) and the post-announcement window (the day of announcement and the next trading day). They then computed the market cleanliness index as the total number of announcements in which a statistically significant informed price movement (IPM) had occurred as a percentage of the total number of announcements in which there had been a statistically significant price change (SA), that is IPM/SA. An IPM is defined as a statistically significant CAR over the two-day period prior to the announcement and in the same direction as the SA, when the CAR over the four-day period is statistically significant.

Dubow and Monteiro's study was for the period 1998 to 2003. They examined two areas. The first was where a merger bid had been announced. Dubow and Monteiro found that IPM had occurred in respect of more than one in five takeover announcements. More recently their data for takeovers and mergers have been updated to include 2004 and 2005 (see Table 9.1). They inferred from this that for a significant pre-announcement abnormal performance to occur, it must have been brought about to some degree by insider dealing, although they also acknowledge that insider dealing may occur without the share price being affected.

Whilst this study provides interesting evidence for the existence of significant price movements ahead of announcements, it probably understates this occurrence for takeovers and mergers because it is using such a short window. A period of two days is clearly insufficient to measure the total share price adjustment prior to a merger announcement when earlier studies reviewed in Chapter 5 have shown that this occurs (and would be expected to occur) over a much longer period, say one month.[1] A debate about this is unnecessary, however, given the poor relationship between the amount of insider dealing transactions and share price movements. Even if an inside dealing transaction is so large as to affect the share price or the volume of trading and this is noticed by investors and the press, the subsequent increase in volume and price will neither amount to, nor actually constitute, insider dealing. It is only in this sense that such data can be used as an indication of insider dealing.

It is also not possible to establish a statistical relationship between the volume of trading and the magnitude of a share price change. The volume of trading may increase on a particular day but there may be little change in the share price. This may simply be because a financial institution has bought, or disposed of, a large block of shares and there is no new information or a change in the perceived value of the stock to significantly affect its price. On the other hand, a large price change may occur without an accompanying increase in the volume of trading, simply because of the release of new information affecting

Table 9.1 Updated market cleanliness data for takeovers and mergers

Year	Number of announcements	Number of IPMs	Market cleanliness %
2000	183	44	24.0
2002	147	37	25.1
2003	160	22	13.8
2004	102	33	32.4
2005	177	42	23.7

1 In the recent criminal cases that came to court, the defendants were accused of dealing in shares in takeover targets many days prior to an announcement.

the security's value or that investors and market makers have simply revised their opinions.

The evidence provided to the courts relating to the behaviour of a security known to have been the subject of insider dealing also suggests that in most cases both the price and the volume of trading are largely unaffected. In other words, the effect will be so small as to be unidentifiable, not least because of the volatility of normal trading activity. In order to identify an inside trade, it would be necessary to be able to predict the amount of trading on a particular day and compare this with the actual amount. As it is not possible to predict so precisely, it is not possible to identify the increase in the volume of trading due to insider dealing.

Dubow and Monteiro also studied FTSE 350 companies' regulatory disclosures. These are trading announcements under such headings as 'trading statement', 'trading update', 'contract award' or 'drilling report'. Dubow and Monteiro's market cleanliness statistics showed that informed price movements had occurred in respect of about one-third of all announcements, that is before FSMA it was 31.3 per cent and after FSMA it was 32.1 per cent. These results are in line with two studies of regulatory announcements relating to profit warnings by Bulkley and Herrerias (2002) and Bulkley *et al.* (2002) who also found a significant amount of abnormal share price performance during the five days prior to the warning announcement.

In my view, insider dealing probably occurs at least on a very minor level in virtually every merger bid and in respect of most other important announcements. I have also argued that it is not possible to infer from these data whether insider dealing and market abuse are increasing or decreasing. There are, however, several factors to suggest that it is likely to increase in the future. The first relates to the accessibility to information and the ease by which a person may trade. Recent developments in technology enable an individual to buy and sell shares more quickly and far more anonymously than before. It is little more than a matter of a quick phone call to a bank. Despite IT efforts to the contrary, it is likely that more individuals have potential access to inside information than ever before. The limiting factor is probably their ability to recognize inside information and how they may profit from it. Running parallel with these changes is the amount of deskilling of jobs, particularly in financial intermediaries, in which there are serious problems relating to breaches of confidential information and the integrity of cheap staff with minimal career prospects and expectations. This has not yet become an area of major concern in share dealing. To counterbalance these developments are the electronic storage of email and other correspondence and the recording of conversations and orders. Whilst in previous decades there was no evidence of the reasons behind a transaction, now there often is.

If this is the case, how often are these incidents investigated? There is little indication of the number of investigations under the post-2000 regime. It has been estimated that before 2000 there was something in the order of two cases a month passed by the LSE to the DTI for further inspection.[2] In the absence of information to the contrary and on the assumption that the level of activity remains about the same, I presume that the FSA investigates a similar number per year.

One of the interesting findings from the analysis of successful prosecutions in Chapter 7 is the relative rarity of market abuse cases other than insider dealing. This is strange given the difficulties of identifying, tracing and obtaining evidence of insider dealing. What makes this particularly strange is that whilst the insider dealer is likely to try to cover his traces, the signs of the hand of the market manipulator are likely to be much more evident, if only in retrospect.

So what are the reasons for the absence of prosecutions for the other forms of market abuse, essentially market manipulation? There can only be two: either that these offences do not exist or that their identification is difficult. In its review of the working of Suspicious Transaction Reports (STR) published in the December 2006 issue of *Market Watch*, the FSA stated that between 1 July 2005 and 31 October 2006 it had received 266 STRs, most of which related to the equity markets: 255 related to insider dealing, 8 to distortion or manipulation, 2 to false and misleading statements and 1 to the scope of the Code. They came from 80 firms, most of these from retail firms including 11 large banks.

Who are the main perpetrators? The general view is that most of the insider dealing is done by those in the city with access to inside information in their professional capacity. As long ago as 1987, *The Financial Times* (2 July) estimated that between a quarter and a half of all insider dealing is attributable to city firms acting as advisers. This estimate is unlikely to have changed. Barnes (1996) found that almost 75 per cent of the rise in a target's share price at the time of a bid occurs before its announcement. When this was analysed between

2 It was reported in a Trade and Industry Committee report to the House of Commons on 2 May 1990 (Trade and Industry Committee 1990) that since May 1988 the LSE had conducted about 240 investigations into possible insider dealing cases and had passed about two a month to the Department of Trade and Industry. Since 1985, 101 cases had been transferred in this way, inspectors being appointed in 41 cases which resulted in 19 prosecutions and ten convictions.

bidders' advising merchant banks, it was found that this occurred significantly earlier in the case of two major advisory firms than others, suggesting their association with the leakage. There is very little academic evidence for other forms of market abuse other than that mentioned in Chapter 5 relating to share support operations.

How can insider dealing and market abuse be regulated?

The way forward according to the FSA is a market abuse regime based on principle-based regulation focusing on compliance monitoring. Compliance monitoring is directed towards all types of financial crime in which market abuse is merely part. Under such a regime, the FSA is attempting to emphasize flexibility in which controls should take into account the size of the financial intermediary, the types of business it does, the types of client the firm has and so on. For instance, if trading volume makes it impossible to look at all trades, the firm should narrow down monitoring to the most likely trades in which insider dealing or market abuse may occur, for example, where a large profit was made or where the price changed significantly on the day's trading. The emphasis is on the awareness by the financial intermediary of the implications of its business.[3] This can only be achieved by education and training.

An important component of the new regime is the STR which is specifically aimed at identifying market abuse and cases of misconduct. STRs should help market practitioners to be proactive in identifying market abuse and cases of misconduct. There are other initiatives. In December 2006 the FSA signed a letter of intent to replace its computer system with a new software system, SABRE II (Surveillance and Business Reporting Engine), which monitors possible market abuse. Whilst SABRE I simply identifies significant changes in share prices and volume of transactions, SABRE II will be a real-time system based on transactions as they occur. The FSA has recently conducted a research project into the standard of controls in firms (Financial Services Authority 2007). It found from its visits to firms that the standard of systems and controls varied enormously. Whilst one firm had failed to comply, about a third had gone beyond the basic requirements or examined in detail how best they could apply the rules to their business operations. Nevertheless, the FSA believes that controls, especially in the area of IT security, can be improved.

3 In such a situation, compliance should track the profits and losses made on clients' accounts. It should be aware that manipulation is possible by investors, especially in the AIM market and with penny shares. Similarly, compliance should be aware of securities affected by Regulatory News statements which could be cross-referenced to client trading.

The regulation of insider dealing and market abuse

It is unlikely that companies and financial intermediaries acting as advisers will be as enthusiastic about their controls as their regulator, the FSA. Insider dealing and market abuse are unlike many other forms of corporate crime and fraud in that their incidence does not occur at the point of control. For instance, it is in most companies' interests to have an effective set of controls in place to prevent them from being the victim of fraud or theft. They are the victims and it is in their power to install systems of prevention and detection to defend themselves from loss. Companies will also try to ensure that their controls are secure in order to protect themselves and their customers from identity theft. The losses that could arise could be huge (Barnes and Webb 2007). However, in the case of insider dealing and market abuse, these incentives are absent. Companies and advising financial intermediaries do not incur losses from insider dealing and market abuse. Market abuse is more likely to be perpetrated by companies and their directors. The cases reported in Chapter 7 demonstrate this. The cases reported there also show insider dealing to be commonly perpetrated by top management and employees of financial intermediaries. There is no suggestion that the companies involved would suffer in any way. The same goes for advisers, brokers and market makers. The reported cases of market abuse in which the FSA took action showed financial intermediaries perpetrating market abuse as part of their business. Of course, financial intermediaries would regard insider dealing as undesirable. More importantly, they would regard it as, possibly, costly – in terms of their reputation – if customers and clients were able to link the insider dealing to them.

The upshot is that there is little incentive for those involved in its control – companies and financial intermediaries – to prevent the occurrence of insider dealing and market abuse: quite the opposite. There is certainly no incentive for them to investigate and initiate a prosecution; say in the way they would in relation to other forms of financial crime such as fraud and theft. On the contrary, it would be more likely to be in their interests to cover it up!

It is necessary, therefore, that regulation is imposed from outside.[4] There are a number of ways by which this may be achieved. For example, the regulators could point out that as the regulations are so voluminous and the penalties so severe, the amount of abuse is minimal. Another approach would be to recognize the difficulties involved and adopt a statutory-based regime in which there are stringent laws and regulations making it easier for investigators

4 Alternatively, we could, of course, revert to when there was no anti-inside trading legislation, admit that it takes place to the benefit of City insiders and forget that ordinary investors and the community at large suffer.

to obtain information and for regulators to prosecute; for example, where the onus is on the defendant to show that they acted properly.

To some extent, the latter represents the present position. Nevertheless, there are ways by which current practice could be improved. Typically, there are many insiders. In some bids there are as many as 1500 named insiders. This is unnecessary. Whilst this is the way of doing business, it will be impossible to prevent leakage. The number of individuals and firms involved needs to be reduced. If this could be achieved, it would then be possible to require companies to have a lead adviser who would be responsible for the confidentiality of the information. The adviser could be severely fined by the FSA if information leaked out and allowed dealers to profit.[5] Alternatively, rather than simply fined, the financial intermediary responsible could be held to be publicly accountable in some way. It is quite possible that the reputational costs involved and the fear of the consequences of censorship would be so great as to be an effective deterrent in both of these approaches.

Concluding points

We should not be fooled into believing that the existence of a vast amount of law and regulations is evidence of protection. On the contrary, it is more likely to suggest the difficulty of the regulators in policing it. The best protection for investors is the scepticism of the press and the market. The maxim 'A fool and his money are soon parted' applies. I have argued that the market is regarded as 'efficient' because it is rational. It is perhaps a more apt to say that its scepticism makes it efficient. Commentators freely believe the market is open to abuse and, whilst it may not be rife, insider dealing is common. Whilst this continues to be said and disbelief about the effectiveness of the control in financial intermediaries remains, there will there be both pressure for, and scope for, improvement.

References

Barnes, P.A. (1996) 'The Regulation of Insider Dealing in the UK. Some Empirical Evidence Concerning Share Prices, Merger Bids and Advising Merchant Banks', *Applied Financial Economics,* 6: 383–391.

Barnes, P.A. and J.Webb (2007) 'Organisational Susceptibility to Fraud and Theft, Organisational Size and the Effectiveness of Management Controls:

5 There are practical problems involved. For example, it may be in the interests of one of those involved to deliberately leak information in an attempt to undermine a deal.

Some UK Evidence', *Managerial and Decision Economics,* 28(3): 181–193.

Bulkley, G. and R. Herrerias (2002) Stock Returns following Profit Warnings, University of Exeter working paper.

Bulkley G., R.D.F. Harris and R. Herrerias (2002) Stock Returns following Profit Warnings: A Test of Models of Behavioural Finance, University of Exeter working paper.

Dubow, B. and N. Monteiro (2006) *Measuring Market Cleanliness,* FSA Occasional Paper 23, London, Financial Services Authority.

Financial Services Authority (2007) 'Thematic Review of Controls over Inside Information Relating to Public Takeovers', *Market Watch,* 21.

Trade and Industry Committee (1990) *Third Report, Company Investigations,* House of Commons Session 1989–90, 2 May 1990, London, HMSO.

Index